LEVANNA

LEVANNA

Interpretation and Controversy in New York Archaeology, 1923–2018

Jack Rossen

ROWMAN & LITTLEFIELD
Lanham • Boulder • New York • London

Published by Rowman & Littlefield
An imprint of The Rowman & Littlefield Publishing Group, Inc.
4501 Forbes Boulevard, Suite 200, Lanham, Maryland 20706
www.rowman.com

6 Tinworth Street, London SE11 5AL, United Kingdom

Copyright © 2019 by The Rowman & Littlefield Publishing Group, Inc.

All rights reserved. No part of this book may be reproduced in any form or by any electronic or mechanical means, including information storage and retrieval systems, without written permission from the publisher, except by a reviewer who may quote passages in a review.

British Library Cataloguing in Publication Information Available

Library of Congress Cataloging-in-Publication Data

Names: Rossen, Jack, author.
Title: Levanna : interpretation and controversy in New York archaeology, 1923–2018 / Jack Rossen.
Description: Lanham : Rowman & Littlefield, 2019. | Includes bibliographical references and index.
Identifiers: LCCN 2019004067| ISBN 9781538128299 (cloth) | ISBN 9781538128305 (electronic) | ISBN 9781538158401 (pbk)
 Subjects: LCSH: Indians of North America—New York (State)—Antiquities. | Algonquin Indians. | Excavations (Archaeology)—New York (State). | New York (State)—Antiquities.
Classification: LCC E78.N7 R84 2019 | DDC 974.7/01—dc23 LC record available at https://lccn.loc.gov/2019004067

CONTENTS

Preface — vii

Acknowledgments — xiii

1 Levanna: A Nexus of Stories and Issues — 1

2 Pulling Down the Pillars: Early Investigations at Levanna (1923–1942) — 11

3 Indigenous Archaeology, the Age of the Haudenosaunee Confederacy, and the Use of Oral Traditions — 45

4 The 2007 to 2009 Levanna Excavations — 65

5 Further Reinterpretation of the Cayuga: The Myers Farm Site — 125

6 Conclusions: Chasing the Ghosts of the Old-Time New York Archaeologists — 159

References — 171

Index — 193

About the Author — 197

PREFACE

I have often told people that the biggest goal for an archaeologist is to find a great story to tell. For an archaeologist, a great story is enveloping: It informs us, mystifies us, forces us to ponder the darker and brighter sides of history and human nature, and brings people, named and unnamed, back to life. The Levanna story fills me with wonder for the recovery of multidimensional and multitemporal puzzles, and it also brings me yearning for the puzzle pieces still missing. Levanna is a story that found me more than I found it. I drove by the site for ten years, barely paying notice to the rusted historical marker. I incorrectly believed published reports of the site destruction by the 1940s from road construction, decades of excavations, the construction of an outdoor museum, and the traffic of thousands of visitors.

It was not until I met Betty Pangborn, a feisty ninety-year-old who became my friend, that Levanna came to my mind in the spring of 2007. I met Betty and many other friends who inhabit this book, including Dan Hill and Donna Silversmith of the Cayuga Nation, through the SHARE Farm project. SHARE stands for Strengthening Haudenosaunee American Relations through Education. It was an audacious community social and cultural experiment where our group of academics and local businesspeople purchased a seventy-acre farm that we ran as an educational center for five years amid the social and political turmoil of a Native land claim. At that time, the Cayuga had owned no land in their Cayuga Lake homeland (now Central New York in the Finger Lakes) since shortly after the American Revolution. We were able to turn over the Cayuga-SHARE Farm to the Cayuga people in 2005, with a big boost from the Onondaga Nation and Haudenosaunee Confederacy.

The Levanna Project would not have occurred without SHARE and our continuing work efforts at the farm. We were able to demonstrate to the Cayuga that we cared about their return to the homeland, and that we were willing to put our hard work and money into it. For me, as the archaeologist in the SHARE group, I also wished to practice what is known as indigenous archaeology. This is archaeology that is a partnership with and a positive force for Native people instead of the negative force it has too often been. Indigenous archaeology is designed to empower Native people and examine—and if necessary, challenge—dominant narratives about history and people. Sometimes what we think or know to be true about the past may just be the echoes of prejudice and the tools of oppression.

A range of archaeologists, from legends to castoffs, were involved with the Levanna site. Arthur C. Parker, a Seneca, director of multiple museums, rising patriarch of New York archaeology, and future president of the Society for American Archaeology (SAA), was the first professional to excavate at Levanna in 1923, along with his principal protégé, William A. Ritchie, later the long-term New York state archaeologist and author of the venerable *The Archaeology of New York State*. In his Levanna letters, Parker sounds articulate, almost regal, as well as authoritarian and dismissive. Ritchie inherited the authoritarian streak and tends to sound combative and defensive as the Levanna feud developed.

The central and most enigmatic figure of the early Levanna excavations is Harrison C. Follett. As the second apprentice/protégé of Parker, he was released from employment at the site when the Great Depression took hold. Follett responded by continuing to work at Levanna on a shoestring budget based on proceeds from an outdoor museum he operated at the site from 1932 to 1941, the onset of American involvement in World War II. He presented the spectacular and then-famous animal effigies as the star attraction of his museum. In return, he was excoriated, shunned, and blacklisted by the professional archaeological community, led by former mentor Parker and former field partner Ritchie.

I spent countless hours with Follett's papers, manuscripts, and letters, trying to breach the inner workings of his mind. I mostly found relentless optimism and years of hard work in archaeology and public relations in the face of persecution, but also dark periods of loneliness, frustration, and anger. Here I explore the animal effigy controversy through the incredible archival record from five sources, including four museums. The story of the quasi-official and sometimes undercover investigation of the Levanna effigies by the SAA is amazing. It does appear that the effigies were the faked enhancement of broken rock earth ovens, but the role of Follett is unclear, especially in comparison with the evidence on some of his cronies. In the final analysis, Levanna represents several major controversies of archaeology then and now. Should archaeology be commercialized? How are sensational claims to be evaluated? How are careers in archaeology created, nurtured, or destroyed? What is the potential role of oral history in archaeological site investigation and presentation? In what ways can modern techniques, cultural attitudes, and analysis specializations help reinterpret a site?

Lost in the intrigue of the 1930s is the fact that Levanna is a real and unusually important site from an underrepresented period known as Owasco (ca AD 900–1300). The Levanna site is indeed the real star of the story. Through a series of landowners, particularly Homer St. Clair, the site was well-preserved and unplowed in a forested zone amid a sea of plowed farm fields. Homer owned the site at the time of my 2007 to 2009 excavations and remembered Follett, the effigies, and many of the characters of the story. Homer's personal archive, kept in a red breadbox, was better than any of the museum collections. Homer became a great friend and supporter and it is my greatest regret that he and Betty Pangborn did not live to see this volume. It is also unfortunate that although it was scanned, the red breadbox of historical treasures was misplaced after Homer's death and no one knows where it is now.

The test excavations of 2007 immediately showed that contrary to published statements, substantial intact deposits were present at Levanna. During the 2008 and 2009 excavations we opened large blocks, and these materials are presented and discussed. Analysis of the materials proceeded gradually through the years and then intensively during the summer of 2016 when I had five stellar full-time student interns in my lab. This was when the new version of Levanna came to life. I make several comparisons of how Levanna was interpreted in the 1930s versus now. In making these contrasts, I took into consideration the cultural backdrop, everyday desperation, and matter-of-fact racism against Native Americans of the Great Depression versus the present-day cultural relativism, systematics, and scientific advances of anthropological archaeology. The Levanna site indeed had hidden stories to tell.

My contacts with farmers in the Levanna area led me to meet Becky and John Binns, owners of the Myers Farm site. Three field seasons (2011, 2013, 2014) at the small and unassuming hilltop site revealed something extraordinary and unprecedented in the region: an undefended feasting ground. This interpretation led me back to two key issues I addressed in my previous book, *Corey Village and the Cayuga World: Implications from Archaeology and Beyond* (Syracuse University Press, 2015). The first is whether the archaeological record matches the reputation of the Cayuga and the Haudenosaunee (Iroquois) Confederacy as relentlessly fierce and warlike. I believe and discuss here that the record does not match the stereotype. At the very least, the Cayuga lived in a peaceful landscape for substantial periods of their history.

The second issue involves the origins of the Haudenosaunee Confederacy itself and the longtime dissonance between the archaeological (ca five-hundred-year-old) and oral tradition (greater than one-thousand-year-old) versions. I discuss this and the relative credibility of oral histories in some detail. The five-hundred-plus year difference is important as the distinction between a confederacy begun just before or as a result of European contact versus a confederacy with much deeper roots. I believe that Levanna and Myers Farm and the peaceful activities and landscapes they represent support a Great Peace brought on by the formation of the confederacy that was substantially earlier than archaeologists have believed.

I have adopted a narrative style for this book, one that includes anecdotes and personal interactions as critical moments of the Levanna Project. It is an attempt to produce a book that is accessible to general readers, but also to present the data for professionals and specialists. Appealing to different audiences can be a tightrope walk, but I feel it is necessary to tell the story in all its dimensions. I hope this style will appeal to graduate and undergraduate faculty, staff, and students of various social sciences, but also to people in general who are interested in history, archaeology, travel, popular culture, and indigenous rights.

My own journey in archaeology has taken me to many places and time periods. I have left New York state, and suspect that this volume closes my door on New York archaeology. My last five years were spent working and performing collaborative archaeology with Native Hawaiians, including leaders of the sovereignty movement, students, and at-risk youth. The experience reinforced my perspective that archaeology is a powerful tool that can produce either great benefit or harm to Native people but is rarely if ever neutral. In the Hawaiian case, indigenous archaeology is reinforcing pride and combating powerful negative stereotypes about ancient Hawaiians that Native youth have internalized.

Presently I work for the nonprofit History Flight in the Republic of Kiribati in the Central Pacific, where we are recovering MIA servicemen from the World War II Battle of Tarawa (November 20–23, 1943). The work is urgent, sad, and emotional as opposed to the joyous curiosity of New York archaeology and the quiet, humble respect of Hawaiian archaeology. The irony is not lost that as a practitioner of indigenous archaeology I long stood with Native people against the excavation of human remains, and now the task is precisely focused on that goal. In this case the work is necessary, and approval is nearly unanimous. The marines of Tarawa lived brief heroic lives that are largely forgotten. May more of the stories be told.

Jack Rossen
Betio Island, Tarawa Atoll,
Republic of Kiribati
November 17, 2018

ACKNOWLEDGMENTS

The Levanna and Myers Farm excavations included six field seasons and tremendous time in the lab and doing archival research. I am enormously grateful to everyone who helped, and all the friendships and collaborations that are represented. Betty Pangburn drove into the Cayuga-SHARE Farm that fateful spring day in 2007, and Bob Deorio gave me his 1973 notes and a shoebox of sherds from Myers Farm.

No research could occur without the enthusiastic support of the local community and landowners. Homer and Randy St. Clair were the stewards of Levanna, and John and Rebecca Binns took great care of Myers Farm. Hans Pecher, a state representative, was a community liaison and frequent visitor. His invitations to give local presentations built support for the research. Without these folks, there are no sites to investigate and no stories to tell.

The teamwork and perseverance of the field crews has my highest gratitude. We had oppressive heat, unpredictable thunderstorms, and the two rainiest summers in central New York history. The Levanna site was excavated from 2007 to 2009. The 2007 season was a pickup crew of volunteers with a steady core: Brad Benjamin, Laura Harrison, Erica Stupp, and Paula Turkon. The 2008 and 2009 seasons were joint archaeological field schools of Tompkins-Cortland County Community

College (TC3) and Ithaca College (IC). The 2008 crew included Omar Carillo, Elisha Chaffee, Lehman Daste, Abby Dubovi, Jessica Flynn, Christine Gorman, Rebecca Grollman, Corinne Hill, Linda Hindall, Ceren Kabukcu, Emma LeClerc, Katie Reynolds, Miriam Rothenberg, John Sheehan, Donna Silversmith, Zac Sims, Jo Speicher, Samantha Strock, Brant Venables (crew chief), Aleta Weaver, and Emily Zepp. The 2009 crew included Jacob Ahola, Elisha Chaffee (crew chief), Silene Binkerd-Dale, Charles Kahan, Corinne Hill, Shawnee Rice, Donna Silversmith, Michael Spears, Samantha Strock, Zach Sundman, Ken Van Vorce, and Jessica Watson.

The Myers Farm site was excavated for three field seasons as joint TC3-IC field schools. The 2011 crew included Ashley Ahouse, Cristin Carlin, Dan Dawson, Sarah Harris, Emma Heath, Brenda Judge, Macy O'Hearn, Lauren Robin, Michael Spears (crew chief), and Sarah Ward. The 2013 crew included Margaret Carleton, Michael Durfee, Molly Heslin, Jennifer McGough, Macy O'Hearn, Tito Reyes, Kayla Sewell, Donna Silversmith, and Xan Jiggetts-O'Neil. The 2014 crew included Alison Armour, Lydia Bailey, Margaret Carleton, Jensen Hurley, Xan Jiggetts-O'Neil, Macy O'Hearn (crew chief), Jeffrey Olson, Donna Silversmith, and Zachary Thomas-Babineau.

The contributing artifact analysts and specialists are the unsung heroes of this project. The summer of 2016 was special, with my lab filled with IC Dana Interns and a Wells College Intern. Much of the analysis was conducted by dedicated students: Alison Armour, Lydia Bailey, Margaret Carleton, Jensen Hurley, Macy O'Hearn, Sarah Ward, and Shannon LaBelle. Other analysts to be thanked are April M. Beisaw, Jessica Watson, Natalie Mueller, and Erica Bucior. Marissa DeMello drew the face pipes. The University of Denver master's thesis of Nina Rogers on the Levanna ceramics is the anchor of the analyses.

Ithaca College, my home for twenty years, provided the lab, field equipment, numerous paid student lab and field internships, and funds for analysis and radiocarbon dates. Matt Gorney and his students at IC Digital Media Services produced the excavation figures. Michael "Bodhi" Rogers produced the topographic map of Levanna and conducted ground-penetrating radar studies of both sites with his IC students.

ACKNOWLEDGMENTS

Indigenous archaeology depends on great relationships, and I am deeply grateful for the friendship and guidance of Dan Hill (Cayuga, Heron Can), Donna Silversmith (Cayuga, Snipe Clan), Chief Sam George (Cayuga, Bear Clan), Corinne Hill (Oneida), Tony Gonyea (Onondaga, Beaver Clan), Freida Jacques (Onondaga, Turtle Clan), Ada Jacques (Onondaga, Turtle Clan), Chief Irving Powless (Onondaga, Beaver Clan), Peter Jemison (Seneca), Rick Hill (Tuscarora), and Rebecca Hawkins (Cherokee). Tadodaho Sidney Hill, the spiritual leader of the Haudenosaunee Confederacy, has long been a great friend and supporter of the project. The Closet Chickens are always my inspiration on how to conduct collaborative and indigenous archaeology!

Ernie Olson and Linda Schwaub were my friends and contacts at Wells College, and Tina Stavenhagen helped organize the TC3 end of the field schools and to Jonathan Lothrop and John Hart at the New York State Museum. I give special thanks to the permissions to use archival materials: to Kathryn Murano at the Rochester Museum and Science Center, Cinda Nofziger at the Bentley Historical Library, University of Michigan, and Tiffany Raymond at Wells College.

Homer St. Clair graciously allowed his personal archive to be scanned and used. Joel Savishinsky contributed his 1968 photo of Sitsa Codzie of the Hare Tribe stringing stone net sinkers.

Last and most important, I thank my wife, Brooke Hansen. Her love, patience, wit, and cooking keep me going through the hardest of times. Here she provided encouragement, and edits, kept me true to the details of the Cayuga-SHARE Farm, Levanna, and Myers Farm stories she witnessed, and suggested other stories I had omitted.

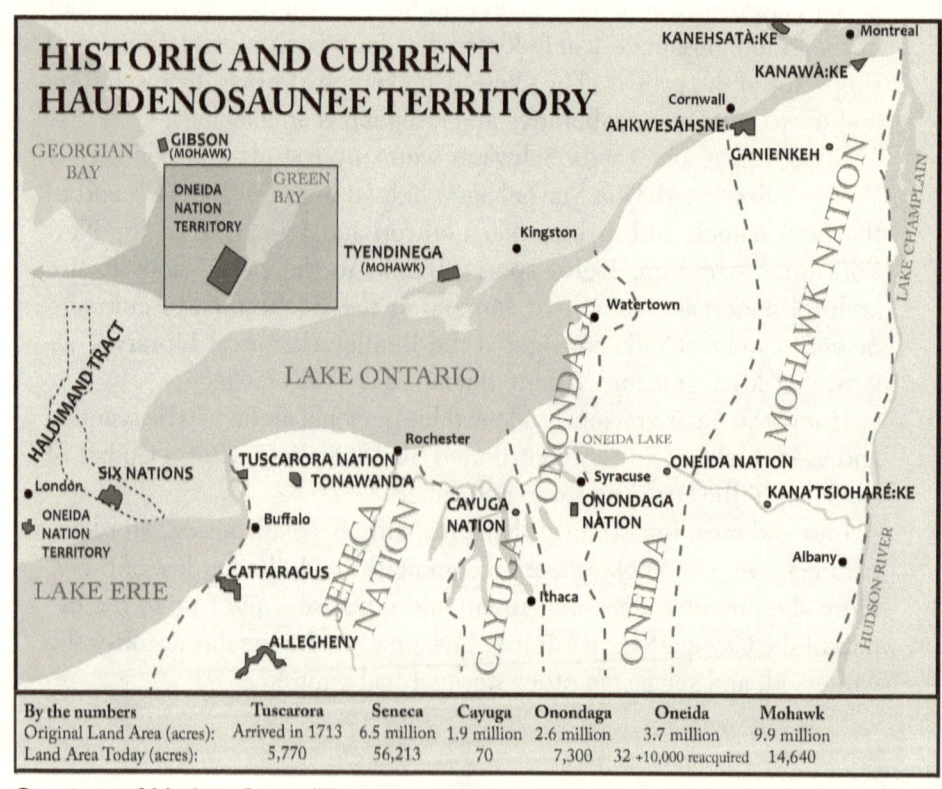

Courtesy of Lindsay Speer/Two Row Wampun Campaign. Honorthetworow.org

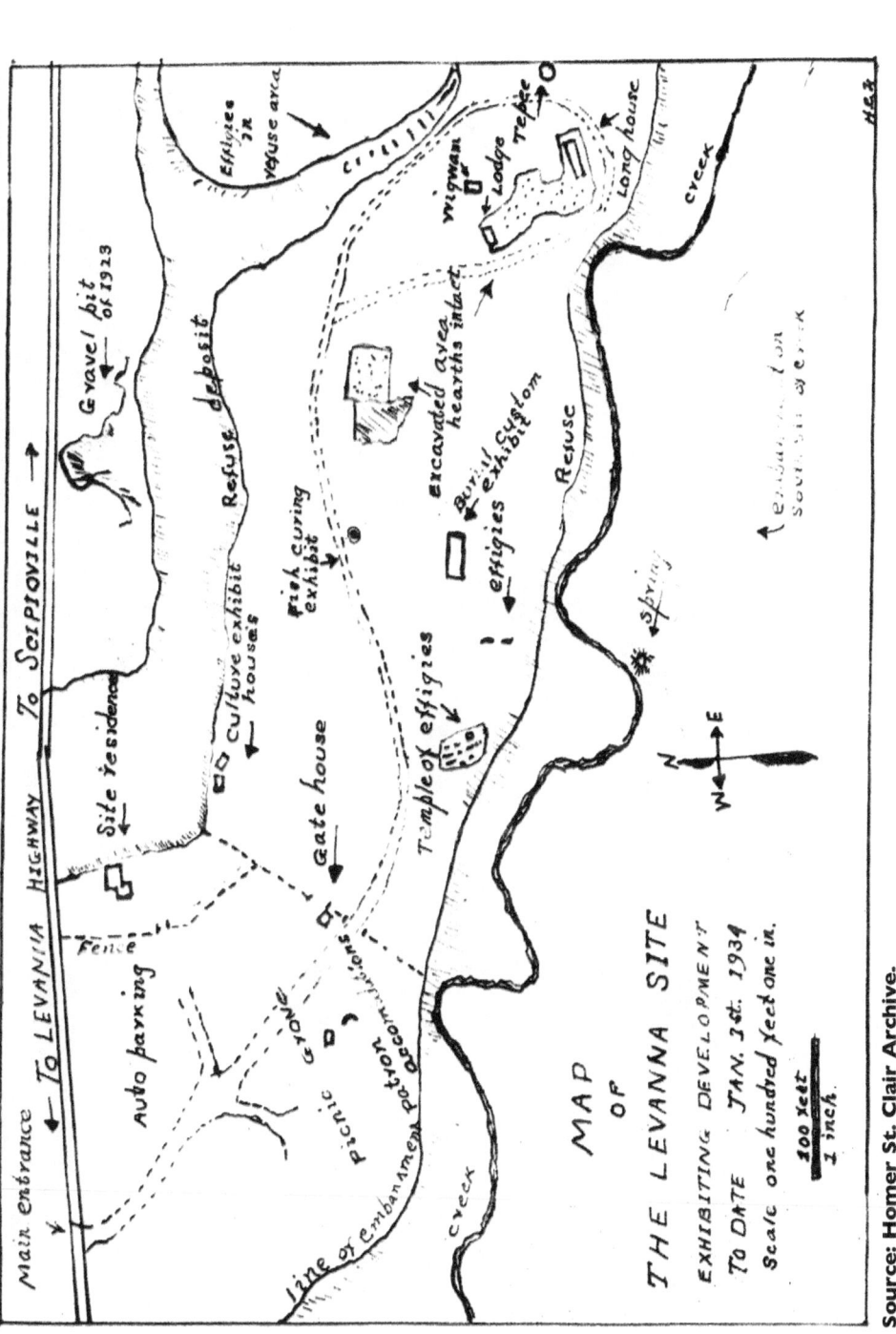

Source: Homer St. Clair Archive.

1

LEVANNA

A Nexus of Stories and Issues

When Betty Pangburn drove into the Cayuga-SHARE Farm driveway in Union Springs, central New York one sunny fall day in 2006, I knew I was in trouble. Betty had just turned ninety, was feeling feisty, and was looking for the Cayuga Indians. She found my wife, Brooke Hansen, first. "When I was a girl, I saw the effigies right over there." She pointed over the woods at the edge of Great Gully to the south toward Levanna. "Someone should look at those." Brooke replied, "You need to talk to my husband; hold on, he's right over there." Betty saw the return of the first Cayuga to the homeland at the Cayuga-SHARE Farm. This was our community project to establish a land base for a people displaced for two hundred years (Hansen and Rossen 2007; Rossen 2006, 2008). Beginning in 2001, the Cayuga-SHARE Farm (Strengthening Haudenosaunee American Relations through Education) was a portal for many projects, including my archaeological research. Betty saw the large stone animal effigies of Levanna as a way for the returning Cayuga to reconnect with their ancient landscape. The effigies had captured her imagination of a lost Native world, and she was in a local minority as a vocal supporter of the Cayuga return. She didn't realize the effigies and Levanna site were long gone and hidden, except for a rusty historic plaque. "You should be digging there," she insisted.

We were doing some routine maintenance work at the Cayuga-SHARE Farm that day, one of many volunteer workdays with our students, helping the Cayuga since we transferred the land to them in December 2005. SHARE was our community organization, founded by local people like Julie and Jim Uticone and academics like myself, Brooke Hansen, and Ernie Olson. We were working in the politically charged atmosphere of the Cayuga Land Claim to educate people about the return of the Cayuga almost two hundred years after their expulsion during and after the Revolutionary War. The seventy-acre organic farm we purchased began as an educational center for events and had just become a homeland foothold for the Cayuga. I had also at that time recently completed excavations at the Corey Village, a sixteenth-century site with strong evidence of medicinal activities, strong enough to suggest that the village was at least partly specialized in healing (Rossen 2015).

Betty was a sweet lady, but I patiently explained that the Levanna site had been mostly dug in the 1920s and '30s and several books stated that the site had been destroyed (Schulenberg 2002, 158). She pushed harder. "That's nonsense. That's where you should be digging." Betty visited the farm many more times, and during the summer of 2007, I conducted test excavations at Levanna to satisfy my curiosity, but mostly to get Betty off my back. It turned out that Betty was right and the books were wrong. Much of the Levanna site was still unusually intact. The Levanna Project turned into three summer field seasons of excavation. It was the jewel of all the sites I investigated in central New York over twenty years of archaeological research there.

Betty's friend Homer St. Clair was the site landowner in 2007, and he remembered the early days of the 1930s Harrison C. Follett excavations. He wooed and married the daughter of Fred Sherman, the landowner when the site was an outdoor museum during the Great Depression. "I wasn't interested much in archaeology. I was interested in other things," Homer told me with a twinkle in his eyes. He showed me the exact locations where the effigies had been and where the old excavations had occurred. One day during the test excavations of 2007, Homer came out of his house with an old red breadbox. "Do you think anyone is interested in this?" His son Randy, who is my age, trailed behind him. "No one is interested in that old stuff, Dad." My heart skipped a few beats when I opened the box and saw the photographs, letters, postcards, and even the original museum guest ledger. This was going to be an extensive archival and ethnohistoric project, too.

The Levanna site, a Native American village in Cayuga County, central New York, was discovered in 1923, during construction of what is now Levanna Road. The site was investigated from 1924 to 1948 and reexcavated by myself from 2007 to 2009. Occupied in the tenth or eleventh century, and then again a second time around AD 1200, it was the location of an outdoor museum from 1932 to 1942. It was an early center for Native cultural expression, with Onondaga and Cayuga holding public dance demonstrations at the site as early as 1932. Investigations were conducted there by the most prominent archaeologists of New York, along with shadowy figures from the fringes and from outside the discipline altogether. In the later investigations of 2007–2009, Levanna became a showcase for efforts in the emerging perspective of indigenous archaeology, a reform movement that places current Native concerns and concepts at the forefront of research and practice. As the new excavations developed, unanticipated issues arose with artifacts (particularly smoking pipes with animals, faces, and figures of Haudenosaunee folklore) that appeared. The site began to have significant implications not only for Cayuga history but also for the origins of the Haudenosaunee Confederacy and present-day Cayuga returning to their homeland.

EARLY INVESTIGATIONS AND ISSUES

Levanna has become a provocative nexus of many major issues that confront all archaeologists and Native Americans. To begin, it is a story of how archaeological sites were treated by researchers in the 1920s and '30s. As the Depression unfolded, Levanna became an outdoor museum, leading to vigorous controversies over the commercialization of science and the authenticity of effigy figures or mosaic stone patterns that were excavated and displayed to the public. Archaeologists labeled the site as "Third Period Algonkian," separating the site and its materials from the present-day Cayuga of the region. This period came to be archaeologically known as "Owasco," after the Lakeside or Owasco site on Owasco Lake in Auburn, New York (Parker 1920). Labels like Owasco became standard in archaeology, providing a wall between past and present Native peoples, an issue that became prominent after the 1990 implementation of cultural affiliation-based repatriation (return of human remains and artifacts to Native tribes) of NAGPRA, the Native American Graves Protection and Repatriation Act.

Other problems with the term Owasco arose through time, based on the chronology of attributes like longhouse architecture, material culture traits, and corn-beans-squash "Three Sisters" plant cultivation. The question was if Owasco really was a unitary cultural phenomenon between AD 900 and 1300, or if Owasco traits emerged at different times in different places (Hart and Brumbach 2003). The earlier question of whether Owasco was Haudenosaunee or Algonquin in linguistic and cultural affiliation, with the term Algonquin implying an in-migration by Iroquoian people and an expulsion of earlier Native peoples, was superseded through time by the notion that infinite cultural variability and numerous migrations and interactions had occurred. This became known as the braided stream, branching tree, or multiscalar model of New York archaeology (Hart and Engelbrecht 2012).

While 1930s archaeologists wrestled with the place of Levanna and its authenticity, Native peoples embraced the location as a showplace for Native culture. The contradictions were numerous, as Onondaga, Seneca, and Cayuga men performed smoke dances alongside the crude and stereotypic displays of a longhouse, wigwams, and human remains. Hollywood actors visited the site to learn how to act in popular western movies. White men posing as Indian chiefs visited the site. At least three site investigators were adopted by the Onondaga or Seneca. Personal conflicts between investigators led to the fracturing of mentor-student relations, exchanges of insults and accusations, a bitter court deposition, and a professional investigation of the authenticity of the site. Even the handling and curation of artifacts were fraught with tension and conflict. Despite an early agreement to house artifacts on site, some were sent by rail to Rochester and others were sold to the National Museum of the American Indian in Washington, D.C. There is evidence that crew members pilfered and sold artifacts, and strong circumstantial evidence that earth ovens and other rock features were enhanced to produce Levanna's famous animal effigies.

Understanding the early archaeology of Levanna requires untangling the knot of stories. How do we make sense of the investigations, cultural labeling, Native involvement, public display, commercialism, and effigy controversy of the era? I will argue that these stories are interrelated and emblematic of major issues that confronted all American archaeology of the 1920s and '30s. They involve the ambiguous and asymmetrical relations between professional archaeologists and amateur collectors, aficionados, Native people, and landowners. These stories also involve the struggle of archaeology to regulate and police itself in order to create and reinforce its legitimacy as a science. Part of this struggle reflected the division between "insider" archaeologists with secure positions at established museums against entrepreneurial "outsider" archaeologists without those advantages. Finally, these early stories speak to the difficulties and developments of public education and Native cultural expression, particularly against the backdrop of the Great Depression. My goal in presenting these stories is to use Levanna as a case study to understand the early twentieth-century growing pains of archaeology and the implications for the present and future of the discipline.

REEXCAVATION OF LEVANNA 2007–2009

The reexcavation of Levanna from 2007 to 2009 brought a different set of issues to the forefront. The newer Levanna Project was a case study in developing indigenous archaeology in New York. Traditional archaeology excluded the interests and wishes of Native people. Arthur C. Parker, one of the first investigators of Levanna, was a Seneca who worked in the margins between museum archaeology and Native culture. However, it was not until the 2000s that a true countermovement known as indigenous archaeology began to develop into a serious minority contingent within the Society for American Archaeology, the professional organization that guides policies, publications, and the national archaeology conference (Watkins 2000). The indigenous archaeology movement involves both Native and non-Native archaeologists such as myself and has become an international phenomenon (Bruchac et al. 2010; Colwell-Chantaphonh and Ferguson 2008; Silliman 2008; Smith and Wobst 2005). It is a multidimensional perspective that values and encourages Native participation and requires the permission and guidance of Native leaders. At its finest, indigenous archaeology shares power with and has positive cultural and practical benefits for Native people. Native excavators such as Donna Silversmith (Cayuga, Snipe Clan) and Corrine Hill (Oneida) were active participants at the new Levanna excavations, while many Haudenosaunee were advisors and guides throughout the research, analysis, and writing.

The new excavations confirmed and debunked aspects of the earlier work. The bear effigy was relocated and investigated. Extensive excavation on both the north and south boundaries of the site failed to produce any evidence of the earlier reported palisade. In general, the site topography previously described as a defensive hilltop could now be described as relatively low-lying and easily accessible from the east and west. A "protolonghouse" consisting of aligned hearths and haphazardly organized posts was excavated, though this structure differs substantially from formally constructed later Haudenosaunee longhouses that are symmetrical with paired posts. The newer excavations were unable to confirm the presence of "lodges" or small round houses of the previous reports.

Rather than label the Levanna site as Algonquin or Owasco, a decision was made that the preponderance of evidence directly linked the site structure and materials to the present-day Cayuga people. A relabeling occurred in referring to the site as Early Cayuga. Artifactually, the new excavations confirmed the known emphasis on fishing. Significantly, modern archaeobotanical analysis shows that corn-based farming was already complementing hunting, fishing, and collecting and management of wild plants by the tenth century. Many smoking pipes (n=270) were recovered with an array of fine designs. Identified to me by Native leaders are Haudenosaunee images of Hado:ih the great healer (a false face image), a flying head, a corn husk person (the little people of Haudenosaunee folklore), a healer wearing a wolf mask, and animals (Canfield 1904; Cusick 2004[1825], 25–26; Johnson 2010[1881]; Schoolcraft 2002[1846], 65–66; for pipe comparisons, see Wonderley 2002, 2005). These can be interpreted as intertribal medicine society pipes, and one pipe stem has a representation of the Tree of Peace, a principle symbol of the Haudenosaunee Confederacy. I was not looking for potential evidence of an early Confederacy, but was thrust into the debate by the emerging archaeological evidence at Levanna.

ORIGINS OF THE HAUDENOSAUNEE CONFEDERACY

The new and unanticipated research path was the potential evidence of an early tenth- or eleventh-century Haudenosaunee Confederacy. There has been substantial discussion and disagreement as to the age and origins of the Confederacy (Bonaparte 2006, 47–52; Fenton 1998, 68–71). The Haudenosaunee themselves have long maintained oral traditions that their Confederacy is more than one thousand years old (Cusick 2004[1825]). In contrast, one argument made by archaeologists is that evidence of smoking trade pipes at the Confederacy edges, between the Seneca to the west and the Mohawk to the east, suggests a functioning Confederacy did not exist before 1650 (Kuhn and Sempowski 2001) or even the 1700s, if it existed at all (Starna 2008). This would make the Confederacy a post-European contact phenomenon.

Can archaeologists find evidence of the age of the Confederacy? What might the emerging Cayuga archaeological record tell us about this controversy? The answer depends on isolating multiple lines of evidence instead of depending on one line such as smoking pipes. Longhouse architecture, the absence of palisades, or other defenses and symbols on artifacts represent other lines of evidence present at Levanna. Since the Confederacy ushered in the Great Peace, it is also important to isolate archaeological attributes or correlates of peacetime versus wartime at both the site and landscape levels.

Levanna was the second of a series of three sites I investigated between 2003 and 2014. As the supposed wartime attributes of Levanna were debunked (by its low-lying position and its lack of a palisade), more attention was brought to the other two sites, a fifteenth-century agricultural station, the Myers Farm site (see chapter 5), and a sixteenth-century village, the Corey Village (Rossen 2015). These sites all failed to express wartime archaeological traits. Indeed the totality of evidence strongly suggests that at least some Haudenosaunee people were living in peaceful conditions from the tenth or sixteenth centuries. The presence of isolated, small, undefended farm stations like Myers Farm in the fifteenth century with its communal feasting contradicts expectations of wartime settlement patterns. As I have previously written, the sixteenth-century Corey site, locally called "the fort," lies on a prominent setting that might be considered defensive with a double earthen embankment and ditch, but only against a steep cliff, while other sides of the site have flat and open access. Close examination of the earthworks and positioning of Corey does not justify its local reputation as a "fort" (Rossen 2015, 180).

ORGANIZATION OF THE BOOK

This book is organized in six chapters. This chapter introduces Levanna as a nexus for various stories and issues regarding the past and present of New York archaeology. Some issues such as representation of Native lifeways and commercialization of archaeology remain through the decades, while some, like the politics of apprenticeship archaeology, fade away and are replaced by interpretive debates about the cultural and regional origins of the Haudenosaunee. Chapter 2 discusses the early archaeological investigations at Levanna from 1923 to World War II, when the site and museum closed. This requires discussion of the cast of characters, personalities and personality conflicts, the details of the effigy controversy, the official investigation, and the activities of Native Americans. In what ways was the Levanna archaeology of that era public or commercial, ethical or immoral, authentic or fraudulent, and intellectually visionary or shortsighted and myopic?

Chapter 3 discusses the intellectual processes of naming, labeling, and renaming surrounding Levanna. This includes the long-standing debate of whether the Haudenosaunee migrated into the region during the first millennium A.D. to displace existing Algonquin tribes, or if they have a long-term, unbroken in situ history of development in what is now New York State. This leads to the debate about the use and implications of the term Owasco as an archaeological time period of about AD 700 to 1300. Archaeologists have recently turned to braided stream, branching tree, and multi-scalar models that emphasize regional cultural variability instead of ethnic and cultural connections with the present-day Haudenosaunee (Hart and Engelbrecht 2012; Miroff and Knapp 2009). In regard to the specific debate of a long-term versus relatively recent Haudenosaunee Confederacy, discussion specifically focuses on how we understand archaeological sites and landscapes as being relatively peaceful or violent and warlike. A key discussion is the use of oral traditions by scholars, particularly in coordination with archaeological information. The final portion of the chapter discusses the reform movement of indigenous archaeology as an attempt to fundamentally change and decolonize the practice, concepts, reporting, and social relations of the venerable discipline. How do indigenous archaeology and the active involvement of Native people refocus interpretations of the past?

Chapter 4 discusses the reinterpretation of the Levanna site, based on the 2007 to 2009 excavations. It is remarkable what can be accomplished by reexcavation of a site thought to have been totally destroyed. Discussed are the newer excavation results in terms of village layout, architecture, and artifacts. Site features like hearths, pits, and posts clarify statements made from the earlier excavations. Analysis results are summarized for a wide variety of artifact types, including ceramics, smoking pipes, chipped stone tools, ground stone, worked bone, fishing gear (net sinkers and hooks), animal bones, and plant remains. The recent excavations and analyses, along with relabeling of the site as "Early Cayuga," lead to a discussion placing Levanna into the Cayuga and Haudenosaunee worlds, with Cayuga referring to a nation and Haudenosaunee referring to the Confederacy the Cayuga belong to, along with the other original member nations (Mohawk, Oneida, Onondaga, and Seneca).

Chapter 5 adds information from excavations of the Myers Farm site. This unusual small site is believed to have been a fifteenth-century agricultural station and communal feasting ground. Though two-hundred fifty years after the later of the two Levanna occupations, the Myers Farm analyzes support and add depth to the Levanna story, particularly in terms of understanding the Cayuga landscape in terms of peaceful interactions.

Chapter 6 considers the lessons from Levanna in terms of the shifting worlds and preoccupations of archaeology and indigenous peoples. How have the parameters of excavation, public display, and ethics changed through time? In what ways is the past reinterpreted by the reinvestigation of the Levanna (and the new investigation of the Myers Farm) site? How do modern analysis techniques, especially faunal and botanical special studies, alter our fundamental understanding of the Cayuga? What were and are the roles of cultural revitalization and the reawakening of Native pride and commitment to their homeland? How does indigenous archaeology, along with a greater appreciation of oral traditions and Native wisdom, affect the way the Levanna past is viewed?

It is proposed that Levanna actually represents a dramatically different past than was previously presented by early investigators. Instead of being Algonquin and non-Haudenosaunee, the new analyses present Levanna as clearly Haudenosaunee, with direct links in architecture, material culture, and symbols. Despite their lack of authenticity, the effigies sparked many people to imagine a lost Native world, but the village must now be reenvisioned without them. Instead of being a wartime palisaded village, the site appears to have been undefended and peaceful. Ethical issues of the past involved commercialization and authenticity, including the strong temptation to sensationalize and alter finds to please the public. Today's ethical issues have shifted to the collaboration with Native people and an emphasis on connections with rather than disconnection between the past and present. Native Americans used the site as an early center of cultural expression, though their activities were set against a stilted and stereotyped backdrop. The Cayuga people were absent from the Cayuga Lake region during the early investigation and museum era, but now are a visible and thriving presence.

2

PULLING DOWN THE PILLARS

Early Investigations at Levanna (1923–1942)

The early investigations at the Levanna site reveal issues that are a microcosm of American archaeology. At its height of public display in the 1930s, Levanna was among the great archaeological attractions in the northeast United States. The cast of characters includes people from all walks of life and various shades of archaeologists: top professionals in the country and state, marginalized mavericks, and amateur opportunists. There were personality clashes, shifting alliances, and bitter emotions, culminating in an official investigation. The site highlighted the controversies of commercialism and tourism, sensationalism and authenticity, and the roles in archaeology of museum professionals, quasiprofessional apprentices, and amateurs. Simultaneously, Native people used, or one could say appropriated, the site as an opportunity for cultural expression and an opportunity to rebuild a nation territory. This chapter attempts to unravel this history and recombine the scattered evidence based on documentary materials.

The archival search for Levanna was as complex as the story itself. The letters of Arthur C. Parker and most of William A. Ritchie's letters, including his court affidavit, are housed at the New York State Museum Archives in Albany, while the correspondence of Harrison C. Follett is split between the Rochester Museum and Science Center and the

Homer St. Clair Archives. The papers of Carter A. Woods and Kerr MacMillan are housed at Wells College Archives in Aurora, New York, only three miles from Levanna. The James B. Griffin Papers are housed at the Bentley Historical Library at the University of Michigan in Ann Arbor. The red breadbox from Homer St. Clair's house held unique items and photos not present in any of the formal archives. As individual archives, each is fragmented and confusing. Only when the pieces from various locations are fit together does a coherent story of Levanna emerge.

CAST OF CHARACTERS IN APPROXIMATE ORDER OF APPEARANCE AT LEVANNA

A brief summary of the personalities of Levanna gives background and depth on the histories of investigations, conflicts, and controversies that follow:

E. H. (Edward) Gohl (1862–1926). A well-known landscape and portrait artist from Auburn, New York, E. H. Gohl had an earnest archaeology collecting interest. He reported several area sites to Arthur C. Parker, including Lakeside (Owasco) and Levanna, often conducting his own ad hoc excavations before Parker arrived. His treatise on "wild westing" discussed the negative effects of Wild West shows on Native people and urged Indians not to participate (Gohl 1914). He was adopted by the Onondaga and awarded the prestigious Cornplanter Medal for Iroquois Research in 1926 (earlier recipients of the award included better-known professionals such as Arthur C. Parker [1916], J. N. B. Hewitt [1914], and William Beauchamp [1906]) (Anonymous 1926; Kelker 1907).

Arthur C. Parker (1881–1955). Parker was a Seneca archaeologist, historian, and folklorist who was trained through the apprentice system at the American Museum of Natural History in New York City under the eminent pioneering archaeologist Frederic Ward Putnam (Colwell-Chantaphonh 2009). Similarly, Harrison C. Follett and William A. Ritchie later became his apprentices. He was the nephew of Ely Parker (1828–1895), who partnered with Lewis Henry Morgan on what is widely considered to be the first anthropological monograph, *League of the Ho-de-no-sau-nee* (Morgan 1851). A. C. Parker was director of the Rochester Municipal Museum during the Levanna period of 1924 to 1945. Biographers have engaged in lively discussion about whether he had an identity conflict between being Seneca and being a professional archaeologist who focused on burial excavation (Colwell-Chanthaphonh 2009; Porter 2001). The 1903 Seneca protests against his burial excavations on the Cattaraugus Reserve are among the earliest documented expressions of Native discontent with archaeology (Colwell-Chanthaphonh 2009, 71–75). His role as the "first indigenous archaeologist" is indeed complex.

Vincent Schaefer (1906–1993). As a teenage companion of Parker at the earliest investigation of Levanna, Schaefer was a young amateur enthusiast of Indian lore and artifacts. He was self-taught and did not complete high school, taking a leave from his machinist apprenticeship at General Electric to work with Parker. His remarkable later accomplishments include being the inventor of cloud seeding and the holder of fourteen patents (Grenander n.d.).

Harrison C. Follett (1872–1954). Follett worked for the Lehigh Valley Railroad, was a local manager for the New York Telephone Company, and was fire chief and mayor of Avon, New York, before apprenticing with Arthur C. Parker (Anonymous 1954a, 1954b; DeOrio 1999). He is the central figure of the triumphs and controversies of the early Levanna investigations: the director of a small group of excavators and the mastermind behind the outdoor museum. He often carried on work alone at the site well into and even through the winter. Many considered Follett to be the last "semiprofessional" archaeologist in New York state, admired by avocational archaeologists searching for greater respect. Avocational archaeologist Robert DeOrio, who collected sites primarily in the 1970s, believes that "Follett never received the acknowledgement and recognition commensurate to his contributions" (DeOrio 1999, 1). Follett was adopted at Levanna by the Onondaga in August 1940 and given the name Ga-hosh-shan-do or "Councilor." His handwritten, unpublished manuscripts on Levanna are a treasure trove of research details, personal troubles with locals, conflicts with other archaeologists, and bitter defense of his impugned integrity. Over five hundred pages of these notes were posthumously condensed and edited, removing "all biographical and personal notes, much controversial material, and a great deal of details on the setting up of the outdoor museum" (Grifone 1957). The result was seven pages long (Follett 1957).

William A. Ritchie (1903–1995). Ritchie was young and inexperienced in his first archaeological field experience at Levanna in 1927. He continued to work there for some time in the early 1930s with Follett, but left the project and a bitter feud developed. According to one source, A. C. Parker divided the excavators into two competing crews to maximize the search for burials (DeOrio 1999, 7). Ritchie swore an affidavit in 1933 and pushed for the investigation against Follett, preventing Levanna from being included in the legitimate archaeological literature of New York. He subsequently served as state archaeologist of New York from 1949 to 1972, conducted more than one hundred excavations, and wrote what is still considered to be the fundamental text on New York archaeology (Ritchie 1981).

No one doing archaeology in the northeast U.S. can avoid tracing the ubiquitous footsteps of Ritchie. I had my archaeological field school on Martha's Vineyard, Massachusetts, where he set the culture history and paradigms (Ritchie 1969). I later worked for the State of Vermont in the Otter Valley of Addison County, where most of the sites I visited had been recorded with Ritchie's chicken-scratch writing on piles of site forms (Rossen 2016). It thus somehow seems natural that I would wind up in central New York at Levanna.

David Sands Titus III (1881–1949). Titus was an unemployed jewelry engraver when he befriended Harrison Follett in the fall of 1932. Follett employed him for the dig, describing him as "eager to do some excavating" (Follett n.d.a., 10, 14). He later sold Levanna artifacts to the National Museum of the American Indian under unclear circumstances.

Harry L. Schoff (1905–1965). A garage and blacksmith shop owner with a lifelong interest in Indians and artifacts, Schoff became a WPA archaeological project director during the Depression and

Figure 2.1a. Levanna postcard, side A. Homer St. Clair Archive.

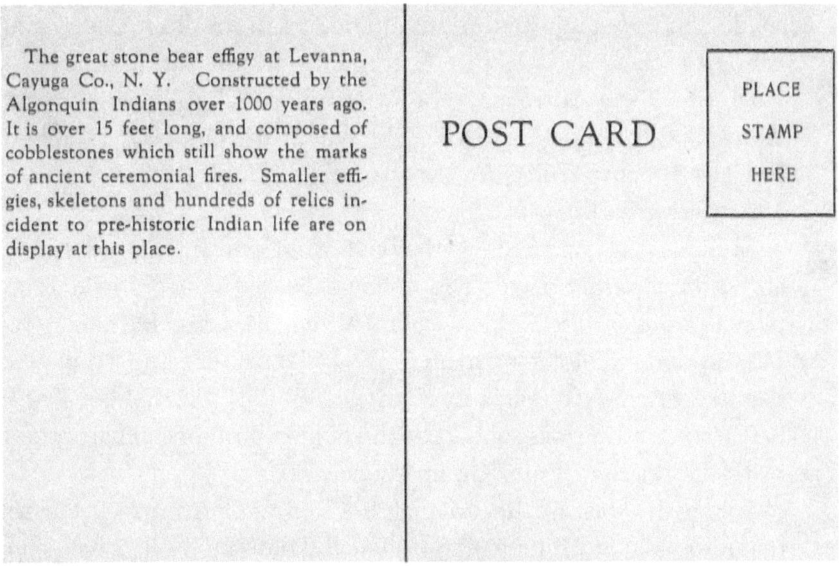

The great stone bear effigy at Levanna, Cayuga Co., N. Y. Constructed by the Algonquin Indians over 1000 years ago. It is over 15 feet long, and composed of cobblestones which still show the marks of ancient ceremonial fires. Smaller effigies, skeletons and hundreds of relics incident to pre-historic Indian life are on display at this place.

POST CARD

PLACE STAMP HERE

Figure 2.1b. Levanna postcard, side B. Homer St. Clair Archive.

conducted excavations in New York, Pennsylvania, Georgia, and Florida (Schoff 1937, 1938, n.d.a, n.d.b; Jeffrey M. Mitchum, personal communication 2010). He came to attention in regard to Levanna as the photographer of the bear effigy postcard (figure 2.1) and probable executor of the fraudulent effigies, perhaps with George B. Selden Jr. He was adopted by the Seneca in 1946 and reportedly given the Indian name "Hud-Goh-So-Do-Neh" or "He Who Hunts and Looks Everywhere as He Travels."

George B. Selden Jr. (1887–1973). Selden Jr. was the youngest child of George B. Selden (1846–1922), a lawyer and inventor who famously patented a light version of the internal combustion engine in 1895. The Selden cars caused a sensation in New York City (Anonymous 1916). During a lengthy lawsuit brought by Henry Ford, plus a series of countersuits, the patent was upheld but finally overturned on appeal in 1911. By then, Selden had made about two hundred thousand dollars in royalties, aside from car sales (Barnes 1981, 14). The Selden Motor Car Company of Rochester, New York, made between 800 and 1,600 cars per year from 1906 to 1914. During World War I, the company switched to Class B heavy trucks for the war effort (Flink 1990; Greenleaf 1961; Stevens 1993).

Much less is known about the well-off Selden Jr. who excavated at Levanna with Follett. The teenage Selden appears in a 1905 photo posing in the Selden car in New York City (Barnes 1981, 10). Selden Jr. along with his brother Henry became employee engineers of the car company (Barnes 1981, 23). The Selden Truck Sales Corporation was sold off by the Selden brothers and absorbed by the Bethlehem Truck Company in 1930.

Selden Jr. was on the original 1927 crew of Arthur C. Parker that also included Ritchie and Follett. By the time Follett had split from Parker and Ritchie and took over at Levanna, Selden Jr. had made his fortune and his company was gone—so he may have been looking for new adventures. William A. Ritchie swore his New York State Court affidavit against Selden Jr. in 1932, accusing him of proposing to reshape the stone heaps at Levanna into animal effigies and other fraudulent activities.

Carter A. Woods (1907–1995). A sociology professor at nearby Wells College in Aurora, New York, for forty-one years (1931–1972), Woods was best known for his theoretical and critical work on culture areas of Native North America (Dieckmann 1995; Woods 1934). He closely observed the Levanna excavations of Follett, and his writings provide unique insights into the history of the controversies and conflicts (Woods and Follett n.d.). Woods was the first author with Follett on at least two unpublished manuscripts, including one for the journal *New York State History* that was blocked on review by Arthur C. Parker. During the prolonged animal effigy crisis, Woods vigorously defended Follett to the bitter end.

Kerr D. MacMillan (1871–1938). MacMillan was the longest tenured president of nearby Wells College (1913–1936). He financially supported the Harrison C. Follett excavations and defended him during the controversies. According to his biography, "He was cautious and slow to take action but was devoted to truth and demanded perfect honesty. A strong and strict man, he had upright moral principles and a decidedly patriarchal view of his college family" (Dieckmann 1995).

Carl E. Guthe (1893–1974). Guthe was a pioneer of American archaeology. He was the first archaeologist hired at the University of Michigan, his alma mater, and director of its Museum of Anthropology. He later was director of the New York State Museum in 1944. He is credited with creating the Society for American Archaeology and its journal, *American Antiquity* (Griffin and Jones 1976). Guthe administered the 1933–1936 investigations into the legitimacy of Levanna and sent investigators, including James B. Griffin, to the site.

James B. Griffin (1905–1997). Among the most distinguished and influential archaeologists of the twentieth century, Griffin was renowned for his work on Hopewell (tribal) and later Mississippian (chiefdom) mound builder cultures of the Mississippi and Ohio Valleys (Griffin 1943, 1952). He was the definer and authority on the Fort Ancient people who lived on the fringes of the great Mississippian chiefdoms. Griffin entered the Levanna story early in his career as a favorite of the older archaeologists and as the designated investigator of the site effigies (he also investigated the related Spanish Hill site). I knew Griffin in my graduate student days as the ever-present, imposing, but kindly man in the front row at every conference. I met and drank beers with him at a conference in 1983. I was a boring companion then, but oh, what questions I would have for him now!

There are others who could be included in this list, but the present cast of characters will suffice to tell the stories of investigation, intrigue, and interpretation of the past at Levanna.

DISCOVERY OF THE LEVANNA SITE

The area surrounding Levanna was devastated by the Sullivan-Clinton Campaign of 1779. As the Revolutionary War ground on and the US Continental Army established the upper hand in military operations, George Washington sent nearly one-third of the army to destroy the Haudenosaunee Confederacy. This scorched earth expedition included the burning of at least forty-three settlements and the destruction of crop fields (Cook 2000 [1887]).

The William Butler detachment of the campaign peeled off from the main force to the west in Seneca territory and burned the Cayuga settlements in the Levanna area, forcing most people to flee northwest to Niagara and Canada while remnant groups stayed behind. Oral traditions include a dramatic recounting of Cayuga women and children hiding in Great Gully (near present-day Union Springs) as soldiers burned the nearby village of Chonodote, known as Peachtown to the Americans, and destroyed a 1,500–peach tree orchard. The Cayuga were spared because their screams echoed off the gorge walls, leading the American soldiers to believe there were warriors threatening ambush. The Great Gully is thus credited with saving the Cayuga people (Tobin 2002). Despite a dominant narrative that the Cayuga were punished for supporting the British during the American Revolution, documents suggest that the Cayuga were primarily neutral, though some may have fought with both sides (Mann 2005, 14, 102–4; Rossen 2015, 199–201). The final Cayuga group left in 1805 when the United States annexed its remaining territory, an act that was contested and legally refuted during the 1980–2005 Cayuga Land Claim (Whiteley 2000).

White settlers arrived nearby and founded the Village of Aurora by 1793, when the Levanna Road was still just an Indian trail between Cayuga and Owasco Lakes (Follett n.d.a., 3, Homer St. Clair Archive). The immediate area of Levanna was not resettled until about 1802. The Levanna archaeological site was discovered during the 1923 removal of gravel, which disturbed seven burials, apparently without artifacts (Follett n.d.a., 3; Ritchie 1928, 6). Edward H. Gohl reported the site to Arthur C. Parker. Harrison Follett wrote that Fred Sherman, the landowner, reinterred the skeletons, but "Mr. Gohl succeeded in finding them" (Follett n.d.a., 3). Gohl was able to define the village site and had "done some puddling in the dump refuse, and had Mr. Sherman plow a few furrows over the top of the site" (Follett n.d.a., 3). The Levanna village was immediately recognized as a rare example of an unplowed site in New York. Cultivation began in fields to the south of the site in 1920 and "the site on the knoll . . . had always been maintained as a wood-lot and cattle pasture which accounts for the nondiscovery prior to this late date of the former occupation by Indians" (Follett n.d.a., 3). In 1923, Arthur C. Parker, accompanied by his wife Anne and Vincent Schaefer, conducted small excavations at the western end of the site.

Parker returned in 1927, along with William A. Ritchie, his brother Donald Ritchie, George B. Selden Jr., and Follett. These excavations were published by William A. Ritchie (1928) in a pamphlet of less than twelve pages of text. He described Levanna as a fishing village with no agriculture, extensive middens, and many post molds that were thought to represent twenty-two small circular lodges. A bed of broken fire-cracked stones was hypothesized to be part of a sweat lodge, and specifically not an effigy or "fancied resemblance to the figure of some animal form . . . this seems unwarranted from critical facts" (Follett n.d.a., 15, figures 2.1 and 2.2). Ritchie described the decorated ceramics and a specific style of projectiles that were to be named Levanna points, bone tools, smoking pipes with fine stamped decorations, fish net sinkers, but only sparse animal bones, indicating limited hunting. Ritchie followed Parker's definition of the site as Third Period Algonkian, a term to be discussed in chapter 3. Based on the six burials discovered at the site, he estimated the village population at two hundred inhabitants for one

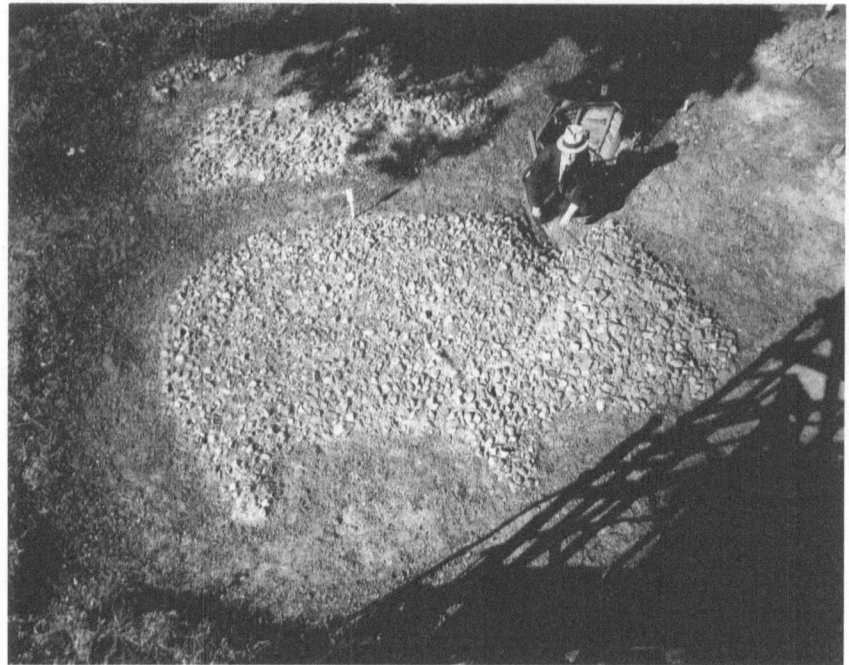

Figure 2.2. Harrison C. Follett with the bear effigy, ca. 1932. Homer St. Clair Archive.

year or fifty shifting inhabitants for four years (Ritchie 1928, 27). No palisade was mentioned, though Ritchie viewed the site as being in a defensive location.

Tensions between Follett and Ritchie date back to their days working together at the Rochester Municipal Museum. Follett writes that he resigned the museum in 1931 because "Ritchie had become so annoying" and jealous. He returned to the museum, only to be laid off as the Depression deepened (Follett 1952, 24–25, handwritten version). Ritchie's monograph on the 1927 Levanna excavations so riled Follett that he wrote a detailed paragraph-by-paragraph critique (Follett 1952, 1–6, typed version). Ritchie returned to Levanna briefly to work with Follett, but left after various squabbles. Follett's notes graphically refer to various arguments about Ritchie's refusal to chop firewood, scaring the neighbor's cattle by shooting at crows, and personal hygiene in the tent:

> A laterine (sic) was established in a wild grape arbor distant a few rods from the tent, but Bill refused its use at night unless Donald accompanied him with a light. It so happened late one evening after Don had returned

that Bill suddenly discovered the urgent call of nature and proposed Don to escort him, which he refused to do and Bill proceeded to utilize a place at the corner of the tent. This act just about resulted in a near midnight riot when he was threatened with by no friendly words to immediately make use of a shovel to obliterate the excretion. (Follett, Vol. 1 handwritten manuscript, Homer St. Clair Archive)

Homer St. Clair also told me this story, along with a story not in the manuscripts that Ritchie had shipped artifacts to Rochester, breaking Follett's agreement with Fred Sherman, the landowner, to keep all artifacts on site. Homer stated that Sherman's cousin worked in the railroad station and reported the breach to Sherman. It is clear from the range of disputes that Ritchie thought of Follett as an untrained amateur while Follett viewed Ritchie as inexperienced and ill-equipped for the rigors of fieldwork. The effigies were uncovered in 1932 after Ritchie left and Follett assumed directorship of the excavations. According to Follett:

> While excavating around the south end which is shown in Mr. Ritchie's drawing as being straight and even across. The southernmost point, in my intention to cut down low enough to have the figure show well in relief it was necessary to excavate several inches deeper than the 1927 trench, therefore the nose was discovered at a greater depth as it naturally dipped down . . . the figure is 17 feet long and nine feet wide (at the) greatest points. . . . The soil which we removed from the bear and the surrounding area was piled up on the east side as a temporary movement upon completion of uncovering the bear this pile of dirt was shoveled over to the south and east and in so doing discovered the figure called the panther, lying parallel to the bear, back to back and 18 inches therefrom, this figure is nine feet in length and five feet at its greatest distance . . . its head is perfect in catlike form the back apparently hunched up in a crouching or springing position . . . the discovery of these figures led us to believe there might be more in the immediate vicinity, therefore the area south of the bear and panther was tested and several beds of stone of the same character as those in the bear and panther was found to exist, then the entire area was relieved of sod and wherever stone was contacted they were carefully exposed and their exact forms left in-tact. (Follett n.d.a., 5, Homer St. Clair Archive)

Follett continued to describe effigies of a "crescent head," a symmetrical bird-like figure with a square body, a bird in flight, another large

Figure 2.3. Salamander effigy, *Syracuse Herald,* **August 23, 1933. Homer St. Clair Archive.**

square figure, a salamander, four crescent-shaped objects he equated with moon phases, a "thunderbird with an eagle-shaped head and outstretched wing," plus another centralized bed of stone he called "the alter" (figure 2.3). All figures were made of fire-cracked rocks smaller than six inches in size. It was noted that large tree roots covered the top portions of some figures and even carried stones up in the tree growth, demonstrating that the stones were not placed recently (Follett n.d.a., 7–9, Homer St. Clair Archive).

> This group of figures forms what we term a temple for some sort of ceremonies. It certainly cannot be in any form a sweat lodge, the arrangement in position the forms and the last figure discovered the thunderbird shows without a question of doubt to anyone with an ordinary degree of intelligence some deliberate intent of the indians in their construction.

Follett's explanation for ceremonialism at the site was an ancient plea for supernatural help in a time of population pressure, resource depletion, food scarcity, and warfare:

> The peoples who inhabited the site had lived here many years increased considerable in population, which require an extraordinary amount of food to supply them. As the demand for food increased and the supply from near by points gradually depleted they became alarmed. In their latter days here they were undoubtedly in fear to make their usual trips to the lake for a supply of fish, owing to the increase in traffic of the enemy upon the lake which was a natural route of travel from the extreme south to the Hudson bay country, this fear is substantiated by their having erected a stockade for protection against marauding enemy tribes. (Follett n.d., 8, Rochester Museum and Science Center Archives)

> That at some time they had been molested is evident by the finding of canabalism (sic) to a small extent in the refuse of the west portion. This prompted the erection of the stockade, and the congregation of all the peoples within the entire stockade section. This also made their trips to the lake for fishing almost prohibitive forcing them to rely on game as a food supply that may to a great extent account for the bear effigy and our theory in connection with it. (Follett 1952, 25, typed version, Homer St. Clair Archive)

The effigies were thus thought to have provided supernatural protection:

> The bird-like figure headed west is supposed to be a message bearer. The thunderbird protecting the group of figures from destruction and also keeping the enemy away from their village to the east, this theory is evidenced by the bird being headed north by east and toward the trail that must be passed near by as an entrance and egress to and from the village. (Follett n.d.a, 9)

Follett was immediately aware of the uniqueness of the effigy claims, realizing they would be challenged. He therefore left unexcavated one figure that came to be known as the thunderbird, with a plan to publicly uncover it. By this time, Follett and Parker were no longer in direct contact:

> A date in Sept. was therefore decided on and an invitation issued especially to Dr. Parker, of Rochester Museum . . . through Mr. Richard

Drummond of Auburn. The public were invited through published notices in all the vicinity papers which was copied by many long distance and far reaching mediums. Dr. Parker failed to come or any of his constituents in so far as is known. Among prominent people present who all signed a document attesting to the form as it was disclosed, are Dr. Bates of Cornell University. President of Oxford College, and his family. Others from N.J. Dr. Woods from Wells College, Mr. Burke Drummond from Auburn. The owner of the property and his family, and a number of local people. Dr. Bates, Dr. Woods, and Mr. Richard Drummond stood over the figure and supervised every move that was made leaving no question whatever that the form exposed is exactly as it was found. As a special request the soil was tested for some distance around the figure to show that there were no other such stone in connection with it. (Follett n.d.c.)

THE OUTDOOR MUSEUM

The discovery and excavation of the stone effigies coincided with the development of Levanna into an outdoor museum (figure 2.4). The Great Depression hit New York museum budgets and staffing hard, and Follett was laid off in 1931. The Levanna Museum was designed to "help defray expenses while we were making excavations" (Follett n.d.a, 1). Exhibits opened in May 1934, and included pole frame reconstructions of a teepee and longhouse, a "culture house" to exhibit artifacts, and exhibits of human remains, including both skulls on shelves and open burials. Follett discussed arranging the open skeletons into various types (flexed, extended, bundle, disarticulated), highlighting deformities and injuries, and including at least one skull from the Lamoka Lake site (Follett n.d.a, 40–41). A reconstructed palisade wound through the site (figure 2.5).

Always, the star attractions were the animal effigies of broken fire-cracked rock. The opening admission charge was fifteen cents per adult, with children free, and this soon was raised to twenty-five cents (equal in value to about $4.25 in 2018 terms). Fred Sherman, the landowner, received one-third the receipts at first and later one-half. According to Follett, the first season "proved a grand success, except from a compensation point of view, due principally to short season and bad weather."

Figure 2.4a. Levanna outdoor museum entrance, ca. 1932. Homer St. Clair Archive.

Figure 2.4b. Culture building. Homer St. Clair Archive.

Figure 2.4c. Temple of Effigies. Homer St. Clair Archive.

Figure 2.4d. Harrison C. Follett. Homer St. Clair Archive.

Figure 2.5. Purported palisade of Levanna, ca. 1932. Homer St. Clair Archive.

In addition to this income, Wells College, under President Kerr MacMillan, contributed fifteen dollars a month ($225 in 2018 terms) to the site excavations.

Follett was a tireless promoter of the Levanna outdoor museum. The Homer St. Clair Archive brims with dozens of undated newspaper clippings of Follett's talks and demonstrations. He spoke at numerous meetings of Rotary Clubs, scout troops, Daughters of the American Revolution, church groups, and county historical societies. Robert DeOrio tallied 129 such events (DeOrio 1999). At the site, there were "archaeological field days," "gala days," "pilgrimages," "wilderness days," and "open house days." These events included speakers and "excavation demonstrations." Organized trips from scout camps and church vacation groups brought large groups of visitors. The 1940 adoption ceremony for Follett held at Levanna was reportedly attended by five hundred paying spectators (not recorded in the ledger).

The Levanna guest ledger was included in the Homer St. Clair Archive. Jensen Hurley conducted a detailed study of the ledger as a summer student intern at Ithaca College. The ledger covers the years

1934 to 1942, with the exception of 1938, and records 8,069 visitors. Follett himself estimated that twelve thousand people had visited Levanna, which is possible given the missing year of records and the known incompleteness of recording, for example, of special events attendees. Most guests arrived from local towns such as Auburn (n=1288) and Ithaca (n=652), but there are also records of individuals visiting from eighteen other states and sixteen foreign countries (see textbox below). The peak years of attendance were 1934 (n=1,640) and 1936 (n=1,635). Many fewer visitors were recorded in 1942, the last year of operation (n=209), and 1940 (n=747). The average recorded number of visitors per year was 897. Daily attendance at the height of popularity was as high as forty people per day. After New York (n=6,637), the most represented states are Pennsylvania (n=282) and New Jersey (n=199). Visitors to the Levanna site were thus heavily regional, which is logical considering its isolated location. The visitors from other states and foreign countries attest to a certain broader level of fame for the museum.

Summary of the Levanna Museum Guest Ledger

Years on record: 1934–1942
8,069 guests on record
Biggest years: 1934 (1,640), 1936 (1,635), 1937 (1,223)
Smallest years: 1942 (209), 1940 (747)
Average distance traveled: 143 miles
Average number of guests per year: 897
Max. range: Cebu, Philippines (8,554 miles)
Min. range: Barber's Corners, NY (.5 miles)
Most highly represented towns/cities: Auburn (1,288 guests), Ithaca (652 guests)
Most highly represented states: NY (6637), PA (282), NJ (199)
16 countries represented
60 people from 15 foreign countries

NOTABLE VISITORS TO LEVANNA

Levanna attracted the rich and famous along with the aspiring rich and famous and other odd characters. Perhaps the most notable visitors were

Douglas Fairbanks Sr. and Mary Pickford, who signed the guest ledger as Mary P. Fairbanks on August 15, 1934, despite a reported separation in 1933 and an impending 1935 divorce (Katchmer 1991, 109, figure 2.6a). They were iconic actors of the silent film era, as well as founding members of the United Artists Studio and the Motion Picture Academy. When they married in 1920, it was said that "everybody's hero married everybody's sweetheart." Among Fairbanks' many performances was a series of more than ten of the earliest western films (Katchmer 1991, 307; Tibbetts and Welsh 2014). Fairbanks played swashbuckling "hardy cowboys, city dudes, outlaws and lawmen, equally at home spurring horses atop Arizona mesas and galloping down Manhattan streets" (Tibbetts 2011, 42). Fairbanks changed the western cowboy character in what has been termed a "Progressive Era" of relatively sympathetic films. Fairbanks "wanted to go on location with Indians . . . (he) embodies all the contradictions and ambivalences of his Westerns" (Katchmer 1991, 109; Tibbetts 2011, 45, 48). Among Pickford's 194 films, she appeared in twenty-nine westerns.

Homer St. Clair remembered the visit of Fairbanks and Pickford to Levanna, telling me that Hollywood had sent them to learn more about Indians for the new talking westerns. However, neither Fairbanks nor Pickford made a successful transition to sound movies after the silent film era ended in 1929. Their careers and indeed marriage were on the wane when they turned up at Levanna, and Fairbanks would be dead in five years.

Chief Ho-To-Pi visited Levanna, was photographed in full regalia, and signed the guest ledger on August 16, 1936 (figure 2.6b). Supposedly an Oklahoma-born Cheyenne chief, Ho-To-Pi was a tenor who studied voice and piano in America and Milan, Italy. He performed numerous concerts "throughout both hemispheres" including church benefits for building funds ("Indian Tenor to Sing for Church Benefit" 1948). At Levanna, he performed "sunset" and "mating" songs, and intoned:

> You want a juicy steak to eat. I will eat a crust of bread and be happy if only there be understanding between us. . . . O Thou eternal mystery behind the sun, guide and protect us this day. . . . You see me put on this headband and are afraid: from your child-books you have learned that feathers mean war. We have never wanted war, only the right to hunt and live in peace. Each feather has a meaning; I do not wear them for show;

through the years I have earned the right to wear them. May good luck and friendship be yours, and may our peoples know each other better. (undated newspaper clipping, Homer St. Clair Archive)

When the chief died in 1973, his true identity emerged, carried in his wallet. He was George Citrulis from Athens, Greece. He was able to pass himself off as an Indian chief successfully for decades because of his dark features, and because of the "feather bonnet tribe" stereotype that homogenized all American Indians (Kleinberg 2010). His presence at Levanna, where forged exhibits of the Native past were displayed, is a double dose of irony. The episode continued a long history of white men "playing Indian" (Deloria 1998) and is particularly reminiscent of subsequent Indian impersonators like Iron Eyes Cody (1904–1999). An Italian-American actor who concealed and denied his true identity, Cody, whose real name was Espera Oscar de Corti, portrayed Indians in more than two hundred films. He became most famous as "the crying Indian" seen by millions in a 1971 "Keep America Beautiful" public service announcement (Waldman 1999; Yamada 2014; for a general history, see Bird 1996).

The Big Swede, from Gillette, Wyoming, signed the Levanna guest ledger on June 25, 1939. In Wyoming, tie hacks or skilled laborers who cut timber to produce railroad ties were nicknamed "Swedes." Tie hacks were part of the colorful lore of the Old West, so we should not be surprised that at least one would turn up at Levanna. Gillette is famous for its tales of the Tongue River Tie Flume, where two men were left alone during the winter of 1912–1913 to tend a railroad camp. One, "the Big Swede," murdered the other and disappeared (Dobson 2015). This event occurred near the height of the American railroad, 1916, when a quarter of a million miles of tracks were in service and maintenance (Bradbury 2005).

Perhaps most interesting was the presence of Native people traveling long hours to Levanna to perform dances. Delegations of Cayuga, Onondaga, and Seneca adopted Levanna as a location of cultural expression. Combined Onondaga and Cayuga dance groups were organized by Cayuga and Onondaga chiefs Jesse Lyon, Ulysses Pierce, Isaac Lyons, Jak Seneca, Reynolds Homer, Oren Lyons (Sr.), and Theodore Talmadge. From the Seneca Cattaraugus Reservation, Clinton Rickard and Joe

Figure 2.6a. Douglas Fairbanks Sr. and Mary Pickford at Levanna, August 15, 1934. Homer St. Clair Archive.

Figure 2.6b. Chief Ho-To-Pi at Levanna, August 16, 1936. Homer St. Clair Archive.

Figure 2.7. Oren Lyons Sr., Nick Thomas, and Percy Smoke at Levanna, August 20, 1936. Homer St. Clair Archive (Follett n.d.c.).

Hemlock led a dance group. Oren Lyons Jr. was surprised and speechless when I presented him with a copy of the photo of his father, Oren Lyons, at Levanna that he had never before seen. He also identified Onondaga dancers Nick Thomas and Percy Smoke in the photo (figure 2.7).

Dancing at Levanna served as a platform for the Cayuga desire to establish a repatriated reservation along the eastern shore of Cayuga Lake. According to an August 21, 1936, newspaper clipping in the Homer St. Clair Archive, "Although a meeting was held after the ceremonial, no action was taken providing for a reservation for the Cayugas, now living in the Cattaraugus Reservation. The Cayugas toured the Finger Lakes region Saturday, supposedly looking for a suitable site" (also see Anonymous 1939).

THE EFFIGIES CONTROVERSY

On March 7, 1933, William A. Ritchie swore an affidavit discussing the reshaping of stone platforms into animal forms or effigies by George Selden, one of Follett's co-workers at Levanna:

> Selden proposed to uncover a certain stone heap which was known to this deponent and to said Selden to have been previously discovered; that said Selden thereafter intended to reshape the heap into the effigy of a bear;

that said Selden further proposed to place certain previously excavated skeletons and artifacts in the adjoining ground and to re-excavate the same . . . that said Selden proposed to announce said skeletons, artifacts and stone heap as new, genuine and original discoveries of said Selden and exhibit the same for financial profit . . . said Selden further stated to this deponent that he desired the deponent to join with him in the said enterprise and asked this deponent to obtain and contribute thereto such skeletal remains, artifacts and other relics as deponent could gather together for the said alleged purpose of burial and re-excavation. (New York State Museum Archives)

In December 1933, Arthur C. Parker was asked to review a manuscript by Follett and Woods for the journal *New York State History*. In a letter to Peter Nelson, the editor, Parker, wrote:

the cloud of suspicion still hovers heavy. Fire beds of broken stone have been found in numerous locations and have even been exposed by the wind and not found to be effigies. However, from a chance heap with extensions from the main deposit, almost any animal can be imagined from amoeba to man. It is all as the imagination is kindled. . . . In my very humble opinion the paper appears like the ingenious, but not too ingenious, attempt of an amateur to present a paper that looks learned but lacks the essential quality of scientific endeavor. I should be very happy if I could believe the statements presented in the Woods-Follett paper . . . if we could actually give credence to Mr. Follett's commercial venture we should feel we had accomplished something. Under the circumstances, however, I must always have grave doubts, even with so able a man as Mr. Woods, Lawyer Drummond and President MacMillan standing by. A clever field man could fool them all. (New York State Museum Archives)

On August 10, 1934, Richard Drummond, the lawyer referred to in the previous quote, wrote to Noah Clarke, then the New York State geologist:

unquestionably we have here an antiquity of great interest and of great scientific value . . . we do feel that we are entitled to ask our own state authorities to regard our effort sympathetically, and at least look at what we have and give us the benefit of advice. Our sacrifices justify this. We have gone about this work very carefully. We have spent some money, and goodness knows that our ideals and ambitions are worthy enough. . . . I am extremely anxious . . . to have you see what there is here and to give us the benefit of your advice and suggestions. Could you come? (New York State Museum Archives)

Parker wrote to Clarke on August 20, 1934:

I have the first photographs of the first appearance and my own eyes are evidence enough. . . . Sometime a fakir (sic) fakes himself to fame and then rests good and meek thereafter, or until another chance be taken. In the meantime it is hard to unscramble the true from the false. (New York State Museum Archives)

Drummond, on behalf of Follett, continued to request an impartial investigation of the effigies. In an October, 24, 1934, follow-up letter to Clarke, Parker continued:

The attitude of the Cayuga group is plainly one on the defensive. I am making no campaign against them and spreading no information not asked for, and I am surely entitled to my opinion and an expression of what I know to be true. Whether any one believes me concerns me not the least. I care not whether any one believes my excavations are genuine or not. Facts speak for themselves and the future will clear the true from the false.

As for an investigation, I have sought to warn Dr. MacMillan, and do it kindly. He prefers to believe Mr. Follett. If he prefers not to believe me, that is his concern, for I have discharged my full duty with good conscience, though it has proven unpleasant for me. It is a matter, as you say, of whom to believe. I certainly will not enter into any discussion to prove that I am honest as compared with Mr. Follett. In my own mind I am satisfied as to the status of Levanna, and how much truth is mixed with falsification. That is my concern and if certain gentlemen desire to believe what I do not believe they may do so.

The unpleasant fact remains, however, that from my standpoint, certain basic things relative to an archaeological situation . . . let us say, have been perverted. I am not content with from the scientific angle, for my life-time effort has been, as you certainly know, to sift out the facts in a methodical way and analyze them for their precise significance. I have sought to recreate the picture of the past, the prehistoric past, and when any anachronism or falsity is injected, the picture fails its purpose. That matters, and when I write or form conclusions about these things, I shall certainly leave out the false—glamorous as it may seem and though it may make the picture more sensational.

I do hope we may not be drawn into a controversy with Judge Drummond who looks through a legal eye or with Dr. MacMillan, who looks through the eye of one who pities the unfortunate and likes to believe them. (New York State Museum Archives)

Clarke visited Levanna and reported to MacMillan:

I shall try to give you my reactions as they occurred to me while on the grounds. Frankly, my first general impression of what is reputed to be a scientific exploration in the interests of archaeological research, was not favorable. . . . I could not countenance the charge of an entrance fee to patrons or warrant the posting of some of the excavations with descriptive labels bearing both bold statements and far-fetched theories in some cases. I also had the feeling that the open graves which Mr. Follett dug and prepared to show the Indian burial customs, savored too strongly of exploitation and had no place here. (New York State Museum Archives)

Clarke measured the stones of the bear effigy and found a discrepancy of ten inches in both total length and width between the 1927 and 1934 appearances (letter from Clarke to Ritchie, June 20, 1936, Rochester Museum and Science Center Archives, figure 2.8):

Figure 2.8. Arthur C. Parker photograph of Levanna rock cluster, 1927. Rochester Museum and Science Center Archives.

The photographs, taken by Mr. Arthur C. Parker on the grounds in 1927, appear to me to show a complete encircling entrenchment around this area of stone, showing no animal effigy form. . . . As you can realize, it is difficult for one to form an opinion of the entire work done on the Levanna site at this time. To pass judgement on a work of this nature, without having observed all the operations at the site from the start, would seem, in my opinion, the height of folly and unfair to the science of archaeology, as well as to the participants in the work.

Correspondence about Levanna and the authenticity of the effigies continued, including aborted attempts to gather groups of archaeologists together to visit the site. A 1933 attempt was unsuccessful, according to an unsigned, handwritten note:

Investigation consisted partly of examination of witnesses, perusal of affidavits of persons known to the committee and in whose truthfulness and integrity the committee has complete confidence, of the examination of newspaper accounts and photographs presumably published by or with the authority of Selden and Follett, and of an attempt on the part of the committee to personally examine the site on the 23rd of March 1933, which the committee was prevented from doing by the presence and unpleasant attitude of Harrison Follett who was at the site and who recognized certain members of the committee. (New York State Museum Archives)

The idea of an independent investigation once again gained momentum on June 20, 1936, when Carl Guthe of the National Research Council wrote to Ritchie:

Throughout the year I have worried from time to time about the Levanna site and the request I received from Dr. MacMillan of Wells College that an attempt be made to investigate the excavations being carried on by our friend Follett. During the spring I made tentative arrangements to have Jimmy Griffin visit the site in the company of two or three other men. . . . It occurred to me this morning that it might be possible for a small group of those who attend the meetings at Rochester to go to the Levanna site and make a sufficiently detailed study to warrant the publication of a brief report in an early issue of "American Antiquity." . . . Surely you could get together quite a group to spend a day down there looking things over. Won't you please think this matter over seriously, because I believe it would be very much to the advantage of American archaeology if we could publish in "American Antiquity" an impartial, objective statement based upon the opinions of a half dozen competent archaeologists. (Rochester Museum and Science Center Archives)

Ritchie quickly replied:

> Both Dr. Parker and I think your suggestion in the Levanna matter is a honey and I have written Olsen, Byers, Johnson and Setzler asking them if they can make the trip. Jimmy has already planned to go and we have arranged for cars. The opinions of these men added to our information and affidavits will just about pull down the pillars of this "Temple of the Idols." (Rochester Museum and Science Center Archives)

Visiting separately from the group, Curtece Aldridge replied:

> We visited Follett, and what a place. Did you suggest, by any chance, that I would believe all that stuff. It's a bit to good and to perfect to exist. How could anyone be taken in. (Rochester Museum and Science Center Archives)

Finally, after years of letter writing and affidavits, James B. Griffin and others were able to visit Levanna on June 19, 1936. Griffin wrote to Guthe about that morning in a letter dated July 18, 1936:

> The purpose of the visit was to determine whether the exhibition of Indian handiwork by the present lessees of the land showed any evidence of non-aboriginal manufacture. The committee felt that the best method of approach would be to appear as a group of tourists for in that way the usual lecture describing the finds would have been heard. However for a number of reasons it was decided to appear as friends of Mr. Olsen and for that reason the party was not treated in the same manner as a group of casual visitors would have been received. We were shown every courtesy and our few questions were answered in a straight forward manner. (New York State Museum Archives)

Griffin summarized what he knew of the site from the Ritchie and Follett reports, then continued:

> It will be noticed that the official report on the site mentions a fancied resemblance to an effigy structure. Certainly then in 1928 when the report

on the site was published no effigy had been found. If this firebed had actually been in the shape of a bear it would have been recognized as such because of its undoubted significance in interpreting the site. Mr. Follett on the other hand maintains that this firebed was at once recognized as an effigy and that he had to threaten one of the workers in 1927 to prevent its destruction. A photograph in the Rochester Municipal Museum which was unfortunately not used in the report clearly shows a trench approximately a foot to a foot and a half deep and about the same width had been dug around the fire bed whose outline conforms to that shown in the report. In this photograph then and in the drawing we find no head and no legs on the fire bed. After the re-opening of the site by Mr. Selden and Mr. Follett this same bed is now revealed as possessing a head and two legs which is interpreted by them as being an aboriginal attempt to form a bear out of a group of fire-cracked rocks. . . .

When I stuck a probe down between surface stones in the center and along the edges of the original fire bed the progress of the probe was consistently interrupted a short distance beneath the surface. This same lack of sub-surface stones was present in the other effigies. This was not the case however when the probe was used to examine the legs of the bear effigy as the probe struck no stones beneath the surface. This same lack of subsurface stones was present in the other effigies. . . . In my opinion, they are not of Indian manufacture. (New York State Museum Archives)

Griffin went on to note that the artifacts at the site are authentic, though he questions the longhouse that was exhibited. "That a long house might be found on a site of this general type is not denied. That this particular structure is a long house is open to some question" (figure 2.9). In his quick-witted and sarcastic style, Griffin concluded:

It seems to me of some interest that witnesses were necessary when the effigies were uncovered. Some thirty to forty years ago a series of "aboriginal" finds were uncovered in Michigan before perfectly reliable witnesses. These finds included clay caskets, cups, tablets, and the Ark of the Covenant, and copper tablets and crowns. These were covered with various letters and inscriptions of Near Eastern alphabets. (Bentley Historical Museum, James Griffin Papers, Box 11)

Thus, the official verdict had come in that the effigies were arranged, probably to enhance the outdoor museum. Who was at the center of

Figure 2.9. Longhouse and teepee reconstructions at Levanna, ca. 1932. Homer St. Clair Archive.

the fraud? Eminent New York archaeologist Robert E. Funk wrote of Levanna that "the charlatans were finally put to rout in a confrontation with Ritchie and officers of the NYSAA (New York State Archaeological Association), but not until one of the schemers threatened Bill with an axe" (Funk 1977, xiv). Robert DeOrio wrote, "It is not our goal to present to the reader a position or opinion on the controversial Levanna effigies. Were they really unearthed, or were they Cardiff-like replications? Is it just possible they were a combination of both?" (DeOrio 1999, 9). Eighty years later it is still difficult to separate the perpetrators from those who were merely taken in by the hoax.

George B. Selden Jr. is named as the perpetrator of the fraudulent effigies in William A. Ritchie's court affidavit, though beyond that document there is no evidence. One other name that comes to the surface in evaluating blame is Harry L. Schoff, the WPA archaeologist and adopted Seneca who took the photo on the bear effigy postcard (figure 2.1). Of the dozens of archival letters in Albany and Rochester pertaining to Levanna, one of the most interesting is a handwritten document from T. Kenneth Wood, a medical doctor and president of the Muncy Historical Society and Museum of History, to William A. Ritchie, dated September 11, 1937. In the letter, Wood described two incidents with Schoff that bothered him:

Incident no. 1: Mr. Schoff, during his stay in Muncy, frequented my home and office very much. One day, he was in my consulting room talking and volunteered the following: "My greatest ambition is to find, associated with an Indian skeleton, some form of pathology; for instance, evidences of arthritis, etc." I said: "how about a gall-stone?" He then questioned me closely as to the "lasting possibilities" of gall-stones in a grave, their structure, how he would know them if he saw them and how one could prove their identity. I told him all that I knew. I did not show him a gall-stone in my desk for perhaps a half hour and when I did, I rolled it across the desk and said; "What is that"? He guessed—"a fossil"? and I answered: 'no a gall-stone". He examined it eagerly and plied me with more questions. Just then I was called to the waiting room for a few minutes and when I came back, Schoff hurriedly took his leave. I casually looked around for "my" gall-stone (which was a prize possession, the largest I had ever seen) and could not find it. It was probably an inch long and ¾" thick, shaped like a symmetrical little barrel with both ends flattened—as if it was the center one of three uniform stones. I should know it among a thousand, however changed by handling.

Incident no. 2. I was calling, professionally, on an old couple named McClintock who granted Mr. Schoff the use of their side-yard for 3 or 4 months as a parking place for his trailer. Mr. and Mrs. S. made their home in a trailer the whole time they were in this vicinity. Old Mrs. McClintock followed me out on the porch and I recalled the Schoff occupation of the yard (this was a couple of months after his departure), of which she said: "Doctor, what do you suppose Schoff was doing with those stones?", pointing to a pile of cobble stone sized stones near by, perhaps 2 bushels of them. "He would make pictures of birds and animals in the snow on the ground beside his trailer and then climb on top of his trailer with his camera and take pictures of them. I asked his wife what he was doing this for and she said he was sending the pictures off in the mail." Mrs. McC. is an innocent-minded old woman and I could see that she was still mystified and I did not undertake to enlighten her though I had my suspicions. I examined the stones and they were of uniform size and likely carried from a nearby stream bed. It was another of Mr. Schoff's ambitions to find, in his excavations, remains of Indian effigies—such as animals or birds or symbolic figures. On the site that he was excavating of *this very period*, he claimed to have found the wide-stretched effigy of a "Thunder Bird," as he called it. Pictures of this find appeared in the local papers over his signature (Fig x). I merely recount these happenings as facts and neither of them may have, in the past or the future, any special significance. (Rochester Museum and Science Center Archives)

Schoff reported the mentioned thirteen-foot wingspan Thunder Bird in Lycoming County, Pennsylvania, writing about his discoveries and himself in the third person (Schoff 1937). Most archaeologists in his day believed the effigies to have been forged. The evidence to this day remains strongly circumstantial. The involvement or level of knowledge of Follett himself remains unclear. Follett remained bitter, and his final reminiscences of the controversy are sad. The last comments on Levanna by Carter Woods are typically bittersweet:

> The Levana Village museum continued to operate until the early forties. The war with gas shortages cut down on the number of visitors and the gate receipts. Mr. Follett was now elderly and in poor health and unable to manage the site. He left to live with a son in Upstate New York. Soon afterwards the site was closed. Attempts were made to interest the Cayuga County Board of Supervisors in taking over the site as a County Museum. But negotiations broke down and nothing happened. As time went on, the culture-house where the artifacts were exhibited was vandalized; several exhibits which were loaned to various organizations were never returned. Without care, the effigies were eroded by the weather. Today, with the exception of a state historical marker near the highway . . . little remains to remind us that on this spot there once lived, a thousand years ago, a large band of Owasco Algonkian Indians. To me, the story of the Levanna Indian Village constitutes an historical and archaeological tragedy. I can only think of what might have been; of a major cultural and educational community resource which has been lost forever. (Woods 1976)

Follett was subject to continuing ridicule. In an August 10, 1936, letter to Ritchie, Griffin referred to Levanna as "Follette's zoo" (James Griffin Papers, Bentley Historical Museum, Box 11), and as Griffin explained in a January 7, 1937, letter to Ritchie:

> Just a note to let you know that the photographs arrived safely and that they will be a big help to me in my work. I am sure I haven't the slightest idea what the grouping of unburned stones can mean, i.e., the ones from the Archaic site at Squawkie Hill. I am sure if Follette (sic) had excavated

the site that the stones would have assumed the shape of a rhinoceros, at least. (Bentley Historical Museum, James Griffin Papers, Box 11)

THE SPANISH HILL SITE

The Levanna effigies were immediately suspicious because of their relative uniqueness. Beyond Schoff's idiosyncratic finds, few other firecracked rock effigies were known in the northeast. Schoff and Donald Cadzow were associated with a series of Pennsylvania sites (Glade's Run Bank, Halls, Muncey, and Athens), all reported only briefly in newspaper articles or newsletters (DeOrio 1999, 8). The reported thunderbirds are particularly suspicious. They are an important symbol in the Pacific Northwest, the American southwest, the Great Lakes, and the Great Plains regions, but not in the northeast, making the symbol an anomaly. However, one other site similar to Levanna was well-reported.

Spanish Hill, in South Waverly, Pennsylvania, is just across the New York state line on a glacial moraine, with broken rock animal effigies remarkably like those of Levanna. Spanish Hill was excavated by Ellsworth Cowles in 1933, almost simultaneous to the uncovering of the Levanna effigies. Cowles was a local amateur archaeologist who was able to prevent the hill from being removed for highway fill. Exhibits about Spanish Hill to this day adorn the Susquehanna River Archaeological Center in Waverly, New York. When I spoke at the center in May 2010 for their "History's Mysteries Lecture Series," local belief in the authenticity of the effigies was strong, and my speaking invitation was based on local interest in Levanna as a comparative case (Rossen 2010).

Spanish Hill has a research and folkloric history even stranger than that of Levanna. Besides the broken stone effigies, unsubstantiated claims for the site have included giant skeletons, horned skeletons, hilltop enclosures, a Spanish occupation, and a Susquehannock village visited in the seventeenth century by Etienne Brule of the Samuel Champlain voyages (Minderhout 2013; Murray 1908; Twigg 2005; Welles 1908). Harrison C. Follett was aware of the Spanish Hill effigies and tried to use them as supporting evidence for Levanna as the controversy burgeoned. He also wrote to Neil Judd in Georgia inquiring about a possible effigy figure in Macon, but was informed it was a clay platform shaped like an eagle within an existing council house (12/5/34 letter from A. Wetmore to H. Follett, Rochester Museum and Science Center Archives). When James B. Griffin examined Spanish Hill in 1931, he declared that it was neither Spanish nor Native American, and that the embankments were the result of white settler field clearing and plowing activities. Ritchie wrote to Griffin on June 9, 1934:

> I thoroughly sympathize with you in the matter of the Spanish Hill business. That crowd of arrogant old women of both sexes is a pain in my rear end too. I am firmly convinced that they don't know yet what it is all about. (James Griffin Papers, Bentley Historical Museum, Box 11)

Griffin later wrote to Ritchie about Spanish Hill: "Nothing comparable has ever been seen before (and I hope not since unto all eternity)" (James Griffin Papers, Bentley Historical Museum, Box 11, March 4, 1937, parentheses in the original).

SUMMARY AND DISCUSSION

The early Levanna investigations offer a fascinating glimpse into the practices, preoccupations, controversies, and interpretations of early twentieth-century archaeology. The discipline included a range of training and expertise and ad hoc efforts at ethics and self-regulation. Commercialism was decried by those in economically secure positions, but there were temptations to sensationalize during hard economic times for those on the professional fringes.

Notable and surprising to me was the role of Native Americans themselves. Regional groups of Cayuga, Onondaga, and Seneca were drawn to the Levanna site as an opportunity for cultural expression. This was a period when Native groups were struggling from national assimilation efforts and invisibility, and when the boarding school era of cultural suppression was strong (Adams 1995; Johansen 2000; Lomawaima and Child 2000). The appearance of Native dancers in Plains Indians headdresses at Levanna is thus indicative of a transitional time when Native people were looking to express themselves utilizing any possible means:

As the American public became infatuated with the Western Indians, they began forming a stereotype image of what a Native American was supposed to look like. Later, films and television would perfect this image that continues to this day. Combinations of Iroquois-style clothing with such elements as a modified Plains headdress began to be worn. The outright use of Plains Indian dress was also coming into practice because it was becoming expected by the public. (Gonyea 1986, 23)

It is thus ironic that visitors to Levanna included stars of Hollywood westerns, a fraudulent Indian chief, and a self-styled or imitating western railroad outlaw.

What attracted tourists to such an isolated attraction? Levanna played to the bloodthirsty savage stereotype and elevated white settlers during the worst economic period of American history. It might even be asked if these stereotypes affected the early interpretations of Harrison C. Follett, which emphasized warfare, starvation, cannibalism, and fear. Crude pole reconstructions of longhouses and tipis implied discomfort and exposure to the harsh elements, and skeletons displayed disease, injury, and disfigurement of young adults and children. Effigy figures were built and interpreted as superstitious and desperate appeals for protection and survival. All aspects of the outdoor museum implied the cultural progress and civilization of the white man, and reinforced the centuries-old idea that humans passed through stages of savagery and barbarism on their way to civilization (Berkhofer 1979). It is extraordinary that the Cayuga, Onondaga, and Seneca brought their desires for cultural expression to the Levanna backdrop. This is especially true for the Cayuga, who tried to use Levanna as a springboard in their quest for a new reservation and return to the homeland after a century and a half of expulsion.

❸

INDIGENOUS ARCHAEOLOGY, THE AGE OF THE HAUDENOSAUNEE CONFEDERACY, AND THE USE OF ORAL TRADITIONS

Winona LaDuke, Native activist, environmentalist, writer, and two-time vice-presidential candidate with Ralph Nadar visited the Cayuga-SHARE Farm in 2003. Winona had learned that our group of college faculty and local citizens had bought a seventy-acre organic farm and were working to give it back to the Cayuga Nation. She told me she was writing a book about Native renaming and reclaiming of places. I wasn't sure our story was worthy of her book, and she hung around for a couple of days, though she didn't take any notes that I saw. We were later surprised when the story appeared (LaDuke 2005, 156–60).

After her time at the farm, I drove Winona to the Onondaga Reserve an hour to the north to meet Tadodaho Sidney Hill. Tadodaho is the traditional title of the spiritual leader of the entire Haudenosaunee (Iroquois) Confederacy. The title Tadodaho dates to the Peacemaker Epic, the seminal story of the Confederacy formation, when the Peacemaker, along with Hiawatha and the woman Jigonsaseh (also Jikonsasay or Jikonsaseh) traveled throughout the lands to unite the original Five Nations (Seneca, Cayuga, Onondaga, Oneida, Mohawk) under the Great Peace. Through a series of displays of magical power, negotiation, and even trickery, the Five Nations were brought from a state of devastating warfare and cannibalism into the Great Peace (Porter 2008, 272–312).

The story is thought of as an ideological power struggle between the genders, specifically between a male cannibal cult and a female corn cult, that explains the origins of the Haudenosaunee matriarchy (Mann 2000, 36). One of the more formidable obstacles was Tadodaho (also Atotáhrho, Adadarho, or Adodaroh), the deformed, insane, and cannibalistic great wizard of Onondaga, who had snakes in his hair and who had murdered Hiawatha's wife and seven daughters out of jealousy and desire. As the snakes were combed out, setting his mind straight, he embraced the Great Peace. The moral of the story is that even the evilest person always has the capability of doing the most good, just as the most depressed person (Hiawatha) can overcome the deepest grief. The title Tadodaho has been handed down for a millennium of generations to the spiritual leader of the Haudenosaunee Confederacy (Porter 2008, 289–312; Tehanetorens 2000, 20–41; Wall 2001, 5–6).

Later that day I took an impromptu car tour of the Onondaga Reserve with the Tadodaho, Turtle Clan Faithkeeper Oren Lyons Jr. (son of Oren Lyons who danced at Levanna in 1936), Faithkeeper Tony Gonyea (faithkeepers keep oral traditions and ritual cycles), and Winona. We pulled up to a pile of building debris and rubble. The Tadodaho said, "This is the most important monument on our land. A person built a smoke shop and refused to share the profits with the nation. This is what had to be done." We sat in stunned silence and contemplated the importance of communal organization and taking down an illicit business for the survival of a proud Haudenosaunee nation.

At some point, Winona began to discuss the importance of names and reclaiming. Referring to Denali in Alaska, named Mount McKinley, she stated, "How can something as powerful and spiritual as a mountain be renamed for something as puny and mortal as a man" (Campbell 2015; National Park Service 2018; von Gelder 2008). Knowing I was an archaeologist, she explained that this idea extends to the past. "Archaic, Woodland, these names disconnect people from their past." For Winona, these were more than names, but connections that were being consciously and systematically severed, and that renaming was a step toward recovering the sacred and promoting cultural survival. For instance, she celebrated in an address to the UN General Assembly when the Queen Charlotte Islands of western Canada were officially renamed Haida Gwaii in 2010: "Those islands never should have been named for one queen." Renaming is a key component of revitalizing Native sovereignty (Dowie 2017).

Winona LaDuke's ideas have implications for a series of concepts, ideas, and debates that affect Haudenosaunee archaeology. The first is how archaeologists develop culture history sequences based on artifact typologies. To what extent do those typologies and culture sequences dehumanize or distract from the real activities and interactions of history? Related to this theme is the question of whether the Haudenosaunee had a long (in situ) cultural development in what is now the northeast United States or if there was an in-migration and displacement of Algonkian-speaking peoples who had inhabited the area. Remember that Arthur C. Parker and William Ritchie referred to the Levanna site as "Third Period Algonkian," which culturally and ethnically separates the site from the present-day Cayuga. The other term is "Owasco," which was widely used for peoples who lived in central New York from about AD 700 to 1300 (Ritchie, Lenig, and Miller 1953).

New themes, debates, and a reform movement in archaeology have created a maelstrom of ideas and arguments. The branching tree or braided stream models have emphasized infinite regional cultural variability instead of cultural continuities between the past and present (Hart and Engelbrecht 2012). Against this backdrop, I have opened new discussion about the discrepancy between archaeological models versus oral traditions of the age of the Haudenosaunee Confederacy (Rossen 2015, 196–99). The central question is, how much value should be given to Native wisdom and oral traditions, and can archaeological evidence be directly compared with oral traditions?

All these themes are relevant to Levanna, once we move past the sensational circus of past investigations and public displays. More than anything, what allows these themes to be addressed is the development of indigenous archaeology. It was the realization of scholars' neglected responsibilities to the living people being studied that was one inspiration for the Cayuga-SHARE Farm Project (see chapter 1). Another idea I have previously discussed is the Haudenosaunee concept that archaeologists do not "find" anything, but, according to the Clan Mothers, things are revealed to the right person when the time is socially or politically correct (Rossen 2008, 2015, 9–10). It is a humbling concept, and modesty is greatly valued by the Haudenosaunee.

INDIGENOUS ARCHAEOLOGY

Indigenous archaeology recognizes the great damage done to Native people by archaeologists, who have excavated their graves without their knowledge, cleansing the land of its identity by removing the ancestors (Benedict 2004; Hill 2006; Anonymous 1986). In Haudenosaunee country, the avoidance of graves is a salient aspect of indigenous archaeology. We also realize that archaeology has stripped Native people of connections to their past in other ways, such as the way ancient people and time periods have been labeled.

Despite the dark history, archaeology is a powerful tool, capable of doing great good as well as harm. Among many possible benefits, archaeology can be a conduit to land rights, repatriation, and renewed pride for Native people (Hansen and Rossen 2007). Native and non-Native scholars doing various versions of indigenous archaeology have constituted only a small minority of practitioners in the SAA. A dissident group within the SAA lobbies for changes in the code of ethics and general practices of the discipline. Indigenous archaeology is slowly effecting broad-ranging behavioral changes in the field, laboratory, and publishing practices of archaeology. Native people are increasingly setting protocols and integrating their perspectives into the practice of all aspects of archaeology, from fieldwork and lab analysis to professional and public presentation to publications. In February 2018, a sign of the continuing advance and broad acceptance of indigenous archaeology was the election of Joe Watkins, the Choctaw archaeologist who coined the term and promoted many of its basic concepts, as president of the SAA (Watkins 2000)!

Indigenous archaeology includes a set of principles and practices designed to reform the discipline. The dark history of archaeology as crudely exploitative of Native peoples and as a support structure for colonialism and imperialism is challenged. Indigenous archaeology varies from place to place, always with an emphasis on involving local communities, based on local history and circumstances (Atalay 2012; Kerber 2006; Silliman 2008). In Cayuga country, the key historical circumstances are the expulsion of the Cayuga people during and following the American Revolution (see chapter 1) and their recent return to the heartland zone east of Cayuga Lake. The Cayuga have no reservation lands and little local support. A regional anti-Indian racist hate group has openly operated for more than two decades (Hansen and Rossen 2007, 2017). Within this situation, the Cayuga are attempting to recapture some semblance of homeland and history.

The fundamental starting point of indigenous archaeology is seeking approval for the excavations from people with a long history of justified mistrust of archaeologists (Benedict 2004). The Cayuga-SHARE Farm aided the development of friendships with Chief Sam George (Cayuga, Bear Clan) and Chief Chuck Jacobs (Cayuga, Heron Clan), who approved, supported, and visited the excavations. At Six Nations Reserve on the Grand River, Chief Blake Bomberry (Cayuga, Turtle Clan) approved the excavations after my visit and presentation in the Cayuga Longhouse in Ontario. The Cayuga-SHARE Farm had greatly increased communication and cooperation between Cayuga at Six Nations and those living in present-day New York.

A partial list of attributes of indigenous archaeology among the Cayuga and Haudenosaunee includes (1) collaboration with Native people, (2) power sharing, (3) expanded identity for the archaeologist(s), (4) a recognition of the power and contributions of oral traditions, (5) a recognition and practice of the Haudenosaunee concept of "good mind," (6) understanding of the Two Row Wampum concept, (7) the recognition of spiritual danger in the excavation and analysis of sites and artifacts, (8) the understanding of archaeologists as conduits (discussed above), and (9) recognition of the inherent problems of understanding and relating the Haudenosaunee past in English. The envisioned culmination is control of cultural resources by Native peoples, organizations, and governments (Rossen 2015, 11–13).

With all these attributes, archaeologists are engaging in a work in progress. Long-term relationships, commitments, and trust must be built. Expanded identity is the idea that archaeologists (particularly non-Native ones) must also be friends and advocates who are active on projects beyond archaeology that benefit Native people (Rossen 2015, 5–6). The good mind and Two Row Wampum are ideas that embody how to interact with other people and the environment (Hill 2013; Thomas 1989). The good mind focuses on maintaining a positive outlook and realizing how your interactions affect others (Jacques 1991).

The Two Row Wampum more specifically addresses Native and non-Native relations that the Haudenosaunee have presented for centuries to arriving outsiders. The original Two Row Wampum was a treaty between the Haudenosaunee and Dutch dated to 1613 and encoded in a wampum belt. Two parallel and horizontal rows of purple beads against a backdrop of white beads are read as an agreement of Native and non-Native people to travel down the river of life side-by-side in mutual friendship and respect without interference (Hansen and Rossen 2017; Hirsch 2014; Rossen 2015, 8; Thomas 1989). The Two Row Wampum further encodes an agreement to work together to take care of the environment (Hill 2013). In a modern interpretation, mutual respect includes understanding the Haudenosaunee idea that spiritual danger is inherent in disturbing the earth and excavating ancient materials, and thus archaeology must be conducted with the good mind and a watchful eye for peril. On occasion during the excavations, Donna Silversmith (Cayuga, Snipe Clan) would exclaim that we were doing "two row archaeology." New ways of doing archaeology led to new perspectives on archaeology from the Cayuga people. The opening paragraph of the Cayuga Nation website includes the statement, "Archeologists have found evidence of Cayuga settlements in many areas surrounding the lake including the present-day villages of Union Springs, Aurora, Cayuga, Seneca Falls, Ithaca and Canoga. Nya:weh. (I am thankful)" (cayuganation.nsn.gov).

I firmly believe that indigenous archaeology is not just politically correct archaeology but is better archaeology. For example, my recent research on agriculture on Hawai'i Island has taught me how difficult it is to understand those field systems without the constant input and commentary of my Native Hawaiian partners, especially regarding sacred landscapes, social organization of labor, and alignments of fields with temples and other aspects of the ancient built environment (Rossen, Pai, and Kalawe 2017a, 2017b). It is the combination of Native wisdom with the Western science and special studies of archaeology that produces a powerful synergy for understanding the past and its applications to the present. The genius of engineering and social organization of labor helps lay to rest ongoing stereotypic representations of the cruel savagery of ancient Hawaiians and their need to be saved and civilized by Europeans. In the Hawai'i case, the ultimate goal is to rebuild ancient agricultural systems and progress to food sovereignty in a place where 90 percent of its food is imported (Rossen at al. 2017). The research supports the grassroots movement toward more indigenous, local, and organic farming ("Facing Hawai'i's Future" 2012). Indigenous archaeology is thus the most direct path to the application of archaeology toward a better future for all humanity.

DEBATES ABOUT CAYUGA ARCHAEOLOGY

In excavating Cayuga sites, I did not seek to enter all the debates discussed here: the nature of typologies, the in-migration versus in situ cultural development debate, the Owasco terminology question, the issue of branching trees and braided streams, and the age and nature of the Haudenosaunee Confederacy. They all found me because Betty Pangburn drove into the Cayuga-SHARE Farm that day in 2006. The remainder of this chapter describes the debates and the place of Levanna within them, as a prelude to discussions of the 2007 to 2009 reexcavation of the site. Winona LaDuke's idea of renaming is indeed much deeper than mere names. What is in a name like Algonkian, Woodland, and Owasco versus Cayuga and Haudenosaunee? Names and how they are used are related to contemporary issues and conceptions of Native historical longevity, cultural survival, revitalization, and repatriation of human remains from museums.

TYPOLOGIES AND OVERLAPS

Artifact typologies are a fundamental part of archaeological analysis and understanding of the past. During the great typological debate of the 1940s, James Ford and Albert Spaulding argued whether typologies represented real mental templates of ancient people or just organizational frameworks for archaeologists (Ford 1954; Ford and Steward 1954; Spaulding 1953, 1954). The importance of typologies to archaeology is multidimensional. Artifact typologies based on artifact styles are used to construct basic cultural chronologies, the foundation of traditional archaeology. Even when archaeologists became dissatisfied with pure chronological approaches to understanding the past in the 1970s, moving to try to understand processes of development, change, and even collapse and reorganization of societies through time (a perspective known as processualism) (Binford 1977), chronologies based on artifact types remained the foundation of the discipline. Persistent problems with typologies included defining the boundaries of types, attempting to understand how they appear and disappear through time, and how to handle artifacts that were between types or altogether anomalous (Adams and Adams 1991). Despite difficulties in constructing and managing artifact typologies, and periods of backlash against their use (Flenniken 1985; Flenniken and Raymond 1986; Young and Bonnichsen 1985), typologies remain a staple of archaeological analysis and interpretation.

In Haudeosaunee Territory, artifact typologies, particularly ceramic style types, are central to the in-situ versus in-migration debate described here (that is, did the Haudenosaunee gradually develop in central New York or migrate in and displace other peoples) and in attempting to understand the connections and relationships between pre-European contact cultures and contemporary people. Archaeologists studying the Haudenosaunee have essentially utilized the same typologies for decades: a ceramic typology developed by Richard S. "Scotty" MacNeish in the 1950s and a projectile point chronology originated by William Ritchie in 1961 (MacNeish 1952; Ritchie 1971). These typologies have been closely examined and details have been critiqued, but their fundamentals remain intact. That is, while particular sherds and projectile points present problems by not fitting the typologies, the vast majority of artifacts fit logically in chronological sequence within these frameworks (Rogers 2014). This is important because a clean temporal break in artifact styles without overlap is necessary to propose an in-migration and population replacement. Recent longitudinal studies of central New York ceramics discovered that types lasted longer and overlapped with each other much more than was previously believed (Hart and Brumbach 2005, 2009).

Artifact styles, particularly of ceramics, have been formally or more often, informally and loosely, associated with ethnicity and identity (Cruz 2011). This approach may be out of style in some areas, but there is precedence in recent regional studies (Birch and Williamson 2013). Ethnoarchaeology, the study of material culture and its patterns among living people, has provided a solid basis for understanding the relationship between artifact styles and ethnicity among living people, with artifacts being styled and decorated as social information and boundary maintenance between social groups (David and Kramer 2001, 168–224; DeBoer 1990; Hodder 1991; Weissner 1983). Within this framework, we used certain artifact styles as indicative of the Cayuga (Pollack 2015; Rossen 2015, 169).

IN-MIGRATION VERSUS IN SITU MODELS OF CULTURAL DEVELOPMENT

The idea of a pre-Iroquoian occupation of what is today central and western New York by Algonkian peoples was developed by Arthur C. Parker by 1919 and promoted by William A. Ritchie in the early 1930s. Ritchie's (1944) *The Pre-Iroquoian Occupations of New York State* was one of the most widely praised and reviewed books of its era (Griffin 1945; Johnson 1944; McKern 1945). The central premise was that a stylistic break in ceramics and other artifacts, along with a discontinuity in settlement patterns, suggested a population replacement at an undetermined but relatively recent point of prehistory. There is also suggestive evidence from historical linguistic geographic areas, showing the Iroquoian speakers of the northeast as an island surrounded by Algic speakers in what is now southern and eastern New York, New England, Canada, and the Great Lakes (Snow 1995). The Haudenosaunee were thus viewed as migrants to central New York who displaced Algic-speaking peoples who had long-inhabited the region (Ritchie 1928, 1932).

During the 1930s and '40s, archaeological sites like Levanna were labeled as "Algonkin" or "Algonkian." Arthur C. Parker referred to Levanna as being associated with the "Third Period Algonkian," the last and most stylistically elaborate expression of Pre-Iroquoian people in New York. It seems noteworthy and ironic that Parker would develop a model of culture history that limited the time depth of his own people in their homeland.

This in-migration and displacement idea fell out of fashion in the 1950s with Richard S. MacNeish's study of ceramic types, which tended to blur the perceived stylistic break (MacNeish 1952; Ritchie and MacNeish 1949). Dean Snow (1995) revived the theory of in-migration of Haudenosaunee groups into the northeast in the 1990s, leading to brisk debate. He readjusted his in-migration hypothesis back in time from AD 1000 to AD 700 based on detailed critiques (Crawford and Smith 1996; Snow 1996).

Today, most archaeologists working in the region follow a more in situ or local development model that grants more continuity and less population replacement through time. However, branching tree, braided stream, and to a lesser extent multiscalar models of culture change have taken another extreme view, that movement of people and ideas was so prevalent that the development of the recognizable Haudenosaunee nations is fundamentally a Contact Period (or European arrival) phenomenon (Parmenter 2010).

At Levanna, the great variety of ceramic styles in a short-term occupation proto-longhouse structure reinforced the idea of long-lived overlapping ceramic styles from a synchronic or slice of time perspective (Rogers 2014). These ceramic styles were thought to be related to different periods, but within the tight stratigraphy and contexts of the Levanna proto-longhouse, it was apparent that they represented styles whose use periods overlapped, even if their periods of greatest popularity were distinctive. For now, it can be stated that the in-migration versus in situ development debate for Haudenosaunee origins is indirectly related to modern issues of land rights and repatriation, and to perspectives that either emphasize or sever past-present connections.

LIFE AND DEATH OF OWASCO

The Levanna site was reclassified into a time period designated as Owasco (AD 900–1300) by Ritchie (1981[1965]; Follett 1957; Ritchie and MacNeish 1949; Schulenberg 2002). The name was derived from the Lakeside site located in Auburn, New York, on Owasco Lake, the type site for a series of dentate stamped ceramic types. This chronological and cultural term was widely used for decades until declared "dead" in 2003 (Hart and Brumbach 2003). According to this line of thinking, the cultural traits defining Owasco, its ceramics, corn-beans-squash agriculture, and longhouse architecture, all appear to have formed or arrived at different time periods (Hart 2008). There is also substantial regional variation between groups that have been placed under the regional and temporal umbrella of the term Owasco. In its place, scholars suggested a concept of branching, braided, or interwoven cultural development that led to a relatively late development of the recognizable Haudenosaunee tribes (Hart and Engelbrecht 2012).

Beyond the issue of whether the time period represented by the term Owasco represents a unified culture, there is another issue. Does the term Owasco disengage past archaeological cultures from the present-day Haudenosaunee, thereby obscuring the connections between past and present? The use of disengaging terms to label archaeological periods may be considered a subnarrative of oppression. The process of renaming is central to recovering sacred meaning and revitalizing cultures (LaDuke 2005). For these reasons, I have come to refer to peacetime sites like Levanna and Myers Farm, in the heart of Cayuga territory with Haudenosaunee art, symbolism, and architecture, as "Early Cayuga."

LONG VERSUS BRIEF CONFEDERACY, WARFARE VERSUS PEACE

There has been substantial discussion and disagreement as to the age and origins of the Haudenosaunee Confederacy, and it has been considered a constant and foundational question in Haudenosaunee historical scholarship (Bonaparte 2006, 47–52; Fenton 1998, 68–71). Different approaches that scholars have taken to the age of the confederacy reflect their attitudes toward cultural evolution and the relative validity of oral accounts and how to handle variations in those accounts. The Haudenosaunee themselves have long maintained oral traditions that their Confederacy is old, over one thousand years in age (Akwesasne Notes 2005; Cusick 2004[1825]; George-Kanentiio 2000, 25–28). Archaeologists have sought evidence beyond the oral traditions (and their written versions) for the age of the confederacy. One argument is that evidence of smoking trade pipes at the Confederacy edges, between the Seneca to the west and the Mohawk to the east, would suggest a functioning Confederacy, and that this evidence did not exist before 1650 (Kuhn and Sempowski 2001). This might make the Confederacy a post-European contact phenomenon.

A significant discrepancy is raised by this perspective. If the confederacy with its Great Peace was formed on the principles of ending centuries of warfare as Europeans arrived, why did a post-contact formation set off a period of aggression against both Natives and Europeans? Was there never truly a Great Peace? Why were the Peacemaker and his companions Hiawatha (a.k.a. Aionwahta or Aionwantha) and Jigonsaseh, supposedly late sixteenth- or early seventeenth-century people by these arguments, not known as historical figures? The confederacy undoubtedly passed through various stages of development and reorganization, so why not view the contact period as one more stage or incarnation of an established confederacy? A confederacy with time depth might better explain the power and organization of the Haudenosaunee as they confidently navigated the tumultuous and fragmenting contact era.

Other archaeologists have accepted a relatively late pre-contact date in the early 1400s, largely based on settlement pattern data showing the development of five site clusters (Snow 1995). Meanwhile, ethnohistorians have matched aspects of oral traditions to astronomical events like eclipses, specifically the black sun that appeared as the Seneca debated in council on joining the confederacy in some versions of the Peacemaker epic (Canfield 1904, 35–40; Wallace and Fadden 1994), to posit earlier dates like AD 1142 (Mann and Fields 1997).

According to oral accounts, "the sun went out and for a little time there was complete darkness . . . when the corn was getting ripe" (Bonaparte 2006, 49). The Cornplanter (William Walker Canfield) version is quite graphic:

> A moan of terrible fear went up from the warriors—men who could meet death on the chase or in the battle with a smile were unnerved by that awful spectacle. They saw a black disc moving forward over the face of an unclouded sun . . . on and on crept that fearful black shadow, eating its way into the disc of the beautiful sun, like a mighty demon that had come to blot out of existence the source of light and warmth and life, while over the fresh and budding earth spread the ghostly gloom that never fails to inspire the most careless observer with awe. The flowers that filled the woods with such profusion closed as though night had suddenly fallen upon them; the warmth and fragrance of the day that had opened with such glory gave way to the damps of evening, while the stars and planets

appeared again in the heavens. Over the whole face of nature was thrown an unearthly, cadaverous hue, and in the sudden chill everything was cold and sodden with the falling dew. (Canfield 1904, 36–38)

The gathered circle of chiefs hastily passed the peace pipe in the darkness, looking up to the sky: "In the light of the twice-dawned day, and in the presence of the sacred dead, who had pointed out . . . the path by which to escape the displeasure of their Father, the Confederacy of the Iroquois was formed" (Canfield 1904, 40).

It is my belief that the eclipse of August 18, 909, best fits the descriptions of the oral traditions and corroborates the tenth- to eleventh-century evidence from Levanna. The mid-August date matches the time "when the corn was high," while the 12:48 p.m. EST occurrence matches the midday schedule of Seneca council meetings. The path of the AD 909 eclipse passed through both Ganondagan, where the Seneca council was held, and Onondaga, where it was also observed.

In 2013, astronomers reenacted the AD 909 eclipse at the Ho Tung Visualization Laboratory at Colgate University. The reenactment, designed by Joe Eakin, their Senior Visualization Designer, exhibited an unusually dramatic darkening and the appearance of stars, matching the oral traditions (Canfield 1904; Rossen 2013; Wallace 1994). However, while intrigued by the black sun story, Native scholars remind us that it does not appear in all versions of the Peacemaker Epic (Richard Hill Sr., personal communication 2013). It has even been suggested that the black sun reference is derived from Jesuit eclipse stories (Bonaparte 2006, 40).

THE USE OF ORAL TRADITIONS BY ARCHAEOLOGISTS

The rejection and use of oral traditions by archaeologists is a complex issue treated in the literature with much angst. According to Roger Echo-Hawk, Pawnee tribal historian and archaeologist: "Through the magic of archaeology, the ancient, abandoned cityscapes were suddenly peopled with Indians. It was a great moment, but it was also a moment in which archaeology explicitly denounced the study of oral traditions" (Echo-Hawk 2009). After excluding oral traditions from research for most of the history of archaeological research, new efforts at coordinating archaeology with oral traditions began in the 1990s, spurred by the passage of the Native America Graves Protection and Repatriation Act (NAGPRA) of 1990 (Anyon et al. 1997; McKeown 1995). NAGPRA forced archaeologists to consult with Native leaders and led to the repatriation for reburial of human remains and artifacts from museum collections. Despite this, there remains a tendency for archaeologists to approach oral tradition and archaeology as multiple pasts that may not be compatible. One distinction is the level of emphasis on time, with oral tradition being much less concerned with absolute and relative dating of events (Anyon et al. 1997, 82–83; Gazin-Schwartz and Holtorf 1999). Scholars also discuss how and under what circumstances archaeology can have relevance to Native people, who already have a culture history, and how archaeologists might run into problems using sensitive sacred information contained in the oral traditions (Anyon et al. 1997). Other issues include the differing nature and structure of archaeology and oral traditions, and perhaps most fundamental of all, questions about the accuracy or historicity of oral traditions.

In casting strong doubts on the historical accuracy of oral traditions, David Henige (1999, 2009) presents issues that include the frailty of human memory and the effects of outside information, especially from European contact. After a global consideration of case studies, Henige states that scholars "underestimate the difficulties and overestimate the need for maintaining consistent content" (Henige 2009, 226). In the specific case of eclipses, he asks, "Why would a society 'encode' or otherwise remember a four-minute-long event, however spectacular, for generation after generation?" (Henige 2009, 216). The conclusion of his study is that scholars must try to corroborate with other lines of data and judge the particular cultural traits of how formally or informally oral traditions were kept and transmitted. Is it true, as Henige states, that, "American Indians do not forget the past so much as they reject—in the context of other needs—the need for memory to be factual" (Henige 2009, 227)? Henige's conclusion is that scholars will ultimately provisionally decide whether or not to believe oral traditions "based on predisposition, experience, authority, and ignorance" (Henige 2009, 227).

Henige would have us downgrade or eliminate the use of oral traditions in research. Yet he asks us to consider the particular circumstances of a culture while making blanket statements about Native American memory and history. Scholars like Henige tend to place written records on a pedestal of reliability above oral traditions. Yet, the dichotomy between "undependable" oral traditions based on shifting memories and "dependable" written history is itself a fabricated academic construct. As indigenous and decolonizing methodologies challenge the status quo of scholarship and gain prominence, one key theme is that books are dangerous as tools of colonialism and oppression for their false aura of stability and infallibility. In both scholarly and legal debates, texts have been falsely privileged as authoritative over oral traditions with greater time depth and resonance (Kovach 2010; L. Smith 2012, 37–39, 48). As we have seen in the history of the Levanna excavations, the veracity of archaeological narratives should also be questioned.

More optimistic archaeologists tend to view oral tradition as "valuable to archaeologists because it offers . . . alternative ideas about the past that counter our tendency to portray everyone in all time as versions of ourselves" (Gazin-Schwartz and Holtorf 1999, 8), or "two separate, but overlapping, ways of knowing the past" (Anyon et al. 1997, 78). According to Teague (1993, 36) in a southern Arizona case study, "oral histories can be shown to conform to archaeological evidence to an extent not easily attributable to the construction of after-the-fact explanation for the presence of numerous ruins throughout the region. These histories reflect direct knowledge of events in prehistoric Arizona." Similarly, Roger Echo-Hawk (2009) concludes, "There is no doubt that a real history is embedded in Native American oral traditions, and that this is the same history that archaeologists study. . . . Since oral traditions and archaeology have inherent limitations, combining them in research can create knowledge that goes beyond what is possible using either source by itself" (also see Echo-Hawk 1997; Ferguson, Watkins, and Pullar 1997, 241).

ORAL TRADITIONS AND ARCHAEOLOGY: THE HAUDENOSAUNEE CASE

The specific circumstances of Haudenosaunee oral traditions and the eclipse story refute some of Henige's negative statements. To begin, oral traditions were kept by specialists, including faithkeepers or "designated rememberers" who were specially trained for accuracy, a practice that continues today (Williams n.d., 110–16). The tradition of memorization goes beyond the faithkeepers to clan mothers, chiefs, and Haudenosaunee people from all walks of life. In 1736, Benjamin Franklin recorded the treaty words of Seneca Chief Kanickhungo:

> We who are now here, are old men, who have the direction of affairs in our own nations, and as we are old, it may be thought that the memory of things may be lost with us, who have, not like you, the art of preserving it by committing all transactions to writing. We nevertheless have methods of transmitting from father to son an account of all these things, whereby you will find the remembrance of them is faithfully preserved, and our succeeding generations are made acquainted with what has passed, that it may not be forgot as long as the earth remains. (Franklin 1938[1736], 7)

In 1912, Seneca Chief John Arthur Gibson prefaced his third recitation of the Peacemaker Epic with

> Don't forget the words he has spoken in front of us who are the elders. This is where they should rest, his words, in the bottom of our hearts, so that, whatever one's age, one will keep remembering the story that he himself, Tekanawita (The Peacemaker) has told. Thereafter the children repeated it, reminding themselves of what he said in front of them. (Gibson et al. 1993)

Europeans likewise noticed the accuracy of Haudenosaunee memory:

> When any Foreign Ambassador comes to them and makes any proposal they contrive to remember every word he says: different people are appointed to learn by heart a separate sentence and no more; so when they come to put it together they know every word of it. (Johnston 1964, 29)

It must be recognized that there are variations in different versions of stories in Haudenosaunee oral tradition. Seneca Chief John Arthur Gibson presented three varying recitations of the Peacemaker Epic, in 1899, 1900, and 1912 (Gibson et al. 1993). However, key themes remain constant in the versions presented by Gibson and others, leaving a coherent epic. Reiteration is a key to keeping oral stories by memory, with an emphasis on the order and principles of the story in spite of variations (Porter 2008). Key stories like the Peacemaker Epic and *Gaiwí:yo*, the Good Message of Handsome Lake, the Seneca prophet who reorganized Haudenosaunee society early in the nineteenth century based on a series of visions, are recited annually in the longhouse to this day (Thomas 1994). Mnemonic devices ranging from condolence canes to wampum belts, which are read bead by bead, aid and supplement these memories (George-Kanentiio 2000, 45–48, 118–19; Tehanetorens 1999; Thomas 1989; Anonymous 1984).

The Peacemaker Epic is recited during trips that retrace the Peacemaker's journey across present-day New York state (ICT Staff 2011). After our purchase of the land that became the Cayuga-SHARE Farm in 2001, our first visit was a busload of Native travelers on the Peacemaker's Journey. Present-day Cayuga territory had been so hostile to Native people, with its visible and active racist hate group, that the Peacemakers Journey group had previously skipped the area. When the busload of Haudenosaunee people disembarked, set up their tents, started playing music and doing traditional dances, we knew the Cayuga-SHARE Farm would take on a life of its own. During their visit we were privileged to witness the recitation of the Cayuga portion of the epic by Mohawk Chief Jake Swamp.

An example of spontaneous and corroborated memory occurred at the Cayuga-SHARE Farm in April 2002 during the visit from Brazil of Yanomami Headman Davi Kopenawa. Davi had come to Ithaca, New York, to speak through a translator at Cornell University. He asked for the return of blood samples of his people. These samples had been collected under fraudulent circumstances during the anthropological research projects of Napoleon Chagnon and James Neel from 1966 to 1976 (Borofsky 2005; Chernela et al. 2002; Turner 2001). Davi explained that many of those people were now deceased but could not travel to the land of the ancestors while their blood remained in research laboratory refrigerators. Most of those samples were finally returned in 2015, primarily because of Davi's persistent quest (Kearns 2015).

Following the Cornell talk, Davi asked about the possibility of meeting some Native leaders of the central New York area. My colleagues and I were able to arrange just such a meeting at the Cayuga-SHARE Farm twenty-four hours later. During the day, we talked and feasted.

The group strolled the short distance to the edge of the Great Gully, where oral tradition states the Cayuga hid in 1779 while the American Army destroyed their villages (Tobin 2002).

Later in the Cayuga-SHARE Farm dining room, the clan mothers and chiefs asked Davi to tell the story of his people. Davi related how his people were killed, given disease, their women were sterilized, and their land was taken and poisoned. Yet they survived. Then Davi asked the Haudenosaunee leaders for their story, which was virtually identical.

During that day, Davi gave Seneca Chief Norman Hill his feather necklace. Cayuga Heron Clan Mother Birdie Hill presented Davi a calico cloth ribbon shirt, the kind worn at ceremonies. At one point of the afternoon, it was decided that Davi should be given an honorary Haudenosaunee name. This was a popular practice in the nineteenth century that continued into the 1930s and 1940s (see chapter 2) but was very unusual in 2002. The chiefs looked at each other. The ceremony had not been done in "a long time" and they were unsure who knew the words. Then in exact unison, four chiefs from different Haudenosuanee nations began a long recitation. I was told the language was probably an old dialect from before the split of the different but mutually intelligible Haudenosaunee languages. The words had been exactly remembered.

A SERIES OF COMPLEX ISSUES FOR ARCHAEOLOGISTS

The fundamentals of academic scholarship itself are challenged by indigenous archaeology and the broader social science movement toward indigenous and decolonizing methodologies (Kovach 2010; Silliman 2008; L. Smith 2012; Smith and Wobst 2005; Watkins 2000). These are theoretical and practical advances that challenge who does research, how that research is conducted, and what we value as evidence. These revolutions in social science affect the Levanna case study in various ways. We first must rescue Levanna from its 1930s interpretations. Then we place our evidence against scholarly debates that have spanned generations. To what extent do artifact typologies represent categories in the ancient human mind? In the Haudenosaunee case, how do artifact typologies reflect either a cultural break (in-migration) or continuity (in situ development)? How do we evaluate evidence for a long versus relatively brief Haudenosaunee Confederacy? What are the indicators of war versus peace in our archaeological record? What is a confederacy artifact? What types of village organization and settlement patterns (including sites of resource procurement and special activities like feasting) indicate wartime and peace?

The coordination of oral traditions and archaeology represents one of the greatest challenges to indigenous archaeologists. Indeed it is considered to be one of the key "stepping stones to common ground" between Native Americans and archaeologists (Swidler et al. 1997). Oral traditions may be used carefully by archaeologists as one line of evidence and as a guide to archaeological investigations. In central New York, this coordination may include finding and investigating particular sites named in the stories, or as in this case, broader topics such as the age and nature of the Confederacy formation.

The archaeological research and analysis must be conducted with a careful eye for archaeological correlates, those relationships between archaeological materials and patterns and their behavioral meanings (Binford 1977, 1980). Archaeologists always aim to minimize the gulf between archaeological data and interpretation, and any coordination with oral traditions must be made with solid archaeological information. Based on this premise, chapters 4 and 5 address the archaeological record and the results from the Levanna and Myers Farm sites, as excavated from 2007 to 2014.

4

THE 2007 TO 2009 LEVANNA EXCAVATIONS

When Donna Silversmith (Cayuga, Snipe Clan) and Corinne Hill (Oneida) arrived to excavate at Levanna in 2008, I knew that our process of indigenous archaeology had advanced a stage. These two represented the Six Nations Reserve within Ontario and an alliance across the international boundary with Cayugas living in New York. Besides being extremely skilled trowel excavators with cultural resource management backgrounds, when the excavation of a longhouse continued toward a poison ivy patch, they were willing to work there! Their presence led to more visits from Haudenosaunee Confederacy leaders like Chief Irving Powless Jr. (telling me it was the first dig he had ever seen) and Faithkeeper Tony Gonyea, both from Onondaga Nation and both with major cultural resource responsibilities.

Donna and Corinne were able to participate in the excavations because the Cayuga-SHARE Farm provided convenient lodging. They brought Native eyes and ears to the site, including a set of protocols and decisions. Later some artifacts, particularly some smoking pipes with images of faces and animals, were photographed to send to a seer at Six Nations Reserve in Ontario as a safety check. The Haudenosaunee have a history of cursed artifacts, like the one that is said to have caused the death of the Seneca prophet Handsome Lake in 1815 (Thomas 1994, 123–24). All artifacts were determined to be safe. We experimented with rubber gloves at the site to prevent direct contact with potentially dangerous artifacts, but abandoned the idea as impractical in the summer heat.

There were bigger questions about the smoking pipes, later interpreted as medicine society pipes (see discussion later in this chapter). There was some commentary at first that they should be immediately reburied. After realizing the potential historical implications, this idea was abandoned. Next came the question of whether they should be photographed. This was the moment in time when Chief Powless visited the excavations with Robert Venables, retired professor of history in the American Indian Program at Cornell University. Mildly irritated at the ongoing question, Chief Powless pulled out his phone and photographed a pipe. "World didn't end." He also addressed the next question, which was if the photos could be shown to the public, expressing the opinion that they should indeed be shown. Ultimately, for publication we jointly decided that drawings were best.

Throughout the excavations of 2008 and 2009, Donna and Corinne made comparisons and contrasts between the hurried and mechanical (often legislated) cultural resource management (CRM) or contract archaeology conducted before construction projects and the slower, more thoughtful and flexible research and field school archaeology at Levanna. Their presence certainly led to an atmosphere of introspection and respect for the site. We listened to it and felt it, noting how important finds came in clusters, and how maybe sometimes little was found for hours if someone on the site was negative or was not maintaining the good mind, the Haudenosaunee concept of keeping positive thoughts and recognizing the impact of behaviors on surrounding people (Jacques 1991; Rossen 2015, 7). We also noticed how the weather or birds might be connected to the crew's personality on a given day. Foremost, they brought practice and calm to an inexperienced student crew and provided visible Native support, with the express permission of both the New York and Six Nations Cayuga.

RESITUATING THE LEVANNA SITE

The new investigations bring an opportunity to resituate Levanna within a cluster of Cayuga sites and resource zones that I have referred to as the Cayuga heartland, their principal settlement area from the tenth to sixteenth centuries (Rossen 2015, 172–85). The Cayuga heartland is a twenty-five-square-mile area halfway up the eastern shore of Cayuga Lake, twenty to twenty-five miles north of present-day Ithaca. This type of site provenience was irrelevant to the 1930s investigators. Levanna is located in the Finger Lakes area of central New York, on a gently sloping rise one and a half miles east of Cayuga Lake. The lake itself lies at an altitude of 380 feet above sea level and 38.1 miles long with a maximum width of 3.5 miles, though mostly it is 1.5 miles wide (Wiegand and Eames 1926, 9).

Five miles to the northwest of Levanna is Union Springs Village, which is notable because of Frontenac Island, the Archaic cemetery excavated by William A. Ritchie (1945). The area between the Union Springs shore and Frontenac Island is shallow and was a rich fishing and wetlands plant zone, including wild rice. Two miles north of Levanna is the Great Gully, the largest drainage, where net fishing could have been conducted and exposed Tully limestone was available for farm hoe blades (Ward 2014a, 2014b). From the Levanna site, it is ten miles to the Onondaga escarpment, the source of high quality chert quarries, although the known locations of these quarries along the escarpment are between fifteen and twenty miles away (Winiarz 2015).

Later key Cayuga sites include the fifteenth-century Myers Farm site (six miles southeast, see chapter 5) and the sixteenth-century Corey Village (eight miles east southeast). A hypothesized string of agricultural station sites like Myers Farm may have stretched to the north to a proximity of three or four miles east of Levanna (figure 4.1). Though most Cayuga sites in this zone are later than Levanna, I believe that Levanna was situated in a well-populated and dynamic area of sites and resource zones. In this scenario, Levanna is a fortuitous case of preservation from a time period with relatively few known contemporary sites.

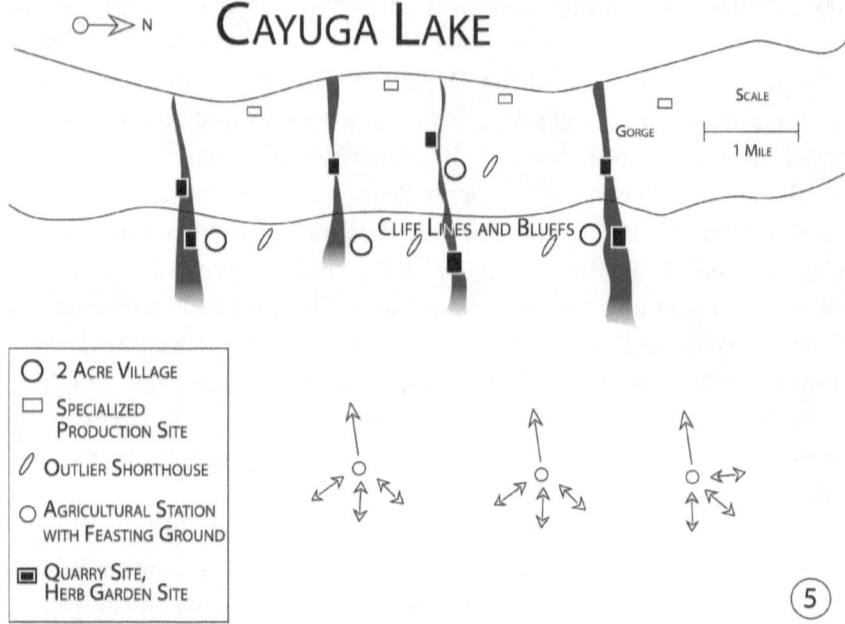

Figure 4.1. Schematic of the Cayuga settlement pattern. Matt Gorney, Digital Media Services, Ithaca College.

EXCAVATIONS AND FEATURES

The Levanna excavations stretched over three summers. The first year entailed three weeks of testing, scattering one by two meter excavations around the site with a few volunteers, ranging from undergraduates to archaeologist friends (11 square meters excavated). The largest crew and excavation effort came in 2008, including a large block (26 square meters excavated). The 2009 field season was slowed by the unusual cold and the rainiest summer in central New York history (25 square meters excavated). A total of sixty-two square meters was excavated to depths ranging from thirty to sixty centimeters in depth in five-centimeter levels. I will describe the excavation and artifact analysis results, along with the interpretations that emerged.

The excavations included one large fifty-four-square meter block and several smaller blocks and test units. The first surprise was that the site was unplowed, with large artifacts such as bone needles and six-inch pottery sherds present in black midden just a few centimeters below the surface. Some features were also visible at the surface, although many were only visible at the base of the shallow black midden, which is twenty to thirty centimeters deep throughout the excavated site area. No stratified evidence of a plowzone is present in most of the research area. This observation agrees with the comments of Homer St. Francis, the site owner at the time of the excavations, who told me his father-in-law Fred Sherman had long protected the site following the 1930s investigations. Sherman refused to plow the site and allowed it to grow into a forested area, today an island of trees within a sea of farm fields. I was indeed skeptical of this statement until the 2007 test excavations were conducted. The one exception, according to Homer, was when his father-in-law became upset that William A. Ritchie broke an agreement to keep the artifacts on site (see chapter 1). At that point in 1932, Sherman plowed a swath of the far eastern site edge. Test excavation units in that area confirmed the story, finding artifacts in a well-defined plowzone. It is likely that without the stewardship of Fred Sherman and later Homer St. Clair, the entire site would have been plowed, and most if not all of the midden and features would have been obliterated.

Large areas of the site were heavily disturbed by the 1920s and 30s excavations of Parker, Ritchie, and Follett. Follett's museum buildings caused further disturbance. These archaeologists also camped on the site, and we found evidence of tent stakes, tin cans, and even a 1932 penny in disturbed site areas. The construction of Levanna Road in 1924 appears to have disturbed the village cemetery, with about seven burials unearthed by Gohl and Parker (see chapter 1). These early archaeologists were interested in burials above all else, along with the earth ovens/effigies. They appear to have been indifferent to some midden and feature zones of the site. Figure 4.2 shows the known extent of the early excavations in relation to the more recent excavations discussed here (Figure 4.3 shows the unit excavation numbers that are referred to). Despite the many years of previous excavation, there were areas of remarkable and unusually intact midden with features such as hearths, pits, and post molds.

The large excavation block is defined by a line of ten superimposed fire hearths, oriented in a northeast-southwest direction (figures 4.4 and 4.5). The hearths overlap to the degree of appearing as a single line across the block prior to excavation. The multiple pits became evident

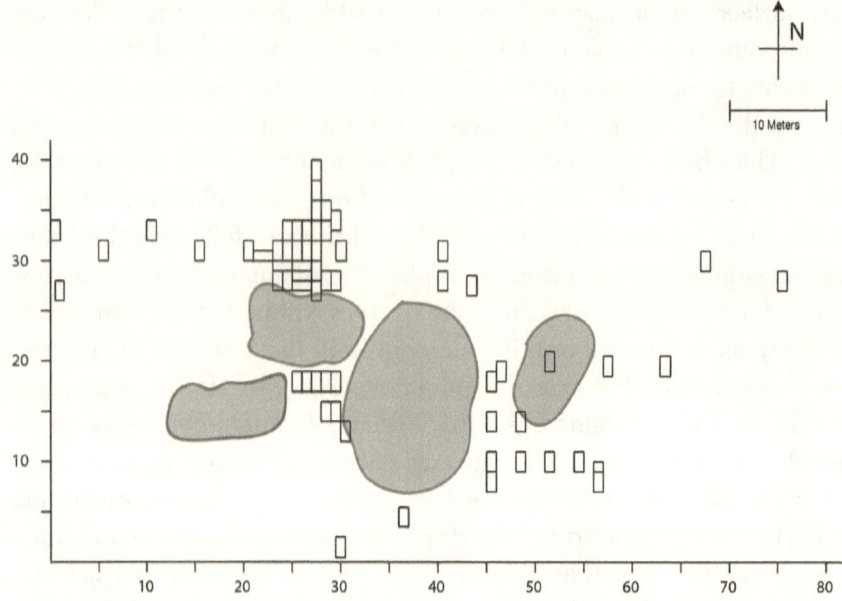

Figure 4.2. Levanna site map. Matt Gorney, Digital Media Services, Ithaca College.

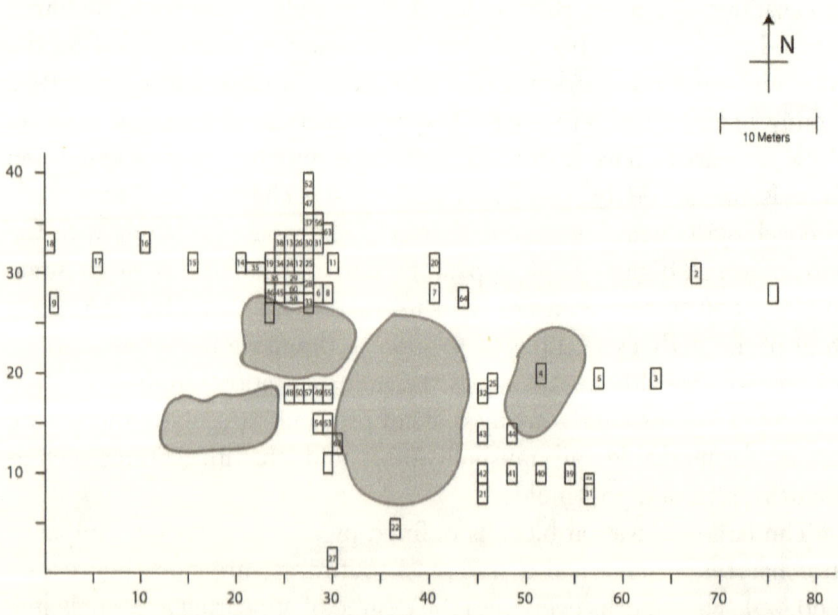

Figure 4.3. Levanna site map with excavation unit numbers. Matt Gorney, Digital Media Services, Ithaca College.

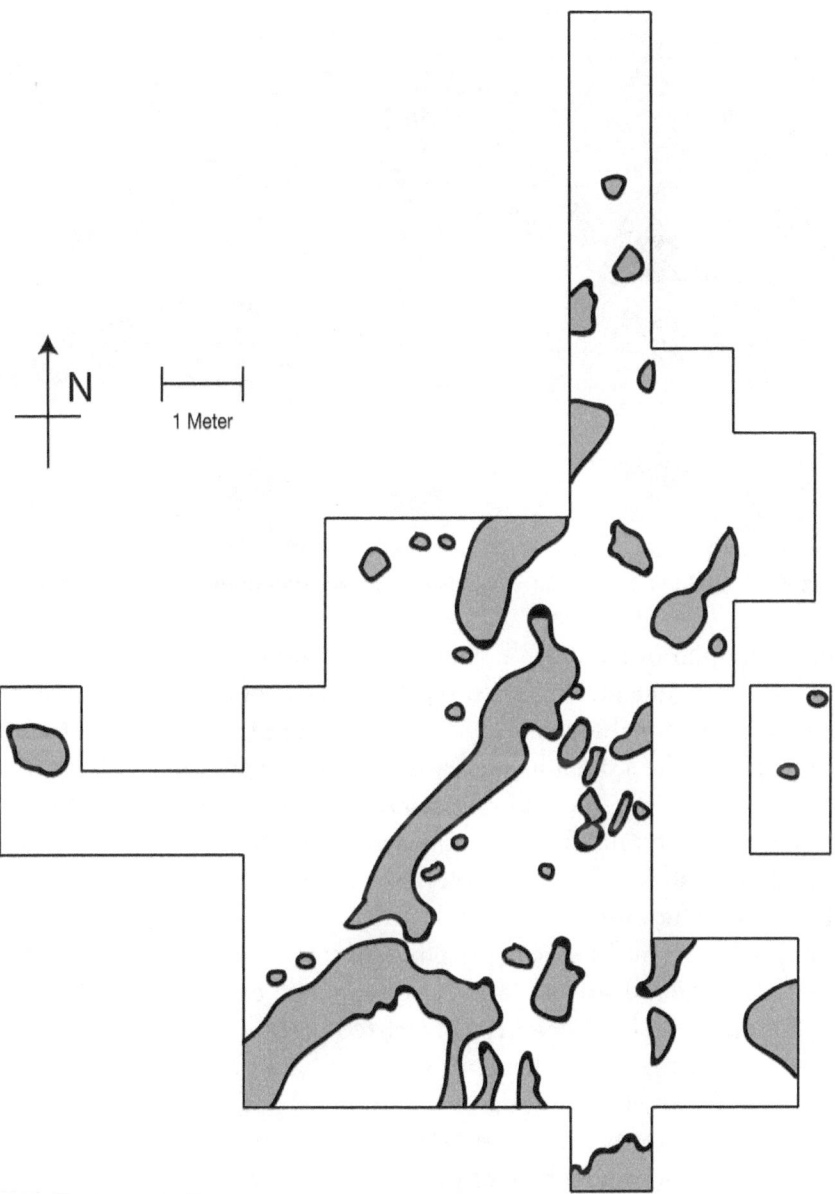

Figure 4.4. Levanna main excavation block features. Matt Gorney, Digital Media Services, Ithaca College.

Figure 4.5. Levanna proto-longhouse excavations underway. Jack Rossen.

on excavation of feature fill. Sixteen post molds are present in a haphazard arrangement. This feature pattern does not represent the classic paired post formal longhouse construction that is well known at later sites such as the sixteenth-century Corey Village (Rossen 2015, 22–27). It appears to represent a less formalized structure. The post mold pattern probably represents a less sturdy structure that was rebuilt several times. This structure will be referred to as a "proto-longhouse." That is, this structure with its aligned hearths represents an early version of the longhouse, including the principles of communal social organization that would be refined and formalized in future centuries.

Pits and occasional hearths and isolated post molds, probably associated with racks and nondomestic structures, are present in the smaller block zones. In all excavations, wall profiles show a shallow black midden twenty to thirty centimeters deep with features and no evidence of plowzone. The proto-longhouse is interrupted at its southwest end by a disturbed area of 1930s excavation. At the northeast end, one meter from the dry creek bank, the line of hearths ends abruptly with a cluster of four post molds, probably the structure entrance. Artifacts within the proto-longhouse area are much smaller and more fragmentary than in surrounding areas, probably due to traffic and trampling within the structure. Nina Rogers noted the small size of pottery sherds in the proto-longhouse during her ceramic analysis. Sherds from the structure average only four centimeters in length, while specimens from elsewhere on the site are two to three times larger on average (Rogers 2014). In performing her ceramic study, Rogers made a far-sighted decision in choosing the importance of the proto-longhouse context over the size of the materials.

Along the site boundaries, we found both intact zones of shallow midden without features and areas disturbed by earlier work. We did not locate any post molds or other indications of a palisade. As discussed in chapter 1, the site location has been mischaracterized as located in a high and defensive position. We found the site to be low-lying and easily accessible from several directions (figure 4.6). The northeast end of the proto-longhouse provided another clear example of how habitation bordered a gently sloping and easily traversed creek bank. It must be concluded that Levanna was low-lying and undefended by a palisade.

In one site area, west of our excavations, with the help of Homer St. Clair's direction, we were able to relocate and reexcavate one of the cracked stone features that were interpreted as animal effigies in the

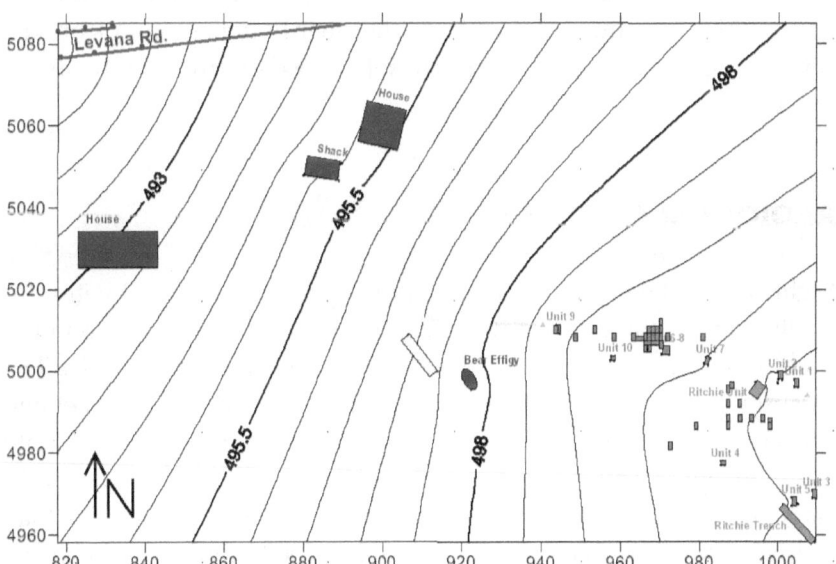

Figure 4.6. Levanna topographic map. Michael Rogers, Physics Department, Ithaca College.

1930s. Although poorly preserved, this concentration of fire-cracked rock had the characteristics of an earth oven. Block samples from midden and all feature fill were collected for water flotation collection of botanical remains and small faunal remains, as discussed here.

TOSS ZONES

The concept of "toss zone" was one of many originated by Lewis R. Binford in his ethnoarchaeological research among the Nunamiut Eskimo of Alaska (Binford 1978, 1983). Binford was dissatisfied with the amount of information that archaeologists were extracting from the ground, and throughout his life introduced a lexicon of "archaeological correlates," or artifact patterns with specific behavioral meanings. Binford was interested in the structure and activities of sites and how they could be read in the archaeological record (David and Kramer 2001, 255–83). He noticed that habitual patterns of disposing waste items, away from a hearth or through a door or hut opening, left distinctive small circular artifact clusters (Binford 1983). The presence of four toss zones outside the proto-longhouse limits (as defined by its post molds), was first noticed from the distributional map of broken ceramic pipes (figure 4.7). Less conspicuous data from the botanical remains confirmed these toss zones.

RADIOCARBON DATES

Eight radiocarbon samples from Levanna provide a range of dates, including one in the ninth century, two in the tenth century, two in the twelfth century and three in the thirteenth century (table 4.1). The earliest dates are from residue on sherds from the Arthur C. Parker and William A. Ritchie excavations (ca. 1924–1928) in the New York State Museum. Janet Shulenberg used the ninth-century dates, along with assays from other sites, to argue that Owasco culture was earlier than had been previously believed (Schulenberg 2002). Parker probably excavated north of the proto-longhouse in the present-day path of Levanna Road and perhaps just to the southwest of the proto-longhouse, where

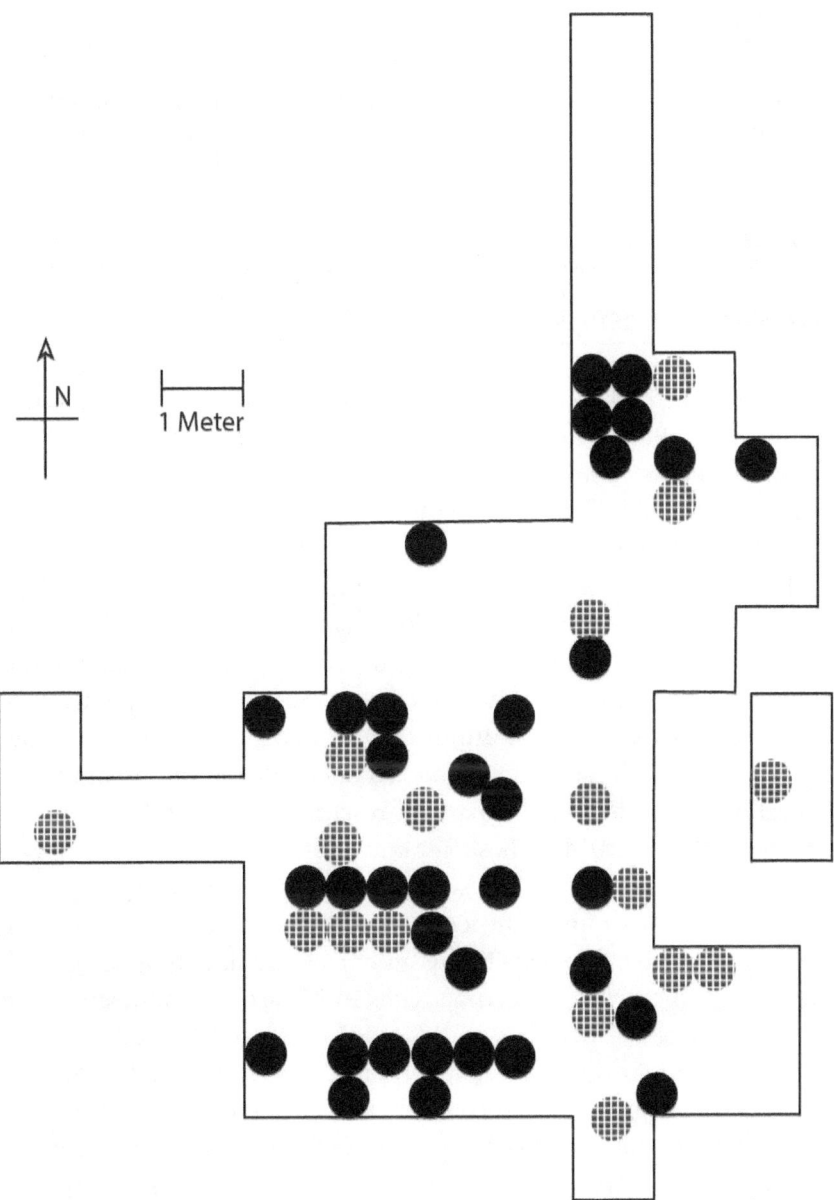

Figure 4.7. Distribution of smoking pipes in and around proto-longhouse, showing toss zones. Matt Gorney, Digital Media Services, Ithaca College.

Table 4.1. Levanna Radiocarbon Dates

	Raw Date BP	Calibrated Date	Provenience
ISGS-A0742	1175+/−30	AD 842+/−45	residue, Parker sherd, NYSM
ISGS-A0754	1115+/−35	AD 928+/−37	residue, Parker sherd, NYSM
GX-28193	1090+/−40	AD 943+/−42	residue, Parker sherd, NYSM
BETA-26418	1910+/−40	AD 1110+/−55	Area 1, Unit 24
ISGS-A3554	840+/−20	AD 1197+/−21	Area 4, Unit 31, Feature 27
ISGS-A3553	835+/−15	AD 1201+/−17	Area 4, Unit 33, Feature 37
UGAMS-21343	800+/−25	AD 1234+/−18	Area 4, Unit 3, Feature 52
BETA-264182	760+/−40	AD 1247+/−23	Area 4, Unit 30

a heavily disturbed area lies. The additional radiocarbon dates are primarily from other areas of the site, with the earliest (AD 1110+/−55) coming from the proto-longhouse.

The shallow midden and integrated features of the site led to two possible conclusions. First, it was possible that the entire site truly dates to the late twelfth/early thirteenth centuries, and New York State Museum dates are incorrect and the additional proto-longhouse date is too early. However, as artifact analysis proceeded, we faced some puzzles of interpretation. In particular, the ceramics and projectile points from different areas of the site were distinctive enough to suspect two occupations. A single occupation was assumed for the entire site when Nina Rogers conducted her master's research on the proto-longhouse ceramics (Rogers 2014). These ceramics generally match the Owasco ceramics from Levanna at the New York State Museum associated with the tenth and eleventh centuries. The early twelfth-century date from the proto-longhouse appears to this author to be a little too late in time. Meanwhile, the tight radiocarbon dates from east and southeast of the proto-longhouse (especially the AD 1197+/−21 and AD 1201 +/−17, in association with more incised ceramics, plus some Madison points mixed in, strongly suggest a second occupation at the cusp of the twelfth and thirteenth centuries. For the purposes of discussing the two occupations moving forward, I will refer to a tenth- to eleventh-century (proto-longhouse) occupation (referred to for the sake of brevity as tenth century) and a second late twelfth/early thirteenth-century occupation (referred to as the late twelfth-century occupation).

Both areas of the site are fine-grained (Binford 1980) in terms of having intact (unplowed) shallow midden, clear feature patterns and identifiable activity areas. From these patterns, the notion of a campsite visited often over several centuries was rejected. The site instead has archaeological correlates that indicate two intensive and relative brief occupations.

SITE ZONES: ONE OR TWO COMPONENTS?

The delineation of components at Levanna is complex and subtle. Radiocarbon dates generally delineate two basic occupations, although there is some overlap in the radiocarbon dates. Feature patterns (post molds, pits, and hearths) and artifact analyses (ceramics, projectile points) support the subtle division into two components. Based in part on the dates, features, and artifacts, as well as the divisions between areas of the site that could be excavated, which were separated from areas that had been excavated in the 1920s through 1940s, seven site areas were defined:

Area 1: Tenth- to twelfth-century component, within the proto-longhouse in the main excavation block (26 square meters excavated).

Area 2: Tenth- to twelfth-century component, outside the proto-longhouse in the main excavation block, including toss zones (21 square meters excavated).

Area 3: Late twelfth- to early thirteenth-century component, a series of units between eight and seventeen meters south of the main excavation block (referred to as south block), including a small eight-meter excavation block (16 square meters excavated).

Area 4: Late twelfth- to early thirteenth-century component, a series of southeast outlier excavation units (21 square meters excavated).

Area 5: One far south outlying excavation unit along the side perimeter (2 square meters excavated).

Area 6: Two far east outlying excavation units outside the site midden (4 square meters excavated).

Area 7: Historic 1930s component, one unit east of the proto-longhouse (2 square meters excavated).

These seven site areas are used as an organizational device to analyze and discuss archaeological materials from different site contexts. In some cases, like ceramics, the site areas were useful in seeing culture change from the tenth to twelfth centuries. In other cases, like botanical remains, there are no substantive differences between areas, except for the Area 7 historic intrusion.

PROJECTILE POINTS

Thirty-six projectile points (including eight tips) were recovered. Projectile points from the site stylistically support the chronological implications of the radiocarbon dates and ceramics that there are two defined cultural components at Levanna (table 4.2). Area 1 and 2, the earlier component, are dominated by Levanna points, plus two Jack's Reef and a single Madison Point. This was the type site for William A. Ritchie's definition of the Levanna point. Ritchie (1928) reported eighteen Levanna points and no other point types. In orthodox typologies, the wider triangular Levanna points are most common around AD 1000 and gradually give way to the finer, slimmer and more aerodynamic Madison triangles by the sixteenth century (figure 4.8). There is a "transitional" point variety, with a size and length-to-width ratio halfway between the two types, that is dominant at the fifteenth-century Myers Farm site (Rossen 2015, see chapter 5). However, Madison

Table 4.2. Recovered Projectile Point Types

Areas 1 and 2: Proto-longhouse and Toss Zones	
Levanna	8
Archaic types	6
Broken/unidentified	6
Jack's Reef	2
Tips	4
Madison	1
Area 3: South Block	
Madison	2
Tip	1
Area 4: Southeast Zone	
Madison	3
Tips	3
Ritchie (1928)	
Levanna	18

Figure 4.8. Levanna site projectile points. Jack Rossen.

points have been found in contexts as early as AD 1200 in low frequency (Ritchie 1971, 34). The Jack's Reef points are most often associated with the tenth and eleventh centuries.

Six Archaic points are present, all from the proto-longhouse excavation block (table 4.2). There is no other evidence of an Archaic component at the site. It is more logical to think of these points as collected or recycled artifacts (Amick 2014; Whyte 2014), possibly from an archaic site less than one mile north near the Great Gully with similar points. Areas 3 and 4, representing the later component, together have five Madison points and four point tips.

Trampling in and around the proto-longhouse is evident in the projectile point collection. Areas 1 and 2 had six broken and thus unidentifiable points, while the other site areas have no broken points. The type differences between Area 1 and 2 and Area 3 and 4 is clear, and the site might appear to show the transition from broader Levanna to slimmer and more aerodynamic Madison points. One problem with this scenario is the Transitional point type known from the fifteen century (see chapter 5) that exhibits measurements halfway between the Levanna and Madison types. Taking the Levanna points at face value would not explain those points at sites like Myers Farm. Finally, the projectile points appear to connect

Areas 1 and 2 more with the previous excavations of Ritchie and Parker because of the dominance of Levanna points in both cases.

OTHER LITHICS TOOLS

Lithic tools other than projectile points were analyzed by Shannon LaBelle (2015), who examined 633 artifacts, 70 percent of which are utilized flakes. These are evenly divided between the two site components, and no significant difference was found between components in terms of nonprojectile point lithic tools. Labelle cataloged side scrapers (n=61), end scrapers (n=20), pottery smoothers and engravers (n=25), burins (n=21), knives (n=20), and drills (n=2). All but eight side and end scrapers have edge angles lower than 35 degrees, with a mean of 20 degrees, suggesting cutting and slicing actions. A substantial percent of tools (46 percent) exhibit obvious evidence of use-wear on tool edges (see following analysis by Michael Spears). Ninety-three tools, including most end and side scrapers, exhibit clear haft marks, indicating their use with bone or wooden handles.

All cherts are Morehouse, from the Onondaga formation, a raw material that is available only at the quarries that line the Onondaga escarpment fifteen miles north of Levanna (LaBelle 2015). In contrast, almost all scrapers at the sixteenth-century Corey Village were made of Seneca chert, the top layer eroded by the glaciers and locally available in streambed cobbles. Seneca is much lower quality because of its erosion state and fracture planes, but was more accessible (Winiarz 2015).

LITHIC MICROSCOPIC USE-WEAR AND POLISH

Michael Spears (2010) conducted a microscopic use-wear analysis of a sample of forty-four lithic tools for an Ithaca College senior honors thesis. Although the different site components had not been identified at the time of this analysis, Spears equally separated his sample into proto-longhouse (earlier component) and areas south and southeast of the proto-longhouse (later component). He focused on expedient tools, especially utilized flakes, that are not normally included in artifact analyses. Spears experimentally created flake pairs and used them on various materials, making fifty strokes each on bone with no meat, bone with meat, tanned leather, fibrous plant, tuber and wood. He microscopically examined both experimental and archaeological use edges at low magnifications ranging from 8 to 30x.

Spears was able to match his experimentally produced use-wear and polish with nineteen of sixty-three use edges, including lithics from both components. Three to four use edges matched well with each category of bone, meat, wood, plant, and tuber. The remaining forty-four use edges could not be confidently matched, suggesting use on other materials. As a pilot study, his conclusion was that greater attention to nonprojectile point lithics such as scrapers and utilized flakes could shed light on a variety of production and processing activities (Spears 2010).

CERAMICS

Ceramics were important to establishing the two components of Levanna. Christina T. "Nina" Rogers conducted a detailed analysis of 150 diagnostic sherds from the proto-longhouse (Rogers 2014). She noted both the strengths and weaknesses of the long-used ceramic typology of Richard S. MacNeish (1952). Documented were both classic "Owasco" types that have long been associated with the tenth century, but also other types that indicated greater temporal overlap and longer use-lives of particular types. Her analysis is indeed a synchronic "slice-of-time" confirmation of the diachronic longitudinal studies of Hart and Brumbach that had similar conclusions (Hart and Brumbach 2005, 2009). Rogers concluded that the ceramics styles melded together in a manner that supported the tenth- or eleventh-century establishment of Haudenosaunee matrilocal settlement. That is, the ceramics indicate that related pottery-making women lived in the proto-longhouse, along with unrelated men who had married in (Rogers 2014, 68–72). This in turn supports the in situ development of the Haudenosaunee back to at least this time or earlier, based on the overlapping presence of earlier Point Peninsula ceramic types (Hart and Brumbach 2005).

Rogers did not see evidence of coiling and believed all the Levanna ceramics she analyzed to have been made with a paddle and anvil technique. This idea was challenged by the petrographic analysis discussed next. The ceramics were certainly open pit-fired, based on the common presence of fire clouding. Just over half of the rim sherds have some form of collar, either an "incipient" collar or a more prominent collar. The process of the gradual development of collared rims is usually portrayed as a temporally linear process. The presence of uncollared, incipient collars and full collared sherds in the same briefly occupied proto-longhouse instead suggests a more dynamic process of stylistic experimentation and use (Rogers 2014).

A wide variety of finishing and decorative techniques are present in this tightly spatially associated collection. Included are cordmarking and cord-wrapped paddle, smoothing, cord-wrapped stick, stamping, dentate, incising and punctation. Some sherds exhibit combinations of techniques. Rogers (2014, 53) illustrated one pot with cord wrapped paddle or cloth impressions on the bottom, oblique cord-wrapped stick in the middle and dentate punctate stamping at the top. Rogers wrote that "whether they used designs popular in the past, or combined types of decorations popular in the past with newer additions such as collars and castellations is an indication of the complexity and thought process of the Levanna people" (Rogers 2014, 54). Rogers concluded:

> The movement towards an elongated collar began in the earliest Point Peninsula (approximately AD 600) Vinette vessels by decorating the collar or adding extra clay to the rims of pots. These additions proceed systematically until they developed into the late Iroquois pots with large collars with castellations. Incipient collars, decorated collars or rims with additional clay added are all prevalent in the Levanna sample, exemplifying the movement from vessels with no collars to large collared pots. Some of the sample have no aspect of collars at all while others have decorated or incipient collars, some with castellations. This makes evident the large variability found inside the synchronic sample. (Rogers 2014, 99)

Rogers compared the 2009 excavated ceramics with Ritchie and Mac-Neish's (1949) analysis of Levanna ceramics, probably from the 1927 excavations. Where Ritchie and MacNeish identified only eight ceramic types, Rogers identified sixteen, plus twenty-five sherds that exhibited

Table 4.3. Levanna Site Map with Excavation Unit Numbers.

Ceramic Types	Rogers 2009 Levanna Sample	Type Percentage (%) Inside Sample	Ritchie and MacNeish Levanna Sample	Type Percentage (%) Inside R&M Sample
Owasco Herringbone	29	19.3%	46	23.9%
Carpenter Brook Cord on Cord	0	0%	50	26.04%
Levanna Cord on Cord	11	7.33%	56	29.18%
Vinette Dentate / Complex Dentate	29	19.33%	0	0%
Two or More Types	25	16.66%	0	0%
Unknown	20	13.33%	0	0%
Owasco Corded Horizontal	6	4%	10	5.2%
Levanna Corded Collar	6	4%	8	4.16%
Owasco Corded Oblique	0	0%	12	6.25%
Canandaigua Plain	2	1.33%	4	1.04%
Owasco Platted	0	0%	6	3.12%
Castle Creek Incised Neck	5	3.33%	0	0%
Owasco Corded Collar	4	2.66%	0	0%
Castle Creek Beaded	4	2.66%	0	0%
Jacks Reef Dentate	2	1.33%	0	0%
Jacks Reef Dentate Collar	2	1.33%	0	0%
Wickham Corded	2	1.33%	0	0%
Point Peninsula Rocker Stamped	1	0.66%	0	0%
Wickham Incised	1	0.66%	0	0%
Wichkham Corded Punctate	1	0.66%	0	0%
Totals	150	100%	192	100%

traits of two or more types (table 4.3, figure 4.9, and 4.10). Another notable difference is that all of Ritchie and MacNeish's sherds were corded, while Rogers found 150 noncorded sherds.

Following the new radiocarbon dates that indicated two occupations at Levanna, Macy O'Hearn examined a similar sample size of 165 sherds from the later, late twelfth-century/early thirteenth-century component (table 4.4). O'Hearn found substantive differences in her ceramics from those analyzed by Rogers. Most notably, the percentage of classic "Owasco" ceramic types increased: Owasco herringbone is present at a rate of 19.3 percent in Rogers earlier sample and 34.5 percent in

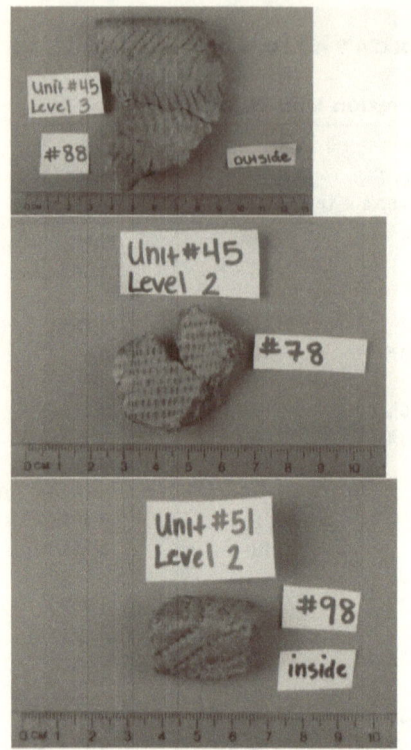
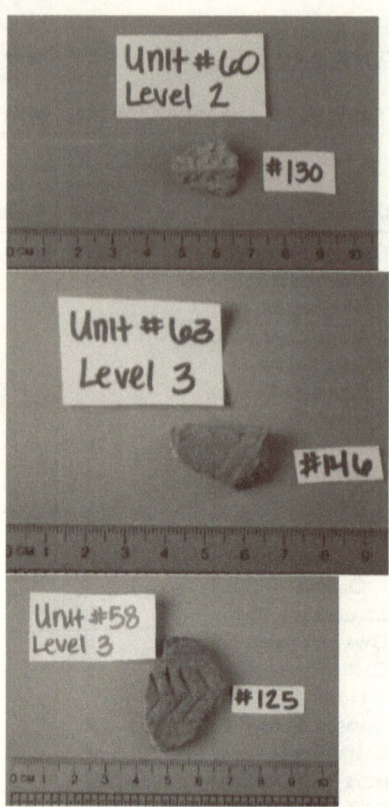

Figure 4.9. Levanna site ceramics. Owasco Herringbone or Carpenter Brook Cord-on-Cord (top left), Castle Creek Beaded rim (top right), Vinette Dentate (middle left), "barbell" design (middle right), Jack's Reef Corded Collar rim (bottom left), rocker stamp smoothed Owasco Herringbone (bottom right). Nina Rogers.

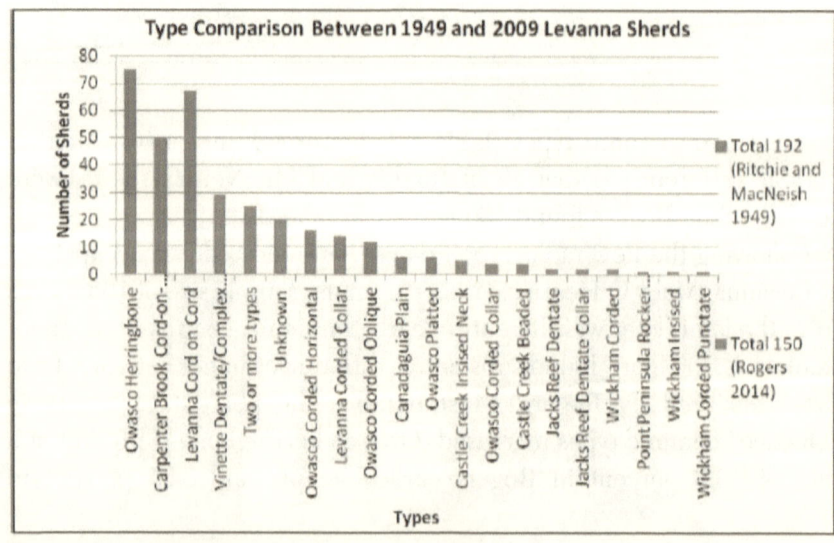

Figure 4.10. Levanna ceramic comparisons.

Table 4.4. Levanna Main Excavation Block Features.

Ceramic Type	Frequency	Percent of Sample
Owasco Herringbone	57	34.5
Owasco Corded Horizontal	37	22.4
Levanna Cord-on-Cord	18	10.9
Carpenter Brook Cord-on-Cord	14	8.5
Wickham Corded Punctate	9	5.5
Vinette Dentate	6	3.6
Barbell described by Nina	5	3.0
Jack's Reef Corded Collar	3	1.8
Kipp Island Crisscross	3	1.8
Owasco Corded Oblique	3	1.8
St. Lawrence Pseudo Scallop Shell	3	1.8
Jack's Reef Dentate Collar	2	1.2
Owasco Platted	2	1.2
Point Peninsula Corded	2	1.2
Jack's Reef Corded	1	0.6
Total	**165**	**100.0**

O'Hearn's later sample, and Owasco Corded Horizontal increased from 4 percent in the early sample to 22.4 percent in the later sample. As expected, the classic Owasco styles are more prevalent in the late 1200s and early 1300s than in the 1000s and 900s. Carpenter Brook Cord-on-Cord, totally absent from the earlier samples (but common in Ritchie and MacNeish's sample, n=50), is present in O'Hearn's later sample (n=14). Furthermore, other types appear in low frequency in O'Hearn's sample, including St. Lawrence Pseudo Scallop Shell (n=3) and Point Peninsula Corded (n=1), with the latter a surviving style of earlier times or a contextually displaced specimen.

O'Hearn noted the common presence of incised decoration alone or in conjunction with traditional cord-marking in her sample, referring to most Owasco Herringbone and Owasco Corded Horizontal sherds:

> According to MacNeish and Ritchie, Owasco Herringbone is characterized by "a corded-herringbone decoration on an outflaring rim (1949, 111)," and Owasco Corded Horizontal is characterized by, "horizontal cord-wrapped stick impressions, with or without oblique corded decorations above the main theme, on outflaring rims (1949, 112)." There is no mention of incising even in the extended descriptions for either of these types. (O'Hearn 2016, 1)

These sherds appear to be a slightly later variant on classic "Owasco" pottery styles, and a precursor to the appearance of fully incised styles that would dominate in Cayuga territory by the fifteenth century (O'Hearn 2013a). Finally, O'Hearn recognized a sample of sherds from Unit 38 that appeared earlier than the rest of her sample, and this unit is indeed from the earlier Area 2 in the southwest toss zone just outside the proto-longhouse. This sample had mistakenly been included in her original analysis.

Both Rogers and O'Hearn noted an unusual design element that is absent from the Ritchie-MacNeish typology. It is the oblique stamping, approximately five millimeters in length, in the shape of a barbell with two small circles connected by a line (Rogers 2014, 86–87). O'Hearn found this design element on five sherds while Rogers noted it on two sherds (figure 4.9). Rogers viewed this as a "more refined dentate stamp." O'Hearn (2016) noted that "individual impressions are often offset from one another, suggesting that the instrument used to make the impressions was a very small stamp rather than a larger cord-wrapped stick or paddle."

CERAMIC PETROGRAPHY

Petrographic analysis of twelve Levanna pottery sherds was conducted by Ammie Chittim (a.k.a. Mitchell) of the University at Buffalo. The sample was chosen to equally include both presumably earlier Point Peninsula and presumably later Owasco styles. Sherds representative of major styles at the site were thin-sectioned and examined for clues to decorative design, construction technique, and temper. Chittim has looked to petrography as a solution to the problems of pottery style typology that were discussed previously (Mitchell 2017). Specifically, the existing pottery typologies based on surface decoration in discreet categories make it difficult to understand culture change and continuity, even though pottery surface styles are assumed to be key indicators of culture and identity. The internal paste of ceramics represents procurement of distant resources, technological choices affecting pottery performance, and possibly ideology based on color selection (Mitchell 2015). Ceramic paste or fabric construction is thus a complex process worthy of analysis, although this type of analysis is only occasionally performed. Chittim describes her methodology:

> Ceramic fabrics were measured with standardized reference aids for the current study (Orton and Hughes 2013) and through the point counting technique described by Stoltman (1989). Point counting is a technique traditionally used by geologists to quantify a rock in an unbiased way. Point counting is conducted using a petrographic microscope, an Advanced Object Guide, and a series of thin sections. Thin sections are produced by cutting narrow sections (c. 10 mm x 10 mm) from a rock or ceramic sherd (Peacock 1970, 379). These sections are ground to 0.03 mm thickness and attached with a resin to a glass microscope slide (Orton and Hughes 2013, 163; Rice 1987, 379). Mineral inclusions at this thinness become translucent and can be identified by their unique optical properties (Freestone 1995, 11). To point count a petrographic slide, one starts in a corner of the sample and moves at a standard interval up and down across the entire sample. (Mitchell 2015, 11)

The analysis grouped the Levanna sherds into three distinctive technological groups. These groups each represent a "ceramic recipe" including specific proportions of angular crushed rock inclusions and rounded sand. Surface treatment and decoration may or may not be part of this recipe, and in this case, Chittim found that the groups cross-cut styles and indeed the presumably earlier Point Peninsula and presumably later Owasco styles. This result supported the stylistic-typological analyses of Rogers and O'Hearn and the notion that styles lasted longer and temporally cross-cut each other more than was previously thought.

Petrographic analysis can distinguish crushed stone used to temper ceramics that cannot otherwise be reliably identified. Two significant groups were identified in the Levanna sample. Group 1 is feldspar-rich (syenite, monzonite gneiss, and [quartz] diorite), while Group 2 is quartz-rich (with high grit content [50–53 percent] granite temper, mixed with low proportions of sand [7 percent].

Ceramics with thicker walls have a lower proportion of crushed rock inclusions, while thinner walled ceramics have a higher proportion of crush rock. Feldspar-bearing stone appears to have been preferred. In the traditional typologies, this might suggest a temporal and technological trend, such as the need for thinner-walled cooking pots as corn became more dietarily important (Hart 2012). In a contemporaneous or synchronic context such as Levanna, there might be technological differences between thinner-walled cooking pots and thicker-walled storage pots. The lack of correlation between style decoration and temper led Chittim to believe that there was a broad similarity in technical knowledge between different potters at the Levanna site that cross-cut pottery styles and broad typological groupings (Mitchell 2015, 2). This supports Rogers' (2014, 68–72) notion that the Levanna ceramics were indicative of an established Haudenosaunee matrilocal social organization with related women potters.

One exception may be incised sherds. The four incised sherds in the petrographic analysis all have moderate to high grit and substantial sand temper. Incised ceramics become dominant by the fifteenth century in Cayuga country, but these sherds raise questions. Is the presence of these incised ceramics at Levanna in the late twelfth century the beginning of a technological transition to thinner cooking pots (Hart 2012), and why is there an apparent connection between technology and style among these sherds that is otherwise absent among Point Peninsula and Owasco ceramics?

The closest igneous or metamorphic outcrops to Levanna are in the Adirondacks and in the Canadian Shield of central and eastern Canada. The closest bedrock sources of syenite, monzonite, and diorite are thus about 220 miles northeast of the site. However, feldspar and quartz-rich stones are locally available in the glacial tills of the site region. Feldspar temper was also identified in the petrographic analysis of the Corey Village ceramics of the fifteenth-century Cayuga site (Stoner 2015, 74). The targeting of feldspar and quartz within the varied glacial tills indicates specific selection and understanding of temper properties.

It is notable that chunks of feldspar and quartz temper were common in the midden deposits (n=785 totaling 5,929 grams). Three adjacent excavation units outside the proto-longhouse contained 1,103 grams or 18.6 percent of the total. It appears that feldspar and quartz for ceramic manufacture were actively collected and crushed in special activity areas.

The petrographic analysis also challenged ideas about pottery manufacture techniques. Where Rogers thought all ceramics from the proto-longhouse were made with the paddle and anvil technique, Chittim sees microscopic evidence of coiling in three-quarters (n=9) of the analyzed sherds, including both Point Peninsula and Owasco vessels. She believes that secondary smoothing on the sherds obscured evidence of coiling and misled analysts into believing the ceramics were paddle and anvil manufactured. Traditional models have assumed that Point Peninsula vessels were created by the coiling technique while Owasco pots were created using the modeling or paddle and anvil method, and this dichotomy was used to support an in-migration model for Owasco/Haudenosaunee groups into present-day New York. A greater prevalence of coiling in both Point Peninsula and Owasco ceramic styles would further support the in situ Haudenosaunee development model.

CERAMIC RESIDUE ANALYSIS

Five Levanna ceramic sherds with visible residue were submitted for residue analysis. The analysis, conducted by Eleanora A. Reber and Didi el-Behaedi (2015) at the University of North Carolina at Wilmington, was a pilot study to assess the potential for this type of analysis of these collections (one Myers Farm site sherd was also included). One fabric-impressed, grit-tempered body sherd from the tenth-century component (Level 3 inside the south end of the proto-longhouse) tested positive for Amyrin and "lots of possible" Friedelin, OL22-26. These compounds are biomarkers for a wide variety of nonconiferous trees and plants. A Levanna sherd from the twelfth-century component (Level 4, Southeast outlier zone) showed a "wide range of Fas in TLE, C14:0-C26:0, and cholesterol (the sterol biomarker RL 314)," meaning the pot contents were "primarily plant, with meat present."

The other three submitted sherds had "no interpretable residue." In these cases, the analysts thought it was possible that "blackened encrustations interpreted as visible residues may have been zones of sooting or reduction of the pottery" (Reber and el-Behaedi 2015). In summary, analysis of residue in ceramics has great potential for taking archaeobotanical and faunal analyses beyond lists of plants and animals utilized toward understanding ancient cooking recipes. In this case, the pilot study was only able to lead to generalized information of plants and meat in the pots submitted for analysis. It is hoped that future studies will produce more specific and definitive results.

SMOKING PIPES

Discarded broken ceramic smoking pipes are common in the midden deposits. These specimens were analyzed by Alison Armour, an Ithaca College student intern. The 181 pipes represent a density of almost three per square meter of excavation. Of the pipe specimens, 59.7 percent (n=108) are bowl fragments and 31.5 percent (n=57) are stem fragments, including 17 with a mouthpiece. The remaining specimens are shoulders (n=9), elbows (n=3), and bases (n=4), including bar bases that would attach to the underside of the bowl. Seventy-five pipe fragments are decorated, including fine dentate stamping (36 percent), punctation (24 percent), and incising (20 percent). Almost half of pipe bowls (44 percent) are undecorated and straight-sided. Decorated bowls include basket type (18 percent), straight-sided (12 percent), straight-sided ring bowls (7.4 percent), bulbar ring bowls (6.5 percent), two square-rimmed or collared bowls (1.9 percent), and one modified trumpet bowl (0.9 percent).

This array of pipes, with finely made and minute decorations and very fine paste, fits the classic definition of Owasco or early Haudenosaunee (see pipes from the contemporary Snell site in the Mohawk Valley [Ritchie, Lenig, and Miller 1953, 73]). Almost all specimens stylistically fit comfortably within the tenth- to twelfth/thirteenth-century time frame of the site occupations. Only three specimens, the two square-rimmed (collared) and the one trumpet bowl, are normally associated with later periods. However, the chronology of pipe styles in Haudenosaunee territory is poorly understood, and assemblages of tenth- and twelfth-century assemblages are virtually nonexistent. In general, the stylistic uniformity of pipe decoration supports the chronology of site components as defined by radiocarbon dates and ceramics. We know that pipes were manufactured at Levanna because of the recovery of unfinished and unfired clay specimens, both bowls and stems, discarded in the Area 4 midden far from the proto-longhouse.

The majority of pipes (n=126 or 68.5 percent) exhibit evidence of use in the form of black staining inside the bowl or stem bore. Only sixteen pipes (8.7 percent) were clearly never used, and another forty-two pipes (22.8 percent) are indeterminate in terms of use.

A spatial analysis of the smoking pipes indicates that these pipes were heavily concentrated in the proto-longhouse and in toss zones just outside the structure (figure 4.7). Pipe smoking was a common activity at the Levanna proto-longhouse, and pipes were commonly broken and discarded there. Perhaps the preponderance of pipes in the earlier component, the proto-longhouse, is indicative of a tenth-century affinity for pipes, followed by a time of lesser use.

Scattered in the small block excavation south of the proto-longhouse, associated with the late twelfth/early thirteenth-century occupation, were only a few smoking pipes, primarily some extraordinary specimens, quite different from the dentate stamped, punctuated, and incised specimens (figure 4.11). One extraordinary afternoon in October 2010, after

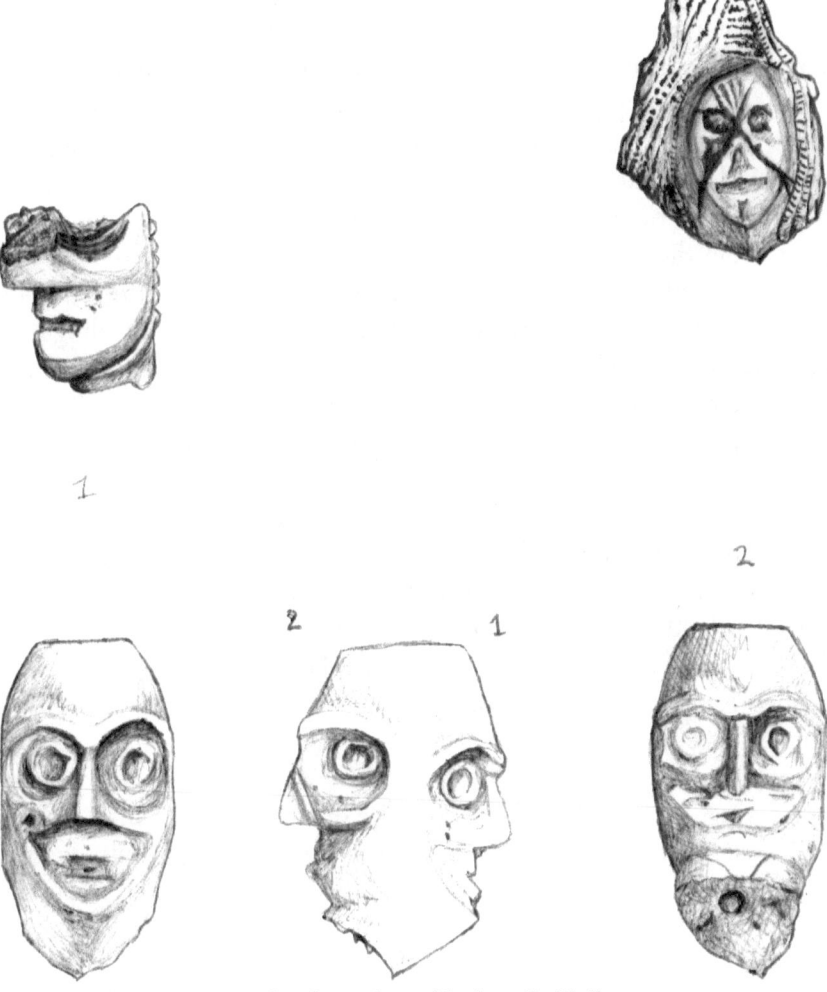

Figure 4.11a. Levanna site face pipes. Marissa DeMello.

speaking at Ganondagan State Park on the Levanna excavations, I sat at the dining room table of Seneca elder Peter Jemison and his relatives with these pipes. The Senecas thought they were indeed extraordinary, and identified Haudenosaunee images of Hado:ih, the great healer (a false face image), a healer wearing a wolf mask, a flying head (a fearsome killer from various folk stories), a cornhusk person (the little people of folklore), and various animals (Canfield 1904; Cusick 2004[1825], 25–26; Johnson 2010[1881]; Schoolcraft 2002[1846], 265–660 for pipe comparison see Wonderly 2002, 2005).

Perhaps the most extraordinary piece is a pipe stem with the design of the Tree of Peace, five ascending chevrons around a vertical line with surrounding rays (Rossen 2015, 175). Years of conversation and discussion with the Haudenosaunee have led to an interpretation of these as medicine society pipes, used in communal and intertribal healing rituals. It was later that the newer radiocarbon dates and ceramic analysis separated the site into two occupations. This new information also separated the effigy pipes from the 181 Owasco-style geometric design pipes from the earlier proto-longhouse area. We began to think about the process of ritualization of pipe smoking, a shift from the common village smoking of the tenth century to a more specialized healing purpose by the end of the twelfth century. My Native friends also believe that medicine society pipes are explicitly confederacy artifacts. That is, these pipes are indicative of an early functioning Haudenosaunee Confederacy with integrated cultural activities.

Smoking pipes continued to be plentiful at the fifteenth-century Myers Farm site (n=51, see chapter 5), but are infrequent at the sixteenth-century Corey Village, where only nine fragments were found (O'Hearn and Ward 2015, 163–64). Similarly, only nine pipe fragments were reported from the excavations and local collections of the seventeenth-century Rogers Farm site, on the western side of Cayuga Lake (Williams-Shuker 2009, 201). It is unclear whether the disparity in smoking pipe frequencies between sites reflects different site activities and functions or if Cayuga pipe smoking declined in the sixteenth and seventeenth centuries. Another fifteen widely scattered sixteenth- to eighteenth-century Cayuga pipes from collectors in the heartland area were described and illustrated by William M. Beauchamp (1898, 112–26). The social and ritual purposes of smoking pipes are further discussed in chapter 5 in connection with the Myers Farm site materials.

FISHNET SINKERS

Net sinkers are among the most numerous artifacts at Levanna. These notched and to varying degree, polished artifacts were analyzed by Jensen Hurley (2016) and Katie Reynolds (2008) (figure 4.12). Harrison Follett's notes indicate that 675 net sinkers were recovered during the 1930s excavations (Follett n.d.a., n.d.b., n.d.c., 14). This discussion includes 313 net sinkers recovered during the 2007–2009 excavations.

Most Levanna net sinkers are between 5.5 and 6 centimeters in length and 4 to 5 centimeters in width and virtually all specimens weigh between 30 and 40 grams. There may have been a degree of standardization in net sinker production, or at least an ideal size and weight. Net

Figure 4.12. Levanna fishnet sinkers. Jack Rossen.

sinkers were recovered in various stages of production, from crude and unpolished to finely polished specimens. To understand the distribution of production stages, net sinkers were placed into smooth (n=156, 49.8 percent), medium (n=118, 37.7 percent), and coarse (n=39, 12.5 percent) categories. Most net sinkers (n=196, 62.6 percent) were recovered from the proto-longhouse tenth-century area. One post mold-like feature just east of the proto-longhouse held nine stacked net sinkers exhibiting a cline in smoothness and polish, with the most crudely worked specimen on top and the most polished at the bottom of the stack.

Sites that are contemporary with Levanna are few and far between. One such site in Schoharie, New York, 115 miles east of Levanna, is the Net Weight site. This is a plowzone site that was surface collected for sixteen years, with its most conspicuous and abundant artifacts being 150 net sinkers identical to the Levanna specimens. Without radiocarbon dates, it was speculated the site dates to the tenth century and I support that estimation (Anderson 2013). This site corroborates the importance of net fishing in the tenth century throughout central New York.

Early Cayuga net sinker technology is not well-understood. Net sinkers tend to be numerous in tenth-century sites and much scarcer later in time. Fishbones are numerous in Cayuga sites from the ten to sixteenth centuries, so it appears that other techniques such as line fishing and traps became more popular. We found that modern metal net sinkers average 41.5 grams, similar to the ideal weight of Levanna specimens. Modern fishnets use floats. Prehistoric net floats were not recovered, probably because they were made of gourd or wood. Along with Neil Patterson, a Tuscarora environmental scientist, we stretched a fishnet with stone net sinkers across nearby Great Gully Creek. Neil was testing water quality based on the diversity of fish species in the creek. In about fifteen minutes, we caught a wide variety of large and small fish, with the largest species being trout and suckers. The efficacy of net fishing near Levanna was well-demonstrated.

Ethnographically, the use of similar stone net sinkers was documented in 1968 by Joel Savishinsky near the village of Colville Lake in the Northwest Territories of Canada. Figure 4.13 shows Sitsa Codzie, a member of the Hare Tribe, photographed by Savishinsky stringing stone net sinkers. The nets were used in the lakes and streams to take whitefish, trout, jackfish (northern pike), and grayling (Joel Savishinsky, personal communication 2015).

Figure 4.13. Sitsa Codzie, Hare Tribe, stringing stone net sinkers, Colville Lake, Northwest Territories, Canada, 1968. Joel Savishinksy.

FAUNAL REMAINS

The 2007 to 2009 Levanna excavations produced a prodigious amount of faunal remains (tables 4.5 and 4.6). On examining the collection, April M. Beisaw of Vassar College estimated there are twenty thousand bones. The analysis was a 10 percent sample by Beisaw, including two lots. Lot 1 is 1,608 bones from the proto-longhouse (tenth century, earlier component) and Lot 2 is 355 bones from Unit 31, emblematic of the late twelfth-century component and the same unit that produced the double-face Hado:i smoking pipe.

Table 4.5. Faunal Remains by Excavation Unit

Unit 1	125	Unit 3	476
Cod	1	Beaver	1
Cotton rat?	2	Cardinal	1
Eastern fox squirrel	7	Chickens and pheasants	2
Fox	1	Eastern fox squirrel	9
Garter snake	2	Garter snake	3
Green frog	28	Ground squirrel	3
Large carnivore	1	Large fish	3
Large mammal	28	Large mammal	86
Medium bird	3	Medium bird	7
Medium fish	13	Medium fish	38
Medium mammal	18	Medium mammal	10
Muskrat	2	Mice and relatives	1
Northern leopard frog	1	Northern leopard frog	24
Partridge	1	Partridge	1
Quail and relatives	2	Quail and relatives	1
Rockfish	1	Rodent	11
Salmonidae?	1	Small bird	1
Salmonids	1	Small fish	93
Small fish	1	Small mammal	166
Small mammal	2	Squirrel	5
Small rodent	1	Tortoise/turtle	1
Tortoise/turtle	1	White-tailed deer	9
White-tailed deer	6	**Unit 5**	**68**
Woodchuck	1	Eastern fox squirrel	9
Unit 2	**35**	King or gopher snake	1
Eastern fox squirrel	4	Large bird	3
Large bird	2	Large mammal	22
Large mammal	10	Medium fish	6
Medium fish	2	Medium mammal	13
Medium mammal	7	Red squirrel	1
Red squirrel	2	Small mammal	7
Small mammal	6	Squirrel	2
Tortoise/turtle	1	White-tailed deer	3
White-tailed deer	1	Woodchuck	1

Unit 24	252
Bobwhite quail	1
Eastern fox squirrel	29
Frog	4
Ground squirrel	2
Large fish	3
Large mammal	51
Medium bird	2
Medium fish	38
Medium mammal	12
Northern leopard frog	3
Partridge	1
Raccoon	4
Red squirrel	2
Rodent	1
Screech owl	1
Small bird	5
Small fish	12
Small mammal	64
Small rodent	3
Tortoise/turtle	2
White-tailed deer	9
Woodchuck	3
Unit 31	**355**
Beaver	2
Eastern fox squirrel	17
Frog	8
Gar fish?	1
Gray fox	2
Ground squirrel	10
Large mammal	83
Medium bird	2
Medium fish	11
Medium mammal	26
Painted turtle	2
Raccoon	1
Red-bellied woodpecker	1
Rodent	12
Small bird	2
Small fish	86
Small mammal	70
Snail	1
Sparrow hawk	2
Squirrel	5
White-tailed deer	6
Wolf or black bear	1
Woodchuck	3
Unit 32	**8**
Beaver	1
Large bird	1
Large mammal	2
Medium bird	1
White-tailed deer	3

Unit 37	80
Canada goose	1
Deer and relatives	1
Eastern fox squirrel	6
Ground squirrel	4
Large bird	1
Large fish	3
Large mammal	15
Medium bird	1
Medium fish	3
Medium mammal	3
Northern leopard frog	1
Small bird	1
Small fish	16
Small mammal	19
Small rodent	3
White-tailed deer	2
Unit 45	**192**
?	1
Eastern fox squirrel	24
Gray fox	1
Large carnivore	1
Large fish	20
Large mammal	26
Medium fish	41
Medium frog	2
Medium mammal	21
Perching bird	1
Pigeon	1
Shore bird	1
Small bird	3
Small carnivore	1
Small fish	4
Small mammal	34
Small rodent	3
Squirrel	2
White-tailed deer	4
Woodchuck	1
Unit 51	**85**
Beaver	1
Eastern fox squirrel	4
Ground squirrel	1
Large bird	3
Large mammal	16
Medium bird	2
Medium fish	1
Medium mammal	22
Pigeon	1
Small fish	12
Small mammal	15
Small rodent	4
Squirrel	1
White-tailed deer	2

(continued)

Table 4.5. Continued

Unit 55	2	Small fish	48
Medium mammal	1	Small frog	1
Perching bird	1	Small mammal	64
Unit 60	250	Small rodent	7
Beaver	1	Squirrel	4
Carnivore	1	Tortoise/turtle	1
Eastern fox squirrel	18	White-tailed deer	9
Ground squirrel	3	**Unit 63**	35
Large bird	3	Eastern fox squirrel	1
Large carnivore	1	Large bird	1
Large fish	5	Large fish	1
Large frog	2	Large mammal	12
Large mammal	29	Marten	1
Meadow vole	2	Medium bird	2
Medium fish	19	Medium mammal	7
Medium mammal	16	Small fish	2
Muskrat	1	Small mammal	6
Northern leopard frog	10	Squirrel	1
Pigeon	1	White-tailed deer	1
Porcupine	1		
Red squirrel	2	**Grand Total**	**1963**
Small bird	1		

Lot 1 bones are from units along the edge or just outside the post mold pattern of the proto-longhouse (Areas 1 and 2), which had the largest concentrations of faunal remains. These materials were either accumulated and buried where the structure wall met the floor or were in the toss zones outside. Faunal remains were concentrated in the same toss areas where broken smoking pipes were concentrated.

Beisaw found the Lot 1 bones to be small, probably due to trampling. Bird and mammal were present in every excavation unit sample, and fish was present in most units. Reptiles and amphibians were most common outside the structure (tables 4.6 and 4.7). Beisaw wrote:

> Recovered species that were likely used for food include the Canada goose, Bobwhite quail, pigeon and partridge. Several elements of perching songbirds were identified, such as the cardinal. These commonly available birds are often considered too small for a food source but their colorful feathers may have been sought after. The same is true for the shorebird (a plover-like species) and the screech owl. (Beisaw 2014, 2)

Table 4.6. Number of Identifiable Specimens (NISP) of Bones Identified to Genus or Genus and Species (NISP estimates the number of individuals of a species that are represented)

Areas 1 and 2 (earlier component)	Count	%
Eastern fox squirrel	111	39.5
Frog	67	23.8
Deer	49	17.4
Woodchuck	6	2.1
Red squirrel	7	2.5
Turtle	6	2.1
Garter snake	5	1.8
Beaver	4	1.4
Raccoon	4	1.4
Muskrat	3	1.1
Partridge	3	1.1
Pigeon	3	1.1
Meadow vole	2	0.7
Gray fox	1	0.4
Bobwhite quail	1	0.4
Canada goose	1	0.4
Cardinal	1	0.4
Cod	1	0.4
King or gopher snake	1	0.4
Marten	1	0.4
Porcupine	1	0.4
Rockfish	1	0.4
Salmonids	1	0.4
Screech owl	1	0.4
Total	281	
Area 4 (later component)	**Count**	**%**
Eastern fox squirrel	17	37.8
Frog	8	17.8
Deer	6	13.3
Woodchuck	3	6.7
Beaver	2	4.4
Gray fox	2	4.4
Painted turtle	2	4.4
Sparrow hawk	2	4.4
Gar fish	1	2.2
Raccoon	1	2.2
Red-bellied woodpecker	1	2.2
Total	45	

Most fish specimens were not identified, but Beisaw did identify cod, salmon, and rockfish. Mammals include marten, raccoon, and gray fox, including charred specimens. Medium-sized rodents identified are woodchuck, muskrat, plus one beaver and one porcupine.

Fox squirrel, red squirrel, and ground squirrel are all present, with fox squirrel being most common. Squirrel bone "showed obvious taphanomic signatures of charring, working, carnivore gnawing and digestive damage." Gnawed bone appears to be evidence of domestic dogs at the site. Beisaw noted an interesting pattern in regard to deer bone:

> The white-tailed deer in this assemblage was almost entirely in the form of foot bones. Four fragment of deer humerus, three fragments of radius, two fragments of cervical vertebrae and one each of tibia, mandible, tooth and antler round out the assemblage of fifty deer specimens. Clearly the removal of heads and feet occurred within or adjacent to the proto-longhouse but meat-bearing elements were disposed of elsewhere. (Beisaw 2014, 4)

Lot 2 included many of the same mammals, rodents, birds, and fish with a few additions: ground squirrel, eastern fox squirrel, woodchuck, raccoon, beaver, fisher (*Martes pennati*), sparrow hawk (*Sparverius?*), red-bellied woodpecker (*Carolinus?*), passenger pigeon (*Migratorius*), frog, painted turtle, water snake (*Natrix sipedon*), and sunfish (*Lepostimes*). White-tailed deer is again present, but only in low frequency.

Beisaw puzzled over two fish specimens. Her email communication lends insight into the difficult and complex process of identifying archaeological faunal remains (figure 4.14):

> There are two fragments of fish mandible that I spent an entire day on—including a trip to the American Museum of Natural History and a dozen emails to experts around the globe. The verdict is this: it looks like a gar (*Lepisosteus?*) but it doesn't match very well in that your specimens have a depression where others have a ridge (figure 4.14). It might be a worked bone—all the smaller teeth and their tooth attachments are missing so being worked makes sense—but this may just be a convenient excuse for why it doesn't match well. Then again there aren't any other gar-like fish that it might be since there aren't any fish quite like the gar. What bothers me the most is that if this is gar it would be huge, easily over one meter in length! (Beisaw, personal communication email 2016)

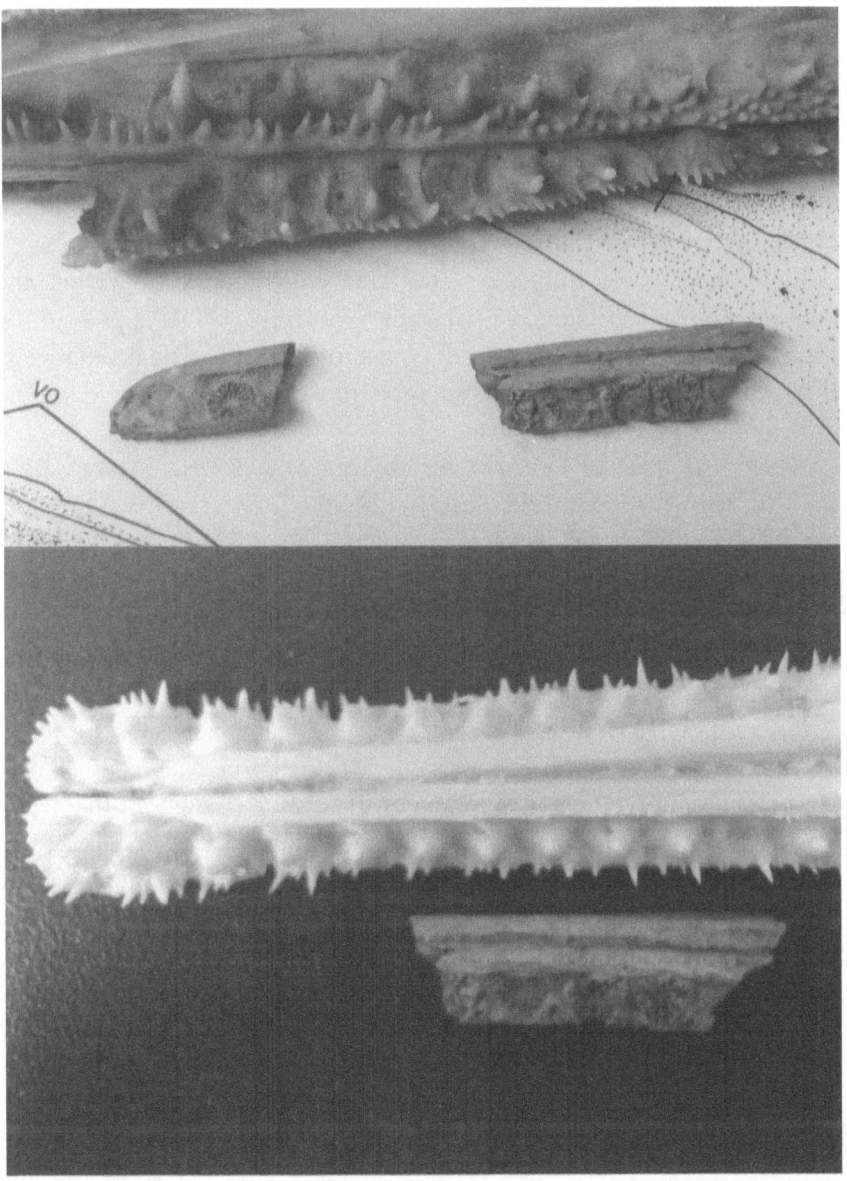

Figure 4.14. Levanna gar fish with comparative collection specimen. April M. Beisaw.

The only gar species in New York is the longnose gar (*Lepisosteus osseus*), which grows to a length of three feet (one meter) and a weight of seven pounds. The New York state record for longnose gar is thirteen pounds, three ounces, from Lake Champlain. The presence of gar at Levanna is interesting because most anglers find it too difficult to catch with a traditional pole, line, and hook. Websites instead recommend hookless rope lures (Carlson, Douglas, and Wright 2016).

In summary, both the earlier and later site components are heavily dominated by small fauna. In particular, squirrel and fish appear to be the primary game sources and deer is infrequent (although relatively few could make a substantial dietary impact). Squirrel could be as prized for its pelt as for its meat.

All tree squirrels at Levanna are fox squirrels (*Sciurus nigere*). Beisaw estimates that the crude meat weight for a fox squirrel would range from 250 to 650 grams (personal communication 2016). Fox squirrels replaced gray squirrels as deciduous forests were cleared for agricultural fields (Moncrief and Dooley 2013). The dominance of eastern fox squirrel at Levanna is thus indirect evidence of substantial farming by the tenth and twelfth centuries.

It is tempting to view the dominance of small fauna at sites like Levanna as a sign of dietary stress, as have some authors (Somerville 2015). This, however, requires a careful definition of stress. Beisaw suggests that if dietary stress occurred because deer were overhunted, then we'd likely see marrow extraction from the deer bone in the collection. Beisaw and myself both believe that the Levanna fauna instead show a dynamic and diverse economy where women and children contributed by trapping and snaring small fauna. This pattern continued for the Cayuga into the sixteenth century, as shown by the Corey Village fauna, which also heavily emphasized fish, rodents, small game, and birds (Beisaw, personal communication 2016; Beisaw 2015; Rossen 2015, 170; Rossen and Beisaw 2016).

WORKED BONE

Worked bone artifacts include needles (n=32), awls (n=21), fishhooks (n=14), pendants (n=5), beads (n=4), harpoons (n=3), effigies (n=2), pins (n=2), and one spoon and dagger. Most specimens are associated with the late twelfth-century component. The large needles found only a few centimeters beneath the surface are one line of evidence that the site was unplowed. The harpoons and fishhooks are suggestive of a gradual shift from net fishing to line and spear techniques after the tenth century. The four beads are tubular. The pendants are bone except for one shell specimen (figure 4.13).

BOTANICAL REMAINS

The subdiscipline of archaeobotany (also known as paleoethnobotany) epitomizes the emergence of modern state-of-the art archaeology. It is based on the simple and elegant technology of water flotation, where soil samples taken during excavation are placed in a machine with agitated water. Materials that sink (heavy fraction) are collected below in fine screen while floating materials (light fraction) are guided through a spout or spillway into a nylon bag or paint strainer. The renowned archaeologist Patty Jo Watson is credited with adapting this geological technique to archaeology. Flotation tanks vary from simple homemade designs to complex air compressor-driven machines, like the Flote-Tech Tank used to process the Levanna and Myers Farm samples (Rossen 1999). There are some trade secrets to effective archaeobotany, including sampling all site contexts (bagging soil from all levels and features like hearths), taking many more samples than will be ultimately analyzed to maintain maximum flexibility as a site becomes better understood, and measuring soil literage as samples are processed, so that botanical densities can be examined and understood.

Once the samples are floated and dried, analysis is a matter of sorting and separating plant remains under the microscope at magnifications of 10 to 30x. Identifications are made from visual memory and comparisons with both modern comparative and archaeological collections. One key aspect of archaeobotany is finding the "literage threshold" of the site. An ideal archaeobotanical site report represents major plant use trends through repetitive finds, along with a maximized overall plant inventory, usually expressed by specimens that only appear in low frequency. Literage thresholds vary greatly in eastern US woodlands sites. Some Late Prehistoric sites in the Ohio Valley, especially Mississippian

Table 4.7. Levanna Site—Water Flotation Samples and Liters Analyzed by Site Area

Site Area	# Samples	Liters
Area 1: inside proto-longhouse	14	149
Area 2: toss zones outside proto-longhouse	9	68
Area 3: block 10 m south of proto-longhouse	3	33
Area 4: southeast outlier zone	7	58
Area 5: far south outlier zone	1	9
Area 6: far east outlier zone	3	13
Area 7: historic intrusion	1	5
Total analyzed samples	38	334

and Fort Ancient sites, may be understood from a couple of hundred liters, depending on the diversity of contexts and number of cultural components at the site, while Archaic sites might require several thousand liters to achieve an acceptable site literage for the purpose of understanding ancient plant use. In the case of Levanna, we achieved a good literage threshold at 334 liters and thirty-eight samples distributed across the seven site areas (table 4.7). That is, we were able to replicate the major plants of the use system and identify a wide range of plants (particularly wild plants that were collected) in low frequency. Once a point was reached where the materials were repetitious, there was confidence in the sample size of the analysis (table 4.8). (At the much smaller, special activity Myers Farm site [chapter 5], the liter threshold and plant use profile were achieved with six samples and 120 liters of floated soil.)

In the case of Levanna, archaeobotany provides a contrast between the impressionistic and ethnocentric 1930s interpretations of the site and reinterpretation based on systematic and scientific data collection and analysis. Once the Levanna site was divided into seven areas or analysis units, based primarily on ceramics analysis, radiocarbon dates, and feature patterns (such as the distinction between being inside the proto-longhouse versus adjacent outside toss zones), and the site was understood in terms of two occupations separated by at least a century, then archaeobotanical analysis could address the basics of plant use (table 4.8). However, the plant profiles are similar in both site components, while different densities and plant species in different site areas suggest some activity differences. There are also surprises such as the presence of wild rice (*Zizania aquatic*) in two samples of the earlier component, one inside the proto-longhouse and one just outside the proto-longhouse in a toss zone.

Archaeobotanical remains also provide crucial evidence on site conditions, contexts, and preservation. The Levanna archaeobotanical remains reinforce the various lines of evidence that the site was unplowed. Samples taken from shallow contexts produced intact carbonized plant remains in a manner that plow zones never do in my long experience. There are no substantive differences between shallow soil samples and deeper samples from pits and hearths across the site.

THE LEVANNA ARCHAEOBOTANICAL ANALYSIS

People living during tenth or eleventh century and cusp of the twelfth and thirteenth centuries at Levanna (the two primary site components) had broadly similar plant use: a mixed economy of cultivated, managed or semi-cultivated, and wild plants. There is also one sample from a feature representing the 1930s historic excavation and museum period (tables 4.7 to 4.9). This spectrum of plant use is common throughout the eastern US woodlands. Even fundamentally agricultural Ohio Valley Mississippian chiefdoms and agricultural tribal groups like Fort Ancient peoples living on their fringes maintained substantive wild plant collecting activities (Rossen 1992; Rossen and Turner, in press).

Table 4.8. Levanna Botanical Remains: Frequencies, Gram Weights, and Ubiquities of General Categories

Category	freq	pct	gm wt	pct
Wood charcoal	9,291	77.2	98.4	97.2
Wild plant seeds	2,157	17.9	—	—
Nutshell/nutmeal	357	3.0	2.5	2.5
Cultigens	182	1.5	0.3	0.3
Unidentified—general seeds	49	0.4	—	—
Total plant remains	12,036	100.0	101.2	100.0

Table 4.9. Levanna Site Botanical Remains by Individual Sample

Sample	Species	freq	gm wt
AREA 1: Inside proto-longhouse (main excavation block).			
Unit 12E Feature 9 Central hearth 11 liters	wood (Am beech 40%, hophornbeam 30%, maple 10%, hickory 10%, red oak 10%)	438	4.6
	hickory (*Carya* sp.)	31	.5
	hickory—nutmeat	1	.0
	acorn (*Quercus* sp.)	4	.0
	corn (*Zea mays*)—kernel fragment	11	.1
	corn—cupule	4	.0
	blackberry/raspberry (*Rubus* sp.)	49	—
	sumac (*Rhus* sp.)	8	—
	amaranth (*Amaranthus* sp.)	2	—
	ground cherry/tomatillo (*Physalis* sp.)	1	—
	unidentified—seed	1	—
Unit 12W Feature 9 Central hearth 18 liters	wood (maple 30%, Am beech 30%, Am chest 20%, w oak 10%, Am elm 10%)	1,120	5.6
	hickory (*Carya* sp.)	28	.4
	butternut (*Juglans cinerea*)	4	.0
	corn (*Zea mays*)—kernel fragment	15	.2
	corn—cupule	2	.0
	bean (*Phaseolus?*)—fragments	2	.0
	gourd—rind (*Lagenaria* sp.)	1	.0
	sumac (*Rhus* sp.)	24	—
	grape (*Vitis* sp.)	5	—
Unit 24E Feature 18 Level 4 West side 11 liters	wood (maple)	217	1.4
	hickory (*Carya* sp.)	10	.1
	corn (*Zea mays*)—kernel fragment	4	.0
	gourd—rind (*Lagenaria* sp.)	1	.0
	blackberry/raspberry (*Rubus* sp.)	12	—
	sumac (*Rhus* sp.)	2	—
	unidentified—general	1	.0
Level 24E Level 3 West side 8 liters	wood (Am beech 50%, unidentified 30%, maple 10%, hickory 10%)	267	3.4
	corn (*Zea mays*)—kernel fragment	6	.0
	corn—cupule	4	.0
	blackberry/raspberry (*Rubus* sp.)	4	—
Unit 24E Level 4 West side 9 liters	wood (hickory 50%, Am beech 50%)	122	1.4
	sumac (*Rhus* sp.)	5	—
	blackberry/raspberry (*Rubus* sp.)	5	—
	unidentified—general	1	.0
	unidentified—seed	1	—
Unit 25W Feature 28 East edge 6 liters	wood (hickory 90%, Am beech 10%)	58	.9
	black walnut (*Juglans nigra*)	1	.0
	corn—cupule	1	.0
	blackberry/raspberry (*Rubus* sp.)	2	—

Sample	Species	freq	gm wt
Unit 25E	wood (hickory 50%, Am beech 50%)	81	1.3
Level 4	hickory (*Carya* sp.)	16	.1
East edge	acorn (*Quercus* sp.)	3	.0
5 liters	corn—cupule	3	.0
	blackberry/raspberry (*Rubus* sp.)	6	—
	sumac (*Rhus* sp.)	3	—
	grape (*Vitis* sp.)	1	—
	cherry (*Prunus* sp.)	1	—
	elderberry (*Sambucus canadensis*)	1	—
	unidentified—seed fragment	1	—
Unit 29	wood (maple 50%, white oak 50%)	14	.1
Level 4	hickory (*Carya* sp.)	2	.0
South center	corn—cupule	2	—
10 liters	blackberry/raspberry (*Rubus* sp.)	54	—
	sumac (*Rhus* sp.)	18	—
Unit 30/26/25	wood (Am beech 40%, hickory 20%, maple 20%, white	69	.7
Feature 31	oak 10%, hophornbeam 10%)		
Central hearth	American chestnut (*Castanea dentata*)	9	.1
4 liters	acorn (*Quercus* sp.)	3	.0
	corn (*Zea mays*)—kernel fragment	1	.0
	corn—cupule	3	.0
	blackberry/raspberry (*Rubus* sp.)	5	—
	sumac (*Rhus* sp.)	5	—
Unit 30	wood (Am beech 35%, maple 15%, hickory 15%, ash	251	3.2
Feature 30	10%, red oak 10%, white oak 5%, Am chestnut 5%,		
North central	hophornbeam 5%)		
hearth	hickory (*Carya* sp.)	18	.1
19 liters	black walnut (*Juglans nigra*)	3	.0
	acorn (*Quercus* sp.)	1	.0
	corn (*Zea mays*)—kernel fragment	4	.0
	corn—cupule	7	.0
	sumac (*Rhus* sp.)	13	—
	blackberry/raspberry (*Rubus* sp.)	1	—
	grape (*Vitis* sp.)	1	—
	unidentified—general (fragments)	6	.0
Unit 36E	wood (Am beech 30%, maple 20%, Am elm 20%	310	3.6
Level 4	ash 10%, white oak 10%, hickory 10%)		
West edge	hickory (*Carya* sp.)	11	.0
13 liters	acorn (*Quercus* sp.)	2	.0
	corn (*Zea mays*)—kernel fragment	1	.0
	corn—cupule	3	.0
	blackberry/raspberry (*Rubus* sp.)	25	—
	sumac (*Rhus* sp.)	13	—
	unidentified—general (fragments)	2	.0

(*continued*)

Table 4.9. *Continued*

Sample	Species	freq	gm wt
Unit 46 Feature 54N Southwest edge 10 liters	wood (Am beech 40%, maple 30%, Am elm 20%, hophornbeam 10%)	161	1.7
	hickory (*Carya* sp.)	6	.0
	butternut (*Juglans cinerea*)	3	.0
	acorn (*Quercus* sp.)	5	.0
	corn (*Zea mays*)—kernel fragment	3	.0
	corn—cupule	2	.0
	blackberry/raspberry (*Rubus* sp.)	19	—
	sumac (*Rhus* sp.)	19	—
	grape (*Vitis* sp.)	4	—
	strawberry (*Fragaria* sp.)	1	—
	unidentified—general (fragments)	9	.0
Unit 60E Feature 64 Southeast edge 13 liters	wood (Am beech 30%, Am elm 30%, slip elm 10% maple 10%, hickory 10%, white oak 10%)	620	1.1
	hickory (*Carya* sp.)	6	.0
	acorn (*Quercus* sp.)	1	.0
	corn (*Zea mays*)—kernel fragment	1	.0
	corn—cupule	4	.0
	blackberry/raspberry (*Rubus* sp.)	34	—
	sumac (*Rhus* sp.)	35	—
	elderberry (*Sambucus canadensis*)	1	—
	unidentified—general (fragments)	2	.0
Unit 60W Feature 66 Southeast edge 11 liters	wood (w oak 30%, Am beech 30%, Am elm 20% maple 10%, Am chestnut 10%)	217	2.5
	hickory (*Carya* sp.)	4	.0
	acorn (*Quercus* sp.)	3	.0
	corn (*Zea mays*)—kernel fragment	1	.0
	corn—cupule	2	.0
	bean (*Phaseolus?*)—fragments	1	.0
	gourd—rind (*Lagenaria* sp.)	2	.0
	wild rice (*Zizania aquatic*)	2	.0
	sumac (*Rhus* sp.)	23	—
	grape (*Vitis* sp.)	1	—
	elderberry (*Sambucus canadensis*)	1	—
AREA 2: Just outside proto-longhouse, toss zones (main excavation block)			
Unit 13 Level 2 NW of longhouse 9 liters	wood (red oak 20%, white oak 20%, maple 20%, hophornbeam 20%, Am beech 10%, Am chestnut 10%)	190	1.6
	hickory (*Carya* sp.)	5	.0
	hazelnut (*Corylus* sp.)	1	.0
	corn (*Zea mays*)—kernel fragment	2	.0
	corn—cupule	7	.0
	blackberry/raspberry (*Rubus* sp.)	7	—
	unidentified—general (fragments)	1	—

Sample	Species	freq	gm wt
Unit 13, Level 4 Feature 14 NW of longhouse 18 liters	wood (Am beech 90%, Am chestnut 5%, red oak 5%) blackberry/raspberry (*Rubus* sp.) sumac (*Rhus* sp.)	177 11 6	2.5 — —
Unit 28 Level 3 E of longhouse 8 liters	wood (Am elm 34%, hickory 33%, Am beech 33%) corn (*Zea mays*)—kernel fragment blackberry/raspberry (*Rubus* sp.) sumac (*Rhus* sp.)	338 1 22 25	3.7 .0 — —
Unit 28 Level 4 E of longhouse 6 liters	wood (Am beech 30%, maple 20%, Am chestnut 20%, hickory 20%, Am elm 10%) hickory (*Carya* sp.) acorn (*Quercus* sp.) corn (*Zea mays*)—kernel fragment corn—cupule blackberry/raspberry (*Rubus* sp.) sumac (*Rhus* sp.) grape (*Vitis* sp.) unidentified—general (amorphous)	332 4 1 5 10 9 45 1 4	4.0 .0 .0 .0 .0 — — — .0
Unit 35 W Level 2 West of longhouse 8 liters	wood (maple 80%, Am chestnut 10%, Am beech 10%) acorn (*Quercus* sp.) corn—cupule blackberry/raspberry (*Rubus* sp.) sumac (*Rhus* sp.) elderberry (*Sambucus canadensis*)	196 2 7 206 18 1	2.0 .0 .0 — — —
Unit 37 Level 3 NW of longhouse 6 liters	wood (American elm) wild rice (*Zizania aquatica*) sunflower (*Helianthus annuus*) pondweed (*Potamogeton* sp.) grape (*Vitis* sp.) unidentified—seed	29 9 3 1 1 2	.3 — — — — —
Unit 37 Level 5 NW of longhouse 4 liters	wood (American beech) hickory (*Carya* sp.) corn—cupule gourd—rind (*Lagenaria* sp.) blackberry/raspberry (*Rubus* sp.) grape (*Vitis* sp.) sumac (*Rhus* sp.)	19 3 1 1 11 2 1	.3 .0 .0 .0 — — —
Unit 56 Level 4 N entrance 5 liters	wood (Am beech 34%, hickory 33%, white oak 33%) hickory (*Carya* sp.) corn (*Zea mays*)—kernel fragment corn—cupule blackberry/raspberry (*Rubus* sp.) grape (*Vitis* sp.) sumac (*Rhus* sp.)	51 1 3 1 29 2 1	.3 .0 .0 .0 — — —

(*continued*)

Table 4.9. Continued

Sample	Species	freq	gm wt
Unit 58	wood (Am chestnut 20%, Am elm 20%, hickory 20%,	53	.7
Feature 63	Am beech 20%, unidentified 20%)		
SE of	hickory (*Carya* sp.)	2	.0
longhouse	corn—cupule	1	.0
4 liters	blackberry/raspberry (*Rubus* sp.)	14	—
	sumac (*Rhus* sp.)	2	—
AREA 3: Excavation block 10 meters south of proto-longhouse			
Unit 48	wood (maple)	530	6.4
Feature 54	corn (*Zea mays*)—kernel fragment	2	.0
14 liters	blackberry/raspberry (*Rubus* sp.)	60	—
	sumac (*Rhus* sp.)	61	—
	grape (*Vitis* sp.)	1	—
	elderberry (*Sambucus canadensis*)	1	—
	unidentified—general	1	.0
Unit 53	wood (maple 50%, hickory 50%)	62	.7
Feature 58	hickory (*Carya* sp.)	1	.0
10 liters	blackberry/raspberry (*Rubus* sp.)	60	—
	sumac (*Rhus* sp.)	36	—
	grape (*Vitis* sp.)	1	—
Units 53—54	wood (Am beech 50%, hickory 30%, hophornbeam 20%)	262	3.4
Feature 67	hickory (*Carya* sp.)	7	.0
9 liters	corn (*Zea mays*)—kernel fragment	5	.0
	blackberry/raspberry (*Rubus* sp.)	41	—
	sumac (*Rhus* sp.)	24	—
	ground cherry (*Physalis* sp.)	22	—
	grape (*Vitis* sp.)	6	—
	unidentified—general	1	.0
AREA 4: Southeast outlier zone			
Unit 5	wood (American beech 85%, American elm 10%, maple 5%)	1,264	19.6
Feature 5	hickory (*Carya* sp.)	1	.0
6 liters	corn (*Zea mays*)—kernel fragment	4	.0
	blackberry/raspberry (*Rubus* sp.)	15	—
	sumac (*Rhus* sp.)	1	—
Unit 21N	wood (American chestnut 50%, American beech 50%)	8	.2
Feature 17	hickory (*Carya* sp.)	22	1.1
11 liters	sunflower (*Helianthus annuus*)	2	—
	squash—seed (*Cucurbita pepo*)	1	—
	grape (*Vitis* sp.)	3	—
	blackberry/raspberry (*Rubus* sp.)	401	—
Unit 21S	wood (Am beech 80%, maple 10%, slippery elm 10%)	51	.3
Feature 17	hickory (*Carya* sp.)	107	2.0
8 liters	sunflower (*Helianthus annuus*)	2	—
	blackberry/raspberry (*Rubus* sp.)	391	—
	grape (*Vitis* sp.)	1	—
	unidentified—general	2	.0

Sample	Species	freq	gm wt
Unit 31	wood (Am beech 80%, white oak 10%, maple 10%)	500	5.5
Feature 27	hickory (*Carya* sp.)	3	.0
7 liters	corn (*Zea mays*)—kernel fragment	1	.0
	corn—cupule	3	.0
	wild bean (*Phaseolus?*)	2	.0
	blackberry/raspberry (*Rubus* sp.)	4	—
	unidentified—general	2	.0
Unit 31A	wood (Am beech 50%, maple 20%, bl walnut 20%,	71	.6
Level 4, 12	sl elm 10%)		
liters	corn—cupule	1	.0
Unit 31A	wood (Am beech 60%, maple 20%, hickory 10%,	304	4.4
Level 5	Am elm 10%)		
8 liters	corn—cupule	1	.0
	blackberry/raspberry (*Rubus* sp.)	7	—
	sunflower (*Helianthus annuus*)	1	—
	pawpaw (*Asimina triloba*)	1	—
	grape (*Vitis* sp.)	1	—
Unit 43	wood (unidentified 70%, Am elm 10%, Am beech 10%,	198	2.3
Feature 45	white oak 10%)		
6 liters	hickory (*Carya* sp.)	1	.0
	corn (*Zea mays*)—kernel fragment	2	.0
	blackberry/raspberry (*Rubus* sp.)	23	—
	sumac (*Rhus* sp.)	10	—
	unidentified—general	2	.0
AREA 5: Far south outlier zone near site edge			
Unit 22	wood (unidentified 50%, Am beech 40%, maple 10%)	109	.8
Level 3	hickory (*Carya* sp.)	2	.0
9 liters	blackberry/raspberry (*Rubus* sp.)	26	—
	sumac (*Rhus* sp.)	2	—
	elderberry (*Sambucus canadensis*)	2	—
Unit 20	wood (Am beech 30%, maple 30%, hophornbeam 20%,	180	1.8
Level 4	American elm 10%, red oak 10%)		
7 liters	hickory (*Carya* sp.)	9	.0
	butternut (*Juglans cinerea*)	3	.0
	corn (*Zea mays*)—kernel fragment	3	.0
	gourd—rind (*Lagenaria* sp.)	1	.0
	blackberry/raspberry (*Rubus* sp.)	7	—
	sumac (*Rhus* sp.)	9	—
	unidentified—general	3	.0
Unit 20	wood (Am beech 30%, Am elm 20%, ash 10%, maple 10%,	61	.6
Feature 18	hophornbeam 10%, white oak 10%, Am chestnut 10%)		
2 liters	blackberry/raspberry (*Rubus* sp.)	3	—
	sumac (*Rhus* sp.)	2	—

(continued)

Table 4.9. Continued

Sample	Species	freq	gm wt
AREA 7: HISTORIC INTRUSION: SE of longhouse			
Unit 63E	wood (eastern redcedar 50%, honey locust 50%)	80	.7
Level 5	barley (*Hordeum vulgare*)	10	—
5 liters	wheat (*Triticum aestivum*)	2	—
	sour cherry (*Prunus cerasus*)	2	—
	plum (*Prunus americana*)	1	—
	corn (*Zea mays*)—kernel	1	.0
	bean (*Phaseolus vulgaris*)	2	.0
	hickory (*Carya* sp.)	1	.0
	grape (*Vitis* sp.)	1	—

WOOD CHARCOAL AND ENVIRONMENTAL RECONSTRUCTION

Like many archaeobotanical assemblages, most Levanna plant remains are wood charcoal fragments (77.2 percent by frequency, 97.2 percent by weight, table 4.11). Most samples have heavily mixed wood charcoal with four to seven species, probably the remains of firewood. In contrast, five proto-longhouse samples with uniform wood charcoal, including one from the eastern edge (Feature 28, hickory), one from the northern edge, one from the west-central interior (Unit 24, Feature 18, maple), and one just outside the northern edge (Unit 37, Feature 39, American beech) come from posts. A charcoal concentration of American beech in Unit 35, Level 2 just west and outside the proto-longhouse may be a fallen and charred maple post.

Wood charcoal and particularly mixed firewood samples are a good indicator of the forest environment during the site occupations. The collection suggests that from the tenth to twelfth centuries there was a mixed hardwood beech-maple-hickory-elm forest near Levanna. There were also chestnuts, hophornbeam, various oaks, ash, slippery elm, and black walnut (table 4.10). As stated earlier the presence of fox squirrels suggests that substantial land clearing for farming had already occurred. The substantial presence of disturbed land plants such as sumac and blackberry that are not present today at the wooded Levanna attests to the edges of the cleared village zone. Wild rice and pondweed indicate that Cayuga Lake had wetland plant communities that have disappeared.

Table 4.10. Wood Charcoal from Levanna Site (historic intrusion sample omitted)

Species	freq	pct	gm wt	pct
American beech (*Fagus grandifolia*)	3,411	38.5	43.2	45.7
Maple (*Acer* sp.)	1,990	22.5	19.3	20.4
Hickory (*Carya* sp.)	1,051	11.9	9.9	10.5
American elm (*Ulmus americana*)	701	7.9	6.1	6.5
Hophornbeam (*Ostrya virginiana*)	470	5.3	6.2	6.6
American chestnut (*Castanea dentata*)	464	5.2	3.4	3.6
White oak group (*Quercus* sp.)	434	4.9	3.4	3.6
Red oak group (*Quercus* sp.)	142	1.6	1.5	1.6
Ash (*Fraxinus* sp.)	100	1.1	0.9	1.0
Slippery elm (*Ulmus rubra*)	74	0.8	0.5	0.5
Black walnut (*Juglans nigra*)	14	0.2	0.1	0.1
Total identified wood charcoal	8,851	100.0	94.5	100.0
Unidentified wood charcoal	272		3.3	
Total wood charcoal	9,123		97.8	

CULTIVATED PLANTS

Corn, sunflower, gourd, and squash were cultivated at Levanna. Of these, corn is by far the most common cultigen (table 4.11). The Levanna corn was an eight-row variety found along the entire eastern US seaboard and known to archaeologists as "Eastern Eight" for its eight rows of kernels around the cob circumference. Other traits of Eastern Eight corn are thick, open cupules (the outermost layer of the cob that holds the kernels) and thick glumes. The cupule bottoms are spongy and segmented.

Because of the positioning of cupules perpendicular to the length of the cob, the long dimension of the cupule is its width and the shorter dimension is its length. The Levanna cupules range in width from 3.3 to 8.2 millimeters with an average width of 5.0 millimeters, while cupule lengths range from 1.5 to 3.5 millimeters with an average of 2.2 millimeters. The width-to-length measurements of cupules range from 1.6 to 3.2 with an average of 2.2. There are no size differences between corn cupules from the different prehistoric site areas. Corn kernels are more fragile than cupules, but a few measurable kernels were recovered. Kernel widths range from 3.8 to 4.5 millimeters and lengths range from 1.2 to 4.0 millimeters. These are low, wide, crescent-shaped kernels that exemplify the Eastern Eight type.

Table 4.11. Food Plant Remains from Levanna (historic intrusion omitted)

Plant Type / Species	freq	gm wt	ubiquity
Cultigens			
corn—kernel fragment	82	.3	.57
corn—cupule (Zea mays)	71	.0	.57
sunflower (Helianthus anuus)	8	—	.11
gourd—rind (Lagenaria sp.)	3	.0	.08
squash—seed (Cucurbita pepo)	1	—	.03
Nutshell			
hickory (Carya sp.)	323	1.4	.70
acorn (Quercus sp.)	23	.0	.27
black walnut (Juglans nigra)	4	.0	.05
butternut (Juglans cinerea)	7	.0	.05
American chestnut (Castanea dentata)	3	.0	.03
hazelnut (Corylus sp.)	1	.0	.03
Wild plant seeds*			
blackberry/raspberry (Rubus sp.)	1,610	—	.95
sumac (Rhus sp.)	412	—	.76
grape (Vitis sp.)	31	—	.48
ground cherry (Physalis sp.)	23	—	.05
wild rice (Zizania aquatica)	11	—	.05
elderberry (Sambucus canadensis)	7	—	.16
cherry (Prunus sp.)	2	—	.05
pondweed (Potamogeton sp.)	1	—	.03
pawpaw (Asimina triloba)	1	—	.03
strawberry (Fragaria sp.)	1	—	.03
Miscellaneous			
unidentified—general	24	.0	
unidentified—seed fragments	5	—	

The small size of both cupules and kernels suggests a relatively undeveloped corn compared with the larger fifteenth-century specimens of Corey, and with Eastern Eight corn found elsewhere in the eastern United States (discussed later). What cannot be controlled for in these measurements is the shrinkage of corn specimens during carbonization, which, as controlled carbonization experiments show, varies greatly depending on the firing circumstances (Rossen and Olsen 1985).

Examining the ratio of corn kernels to cupules in individual samples can sometimes help understand plant-related activities. Kernels are edible food waste, while cupules are an inedible product of food processing. It is thus interesting that two samples from Unit 12, Feature 9, a central fire hearth of the proto-longhouse, have far more kernels (n=26) than cupules (n=6), while samples from the toss zones just outside the proto-longhouse (such as Unit 12, Level 2 and Unit 28, Level 4) tend to have more cupules (n=17) than kernels (n=9). Food processing debris may been tossed out of the house more than actual food waste that was disposed in the fire hearth.

Sunflower (*Helianthus anuus*), gourd (*Lagenaria* sp.), and squash (*Cucurbita pepo*) were recovered in trace amounts, demonstrating the importance of large flotation collection and analysis efforts (tables 4.10 and 4.12). These three plants can be traced back to the Middle and Late Archaic periods (ca. 7,500-5,000 B.P.) throughout the eastern US woodlands, when hunter-gatherers focused on collecting nuts and wetlands plants (Rossen, in press; Smith 2009, 2011). Weedy dryland annuals including sunflower were also collected and became more important as wetlands receded during the peak of the Hypsithermal Drying Period.

As early as 5,000 BP, a cultivated version of sunflower was developed within a complex of native starchy and (in the case of sunflower) oily seeded plants of the so-called Eastern Agricultural Complex (EAC). The EAC was really a low-level horticultural or gardening complex that predated the introduction into the eastern United States of corn from Mexico by at least three thousand years (Asch and Asch 1985; Rossen 2000, in press; Schroeder 2007; Simpson and Mocas, in press; Smith 2009, 2011; Stafford and Mocas 2009, 490). The EAC stretched from Pennsylvania in the north through much of the southeastern and midwestern United States, as defined by archaeological evidence of increased seed sizes and the presence of plants far outside their natural range. There is not yet evidence of cultivated EAC plants north of Pennsylvania (McConaughy 2008). In the case of sunflower, early cultivation was defined by the legendary archaeobotanist Richard Yarnell, who compiled seed sizes from a variety of Kentucky sites (Yarnell 1978).

Eight sunflower seeds were recovered from four samples. Three seeds are from two samples of the tenth century Area 2, the toss zones just outside the proto-longhouse. The other five seeds are from three samples of the twelfth-century Area 4 southeast outlier units. Four of these are split between the two samples from Unit 21, Feature 17, a trash pit.

The wild range of sunflower encompasses the Colorado Plateau and Great Plains from southcentral Canada to Texas. It is not native to the eastern United States (McAssey et al. 2016; Yarnell 1978, 290).

According to Yarnell's (1978) classic sunflower study, early wild seeds measured about 4.5 to 5.0 millimeters in length, with larger seeds (5.1 to 12 millimeters) representing the processes of cultivation and domestication. The Levanna seeds from Area 2 range from 5.5 to 6.5 millimeters with an average length of 6.0 millimeters. The later Area 4 seeds range from 4.9 to 5.6 millimeters with an average of 5.3 millimeters. As always, shrinkage due to carbonization can complicate this discussion. The Levanna sunflower seeds are relatively small in size but within the range of cultivation, though they are much small than contemporary cultivated sunflowers from the Ohio Valley.

Squash and gourd were apparently cultivated within a hunting-gathering lifeway by Middle Archaic times (ca. 7,500 BP). Early versions of these plants were used for containers, fish floats, and edible seeds (Hart, Daniels, and Sheviak 2004; Hudson 2004). DNA evidence suggests that gourds, which have no wild American plant relatives, were introduced throughout North America from Africa by transoceanic drift, and that both squash and gourds were domesticated several times at different places in North America (Kistler et al. 2014). The unusually early cultivation of both squash and gourd may have been stimulated as early as 8,000 BP by food scarcity caused by the disappearance of the great megafauna (including mastodons and mammoths) who maintained disturbed habitat and distributed seeds (Kistler et al. 2015). Three gourd rind specimens are dispersed in three samples, including one sample and seed each from a central hearth of the proto-longhouse, the toss area just northwest of it, a far east outlier unit. One squash seed was recovered from Unit 21, Feature 17 of Area 4, the southeast outlier zone.

Tobacco (*Nicotiana* sp., probably *N. rustica*) was not directly recovered through water flotation, but the frequency of smoking pipes indicates it was present. The seeds are minute and are only rarely and fortuitously recovered, especially since the seed themselves are not utilized, so they are less likely to be carbonized and deposited in sites (of approximately three hundred sites I have analyzed, tobacco has appeared in three, including one seed from the Corey Village).

Tobacco is probably native to the eastern Andean slopes of South America (Wilbert 1987), although there are indigenous North American varieties (Haberman 1984). The earliest eastern US tobacco appears in Middle Woodland sites of Illinois (ca. AD 200) near the confluence of the Illinois and Mississippi Rivers (Asch and Asch 1985; Johannessen 1984; Wagner 2000). There is Haudenosaunee folklore about the origin of tobacco. The story describes the passing of a boat near a river bank filled with dangerous medicine men and "strange beings," who were decoyed into a council house, killed, and burned, saving the community. The first tobacco plants rose from the ashes of their dead (Smith 1994[1883], 37).

Tobacco smoking facilitated communication, making strangers into kin, and as discussed earlier was used in medicinal ceremonies (Drooker 2004, 78; Mann 2004, 172). There was a wide variety of plants and mixtures used in smoking pipes, including sumacs (*Rhus* sp.), laurels (*Kelma* sp.), arrow root (*Viburnum* sp.) and dogwoods (*Cornus* sp.), but tobacco was the foundation of the mixtures in both secular and sacred smoking (Rutsch 1973, 31–33).

According to an early twentieth century report by Ralph Linton, the Cayuga kept tobacco beds that were "lightly manured from time to time, but were not cultivated, and the plants were left to propagate themselves. The leaves were gathered, but the stems, with the seed pods, were left standing in the patch. The Seneca, another tribe of the Iroquois confederacy, simply scattered the seeds on the ground and had a religious prohibition against cultivating the plant" (Linton 1924, 3–4). These practices appear to refer to a process of incipient cultivation known as "extension of collecting" (Harlan 1992, 41–43), a practice widely used by Native American peoples on highly valued "specialty plants"—that is, scarce plants with highly specialized uses (Asch 1994).

A COMMENT ON EASTERN EIGHT CORN-BASED AGRICULTURE

Elsewhere in the eastern United States and contemporary to Levanna, Eastern Eight corn is associated with the Fort Ancient of Kentucky and Ohio and the Monongahela of Pennsylvania (Means 2007; Rossen 1992; Rossen and Turner, in press; Rossen and Edging 1987). These are both advanced tribal groups who were heterarchical; that is, they primarily lived at the large village level of social and political organization and did not have advanced centralized authority. It has been sometimes assumed that the development of agriculture required centralized authority to manage labor and harvests, but the point at which agricultural intensification pushes political centralization is not always clear. My studies of early agriculture in northern Peru show that a change from family garden plots to multifamily farming and irrigation canals with their high maintenance requirements only spurred political centralization several thousand years after agricultural economies were established (Rossen 2011a, 2011b).

The Haudenosaunee took an alternate path to governance and agriculture by developing a confederacy of linked, parallel, yet independent peoples governed by clan mothers and chiefs. Agriculture was conducted and controlled by women within what has been referred to as the "woods and clearing model" (Rossen 2015, 184–85). A basic simplification of the model is that women controlled or even owned the village while men were primarily in the woods for hunting activities. There were also collaborative activities such as fishing. Agriculture would have become a communal multifamily endeavor as the longhouse social order developed. Levanna is a fascinating case study in the parallel developments of social organization and agriculture because of its proto-longhouse, possibly a prototype of the later more formalized longhouse and gendered social organization.

MANAGED WILD PLANTS

Wild rice (*Zizania aquatica*) was a surprising discovery in two samples (one inside the proto-longhouse and one just outside in a toss zone). Wild rice is absent from Cayuga Lake today, but it would have been associated with shallow and marshy areas of Cayuga Lake, which is hundreds of feet deep in most places. The southern end of the lake, near present-day Ithaca, is a shelf that would have been an ideal habitat for wild rice, and nearer Levanna, the area between Aurora Village and Frontenac Island is shallow. These swampy areas were cleared early in historic times. Wild rice would have been collected in canoes using paddles, along with a technology for roasting the grains (LaDuke 2005).

Wild rice is listed as present but rare in an early twentieth-century floral catalog of Cayuga Lake (Wiegand and Eames 1926, 82). Wild rice is not mentioned in F. W. Waugh's classic (1916) discussion of Iroquois (Haudenosaunee) foods and food preparation. Arthur C. Parker did briefly discuss wild rice: "It was little used by the Iroquois . . . although there are records of its employment. The Seneca some forty years ago gathered a great quantity of it but the writer does not know of its use subsequently" (Parker 1910, 109). This would refer to an activity that occurred about 1870. The Great Lakes tribes like the Ashinaabe are known for their extensive management of the wild rice lakes to ensure healthy stands and continued availability (LaDuke 2005, 167–90). It is reasonable to assume that the Cayuga would have treated the wild rice stands of Cayuga Lake in a similar manner.

Sumac (*Rhus* sp.) produces edible berries that are easily dried and stored. The plant is best known for its use in a high vitamin C tea and as a flavoring for stews (Gilmore 1931, 47–48). I long ago argued that sumac has been overlooked as a possible protected or encouraged plant, because sumac exhibits characteristics that would favor management and systematic exploitation over simple gathering (Rossen 1992, 196–98). Sumac grows well and spreads rapidly in disturbed land, and experimentation revealed it is easily grown from seeds, and new plants survive the first winter at a 70 percent success rate (Smith 1970, 51–60). Mature plants are easily transplanted to clearings, where they reproduce more readily. Sumac does not produce significant harvests until the second to fourth year, and peak productivity is the seventh year. A managed stand of sumac trees of various ages produces reliable harvests of more than ninety kilograms per hectare (Smith 1970, 19–20). The case for management of sumac is circumstantial, considering its botanical attributes, frequency, and dietary importance at Levanna, Myers Farm, Corey Village, and elsewhere (Rossen 2015, 159).

WILD FRUITS AND BERRIES

Almost all eastern woodlands Native populations collected, fire dried, and stored seasonally available fruits and berries (Bartram 1955[1791], 321; Swanton 1946, 606). The list from Levanna is impressive: blackberry/raspberry (*Rubus* sp.), grape (*Vitis* sp.), elderberry (*Sambucus canadensis*), cherry (*Prunus* sp.), pawpaw (*Asimina triloba*), and strawberry (*Fragaria* sp.) (table 4.12). In addition to these fruits and berries, the wetlands plant pondweed (*Potamogeton* sp.) is present, possibly as a by-product of wild rice collection.

Some but not all of the blackberry/raspberry and sumac seeds are desiccated and not carbonized. In many samples, both desiccated and carbonized seeds were recovered together. I spent much time pondering if these desiccated seeds are modern intrusions, part of a natural "seed carpet" of the site, or representing unusual preservation of botanical remains. Usually, only carbonized materials are considered archaeological, and all other reported materials here are carbonized. To begin, it is clear that blackberries, raspberries, and sumac were heavily utilized by Cayuga people, regardless of the disposition of the desiccated specimens. These plants are associated with disturbed land, particularly forest edge zones and clearings, and were not seen during excavations at the site, which has long been wooded. The strawberry festival occurs every spring as the first celebration of the annual ritual cycle (Smith 1994[1883], 82).

Botanical densities, particularly seed frequency per liter of floated soil measured across the site in various contexts, has been used to distinguish seed carpets (the result of natural seed rain) from cultural deposits (Rossen, Planella, and Stehberg 2010). Natural seed carpets tend to produce uniform frequencies across a site. The seed densities of Levanna do not show this type of uniformity in seed density (table 4.12). For blackberry/raspberry, Area 2 toss zones have more than double the density of (Area 1) interior proto-longhouse samples. Even more striking, samples from Area 4, the southeast outlier zone, have more than three times the density of the proto-longhouse toss zones, and more than seven times the density of interior proto-longhouse samples (table 4.12). In the case of sumac, densities are highest in the proto-longhouse and toss zone samples (Areas 1 and 2), which are five to seven times higher than in samples from the southeast outlier (Area 4) zone. The blackberry/raspberry and sumac seed densities from Area 1 and Area 4 (with the highest archaeobotanical samples) are not uniform across the site and do not match each other, suggesting cultural patterning and some preservation of ancient desiccated plant remains.

The pawpaw seed from Area 4, the southeast outlier zone, is notable. Pawpaw is a small tree that is common in the Southeast, with a natural

Table 4.12. Botanical Remains: Density per Liter of Floated Soil for Key Species (frequency except where noted)

SITE AREA	1	2	3	4	5	6	7
blackberry / raspberry	2.0	4.5	4.9	14.5	2.9	1.6	—
sumac	1.1	1.4	3.7	0.2	0.2	0.9	—
corn—kernel	0.3	0.2	0.2	0.1	—	0.8	0.2
Corn—cupule	0.3	0.4	—	0.1	—	0.2	—
Corn—all	0.6	0.6	0.2	0.2	—	0.9	0.2
nuts	1.1	1.1	0.2	2.3	0.2	1.7	0.2
wood (frequency)	26.6	20.4	25.9	41.1	9.3	43.0	16.0
wood (gram weight	0.2	0.2	0.3	0.6	0.1	0.4	0.1

range extending north to central Pennsylvania, extreme western New York, along the shores of Lake Ontario, and southern Ontario Province in Canada (Little 2004). The creamy fruit has been compared in some respects to bananas and mangos. Pawpaw was also recovered at the sixteenth-century Corey Village site and is considered to be outside its natural range at both central New York sites. These are either cases of exchange, procurement during travel, or most likely in my opinion, planting to extend the natural range (Rossen 2015, 160).

In summary, the botanical remains from Levanna show a vibrant and varied mixed economy of cultivated plants, managed and manipulated wild resources, and wild plants, especially fruits and berries. The cultivated plants include food and nonfood species like gourd that provided utensils and supported fishing. Corn was introduced into the northeast from Mexico via the Ohio Valley and sunflower was introduced from the Colorado Plateau. Wild rice and sumac populations were probably managed to protect and maximize these food sources. Pawpaw is a possible case of planting to extend the natural range of the tree.

OTHER ASSEMBLAGES: GORGET, HOE BLADES, CALCITE, AND TEMPER

One banded green slate gorget was recovered. Gorgets with two drilled holes were worn as symbols of power and status. Two conjoining fragments were recovered from different excavation units in the southern end of the proto-longhouse (figure 4.15). New York sources of green banded slate are located in seven counties (Columbia, Dutchess,

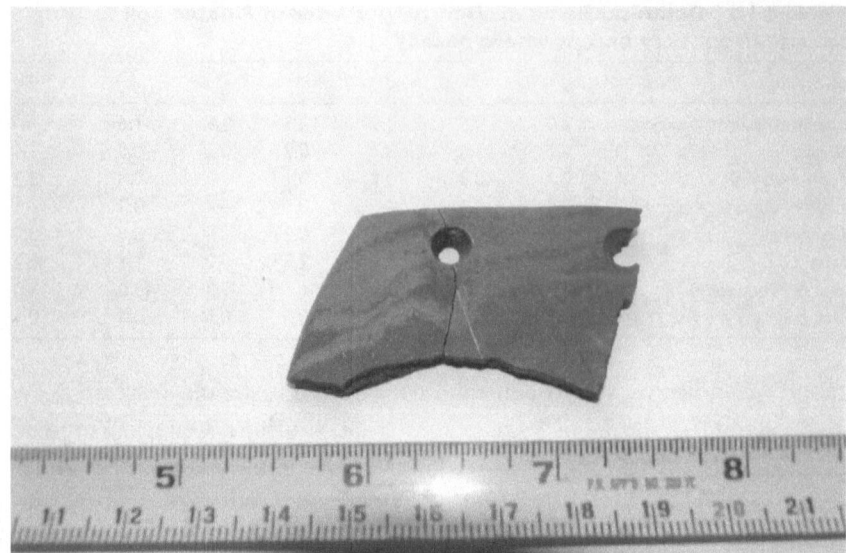

Figure 4.15. Levanna gorget. Jack Rossen.

Greene, Rensselaer, Saratoga, Ulster, Washington) along or near the western bank of the Hudson River in eastern and southeastern New York (Van Diver 1985; US Geological Survey 2007). A similar gorget was recovered at the contemporary Turnbull site in the middle Mohawk Valley (Ritchie, Lenig and Miller 1953, 91).

Four hoe blades were recovered, all from the eastern and western outlying excavation units at the site peripheries. These are made of Tully Limestone, exposed and available in the many Cayuga Lake gorges. The low frequency of hoe blades contrasts with the high frequency found at the much smaller Myers Farm site (n=45). Hoe blades are discussed in detail in chapter 5.

Fragments of temper, the crushed granitic stone mixed with clay in the production of ceramics to improve stability during firing, are present throughout the site. The ubiquity of this material, with ten to forty grams present in nearly all levels, attests to the constant production of ceramics at the settlement. Eight concentrations of one hundred to almost four hundred grams were recorded, including six in the various toss zones surrounding the proto-longhouse. The remaining three concentrations are in Area 4, the southeast outlier zone. Crushing stone in preparation for ceramic production was one activity conducted in or near the proto-longhouse.

Chalky calcite or calcium carbonate (CaCo3) was utilized at Levanna during both site occupations, but probably more heavily during the later, twelfth-century settlement. Calcite could be used as a white pigment, or to soak dried corn to soften it (Parker 1910, 51, 69; Waugh 1916, 62). Calcium carbonate or lye solutions were also used to soak bitternut hickory and acorn to leach bitter tannins (Parker 1910, 99–101; Waugh 1916, 122). The exact use at Levanna is not known. Both calcite and granitic temper may have been procured at the Onondaga Escarpment chert quarries in coordination with the collection of high-quality cherts (Boggs 2006; Lajewski et al. 2003).

Calcite is present in all site areas, but is most plentiful both by quantity and ubiquity in Area 4, the twelfth-century southeast outlier zone. Frequencies per excavation level vary from one to sixteen fragments and from five to 320 grams in weight. Eight site excavation levels contain notable concentrations of more than one hundred grams, with four such concentrations in the twelfth-century Area 4 (Unit 31N, Level 2; Unit 42S, Level 3; and Unit 44S, Level 2). Smaller calcite amounts are commonly present in (n=13 levels) and around the proto-longhouse in toss zones (n=14 levels).

SUMMARY OF THE 2007 TO 2009 LEVANNA EXCAVATIONS

For two brief periods, perhaps twenty to thirty years each, one in the tenth or eleventh century and again at the cusp of the twelfth and thirteenth centuries, Levanna was a bustling village. Cultural patterns of the Cayuga people were being established, including the gradual development of longhouse architecture, matrilocality, a diverse food economy including corn-based agriculture and wild plant management and collecting, along with hunting, trapping, and snaring of a wide variety of mammals and birds. Pelt-bearing squirrels were valuable and are prominent in the site. Fishing gear was complex, including nets, harpoons, fishhooks for pole and line, and perhaps net lures. All indications are that the low-lying village lived in peace, with open access from at least two directions and without defensive palisades. Ceramics indicate a range of artistic expression, including use of older decorative (Point Peninsula-like) traditions and the development of newer (Owasco-like) traditions and the beginnings of incised decoration motifs that would later become dominant. Smoking pipes suggest both secular and sacred tobacco smoking. Formal Haudenosaunee traditions such as longhouse construction and matrilocality along with images of Haudenosaunee healers and folkloric images on pipes support direct connection with Cayuga people and the present-day Haudenosaunee Confederacy.

This peaceful and dynamic view of Levanna starkly contrasts with the view that was promoted at the Levanna Museum during the 1930s. Levanna people were displayed as Algonkian people, different and disconnected from the present-day Cayuga of the area. The earlier view of Levanna centered around warfare, fear, deprivation, defense, and animistic, superstitious ritual. Modern excavation techniques, artifact analysis, and special studies have indeed forced a substantial reevaluation and reinterpretation of Levanna.

5

FURTHER REINTERPRETATION OF THE CAYUGA

The Myers Farm Site

Adelaide "Ada" Jacques took up pottery design and manufacture late in her sixties. A child of the boarding school era, she loved to tell the funny and tragic stories of life at the Onondaga Reservation. One story I remember well is how as a young girl she would place the apple on her father's head for arrow shooting in one of the last Indian shows. She was a modern potter, making beautiful raku and impressionistic pieces. Her ceramics were exhibited in museums throughout central New York, including the Everson Museum of Art (Syracuse), the Iroquois Museum (Howe's Cave), and the Dowd Fine Art Gallery (Cortland) (Anonymous 2016).

I was especially interested in Ada's traditional pots, which were primarily blackwares with incised designs and collared rims, and I bought and was gifted several over the years. Ada told me that the designs and pottery shapes were passed down in the family, plus there were designs that came to her in dreams. She also made traditional fabric-impressed and cord-wrapped paddle wares. Ada discussed techniques for producing the blackware surface, such as refiring the pot a second time in a barrel filled with brush. The matches between her ceramic designs and the sixteenth-century Cayuga archaeological specimens from the Corey Village were striking. The Cayuga of course were close neighbors of the

Onondaga and co-members of the Haudenosaunee Confederacy. I remember not buying one of Ada's blackware pots because I had not seen the design at Corey, only to have the incised pattern show up at the site excavations shortly after.

I asked Ada to replicate the complete but heavily fragmented pot found at the Myers Farms site, which is discussed later. She took home the refitted and glued archaeological specimen, but was troubled by the inverted shoulder of the pot. According to Ada, it was not "made correctly," and so when she produced her replica, it had the standard collared rim and bulging rounded body of the ceramics she knew. Ada had a firm notion of how traditional pottery (in her case, of course, Onondaga pottery) should and should not be designed. Our conversations helped me understand how the tenth- and twelfth-century Levanna ceramics (Rogers 2014), the fifteenth-century Myers Farm ceramics to be discussed next (O'Hearn 2013a), and the sixteenth-century Corey ceramics (Pollack 2015) represent evolving Haudenosaunee mental templates and identities. Though she came to ceramics relatively late in life, Ada embodied and internalized Native identity and the meaning and importance of producing material culture.

THE MYERS FARM SITE

Unlike Levanna, the archaeological site that came to be known as Myers Farm did not have a long history of investigation. Ten miles south southeast of Levanna and five miles east of Cayuga Lake, Myers Farm is a small and inconspicuous hilltop site. It was recorded and collected by Robert DeOrio, an avocational archaeologist who was alerted to the site in 1973 by David Myers, a local farmer (Niemczycki 1984). DeOrio's amateur work was inspired by his hero Harrison C. Follett (DeOrio 1999). When I met with Bob in early 2011 at his Auburn, New York, house to discuss my interest in the site, he pulled a shoebox of pottery sherds from the site off a shelf. The site was mysterious, with unusual decorated sherds. Even the site size was unknown. It was thought to be a two-acre village site like Levanna and Corey, because that was the presumed Cayuga settlement pattern. In a warfare landscape, people would be garrisoned in defended villages with open space or "no man's land" between. In Mary Ann Palmer Niemczycki's broad study of the locations and ceramics of Cayuga and Seneca sites, the site appears on maps under two names: Myers Farm and Damyer, a transposition of David Myers, and is classified as "transitional" between Owasco and Iroquois (Niemczycki 1984, 22, 42). Unlike most sites in her volume, no description or discussion of site size or ceramics is presented.

It did not take long to challenge the presumed nature of Myers Farm. With the blessing of landowners John and Rebecca Binns (David Myers's daughter), and helped by my Ithaca College students, we thrashed around and shovel tested in the eight-foot-high hayfield, unable to relocate the site. Finally, after John had cut the hay and only a few days before my scheduled archaeological field school, we found a small elliptical black midden area, barely thirty by twenty meters (figures 5.1 and 5.2). Could this be a portion of the two-acre village that DeOrio had documented? Over three field seasons (2011, 2013, 2014), we discovered that this was the entire site, that Myers Farm was indeed a very small and undefended site surrounded now and then by agricultural fields. Despite its size, the site had a heavy density of artifacts and a fine-grained pattern of features (pits and post molds). We came to label it as an agricultural station and feasting ground (Rossen 2015, 176–80).

Figure 5.1. General view of the Myers Farm site. Jack Rossen.

Figure 5.2. Myers Farm main excavation block. Jack Rossen.

EXCAVATIONS AND RADIOCARBON DATING

Over three six-week field seasons, a total of sixty-six square meters was excavated. This includes twelve square meters excavated outside the black midden zone. The results are excavation of about 70 percent of the black zone (figure 5.3). The site has a well-defined thirty-centimeter plowzone. However, because of the site use as a hayfield beginning in the early 1970s, it was only plowed on average once every six or seven years. Thus, in contrast with some area sites that have been plowed hundreds of times, Myers Farm was only plowed about six or seven times. The relatively light damage from plowing was evident from the relatively large pottery sherds, smoking pipe fragments, and faunal remains that were recovered from plowzone deposits.

Beneath the plowzone at Myers Farm are well-defined features. Most dramatic is a large circular cooking pit that is 140 centimeters in diameter and 81 centimeters deep, labeled Feature 3 (figure 5.4). This feature became evident at the base of plowzone as a black circle with a bright red surrounding ring. The pit was lined by twenty-seven broken and exhausted limestone hoe blades and stratified from many

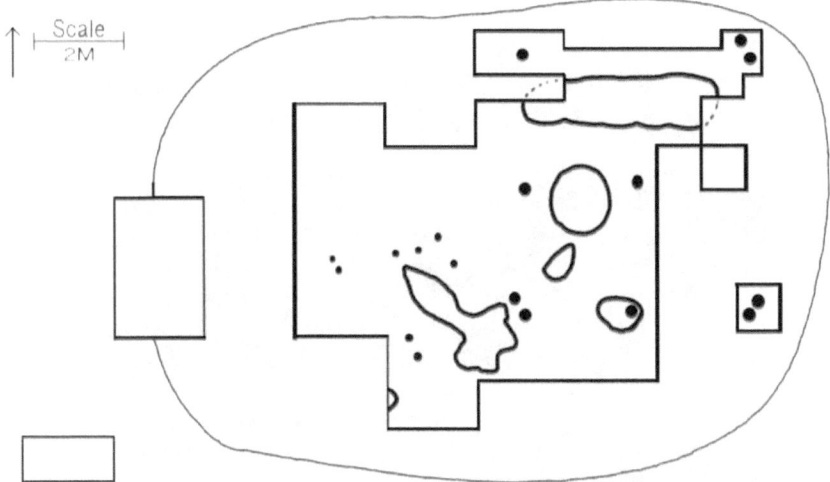

Figure 5.3. Myers Farm site map. Matt Gorney, Digital Media Services, Ithaca College.

episodes of cooking and refuse deposition. Charcoal lenses throughout the pit produced an abundance of faunal and botanical remains. A complete broken pot was recovered at a depth of fifty centimeters. The pit bottom contained a particularly dense twenty-centimeter charcoal layer. This pit was excavated in ten-centimeter levels and was completely collected for water flotation to recover botanical remains, fine faunal materials, and small artifacts. A radiocarbon sample of nutshell from sixty-five centimeters yielded a date of 400+/–20 BP, calibrating to AD 1466+/–18 (ISGS-A2591). This date exactly matches the artifact styles at the site.

Further excavations showed that the pit was inside a rectangular structure oriented in cardinal directions, six meters east-west and six meters, thirty centimeters north-south. This structure was defined by eleven wall posts and one interior center post. Double posts were defined at three of the four corners. At the northwest corner, only one post could be defined. Along the northern interior of the structure is a thirty-centimeter deep step or shelf, suggesting a subterranean floor (figure 5.5). This is quite unusual in Cayuga country, where most structures are variations on the paired-post longhouse with a row of central fire hearths. I interpret this structure as a cookhouse, still a feature of Haudenosaunee life today.

Figure 5.4 (a–c). Feature 3, the large cooking pit. Jack Rossen.

Figure 5.5. Steps into the Myers Farm cookhouse. Jack Rossen.

Two other smaller pits without signs of burning are present in the structure, probably storage pits. Just outside the southwest corner of the structure, a honeycombed network of overlapping and integrated storage pits was encountered. Though the site has a high artifact density throughout the black zone, there are no other features besides these, particularly in substantial excavation west of the structure. This fine-grained pattern leaves a strong impression of well-organized activities.

Surrounding the black zone of plowed midden and features is the four-acre hayfield. Michael "Bodhi" Rogers of Ithaca College brought his student team to the site for weeks of ground-penetrating radar (GPR) during the 2012 and 2014 field seasons. It was hoped we could find signs of the surrounding ancient agricultural fields that we believe were there. Excavation of anomalies in the GPR data outside the black zone were conducted, but no features were identified. Excavations scattered around outside the black zone showed only light brown plowzone and subsoil with well-defined parallel plow furrows. Six limestone hoe blades and chert flakes were the only artifacts recovered from these excavation units. The GPR, twelve meters of excavations and extensive shovel testing provided two important results. First, the black zone was not merely one of several "hot spots" or activity zones of a larger village site as we originally supposed. Second, there is no evidence of a wall or palisade protecting the site. Despite its hilltop location, it was concluded that Myers Farm was small and undefended.

CERAMICS

An ongoing discussion in the analysis of archaeological ceramics that is particularly relevant to the Myers Farm site is the relationship of pottery decoration to ethnic groups and identity. This is a complex debate about whether or not "pots are people" (Cruz 2011). In Haudenosaunee archaeology, the recent trend is to recognize that differences in pottery decoration styles represent regional and community differences that "reflect expressions of ethnicity" (Birch and Williamson 2013, 129). Even in arguing that Haudenosaunee pottery types do not match ethnic identities, scholars attach those types to ethnic groups within social network analyses (Hart and Engelbrecht 2011). Ethnoarchaeological studies tend to confirm that ceramic styles are "past choices, made at some time in the past by a social, though not necessarily an 'ethnic' group [that] is reaffirmed and inculcated through apprenticeship" (David and Kramer 2001, 148–49). In this sense, ceramics and existing ceramic typologies suggest social connections and interactions within and between regions that are traditionally associated with various Haudenosaunee peoples and their neighbors (see Pollack 2015; Rossen 2015, 169).

The Myers Farm excavations produced more than 1,500 ceramic sherds. Features produced the largest materials, including one complete pot from the cooking pit. Macy O'Hearn (2013a, 2013b) conducted an analysis of seventy-nine representative decorated sherds and the complete pot. She noted cordmarking, incising, notching, and dentate stamping forms of decoration and was able to place them into twelve ceramic types from Richard S. MacNeish's classic (1952) ceramic typology (table 5.1). The collection includes types that are known as local Cayuga types, but also, surprisingly, nonlocal types that are diagnostic of the Seneca, Onondaga, Mohawk, and Neutral Nations.

Local Cayuga ceramic types are Richmond Incised (n=29), Cayuga Horizontal (n=13), Hummel Corded (n=6) and Ithaca Linear (n=2). O'Hearn noted the difficulties of distinguishing between the Rich-

Table 5.1. Myers Farm Decorated Ceramics (after O'Hearn 2013)

Ceramic Type	freq	Cultural Affiliation
Richmond incised	31	Cayuga
Cayuga horizontal	13	Cayuga
Hummel corded	6	Cayuga
Ithaca linear	2	Cayuga
Sparta dentate	13	Senecca
Dutch hollow	7	Senecca
Swarthout dentate	2	St. Lawrence, Onodaga
Otsungo notched	1	Mohawk
Lawson incised	1	Neutral (Ontario)
Uren dentate	1	Neutral (Ontario)
Ripley triangular	1	Neutral (Ontario)
Iroquois linear	1	(unusual paste and color)

mond Incised and Cayuga Horizontal types. The two types grade into each other, leading O'Hearn to classify some sherds as "transitional" between the types.

Nonlocal types make up 36 percent of the decorated ceramics that O'Hearn analyzed. These types typically represent the Seneca to the west, the Onondaga and Mohawk to the north and east, and the Neutrals to the north along Lake Erie in present-day Canada. The types are Sparta Dentate (n=15, Seneca), Dutch Hollow (n=7, Seneca), Swarthout Dentate (n=2, Onondaga, specifically Onondaga and Madison Counties, New York, and also the St. Lawrence region of Canada), Iroquois Linear (n=2, a widespread New York, Ontario, and Pennsylvania type), Otsungo Notched (n=1, Mohawk), Lawson Incised (n=1, Neutral), Ripley Triangualar (n=1, Neutral), and Uren Dentate (n=1, Neutral) (MacNeish 1952, 14, 19, 20, 75–76; figure 5.6). Some of these types may have broader geographic distributions than have been previously recognized. For example, the Dutch Hollow type has appeared at other Cayuga sites such as Corey Village and the Ripley Triangular type was recovered at Indian Fort Road, a Cayuga village on the western side of Cayuga Lake near Trumansburg, New York (Baugher and Clark 1998). The three Neutral types are previously undocumented in Cayuga Territory.

Distribution maps for local versus nonlocal ceramics show differences. Local ceramics are concentrated south of the cookhouse while nonlocal ceramics are concentrated in and around the cookhouse itself (figure 5.7). These distributions are suggestive of activity areas, perhaps

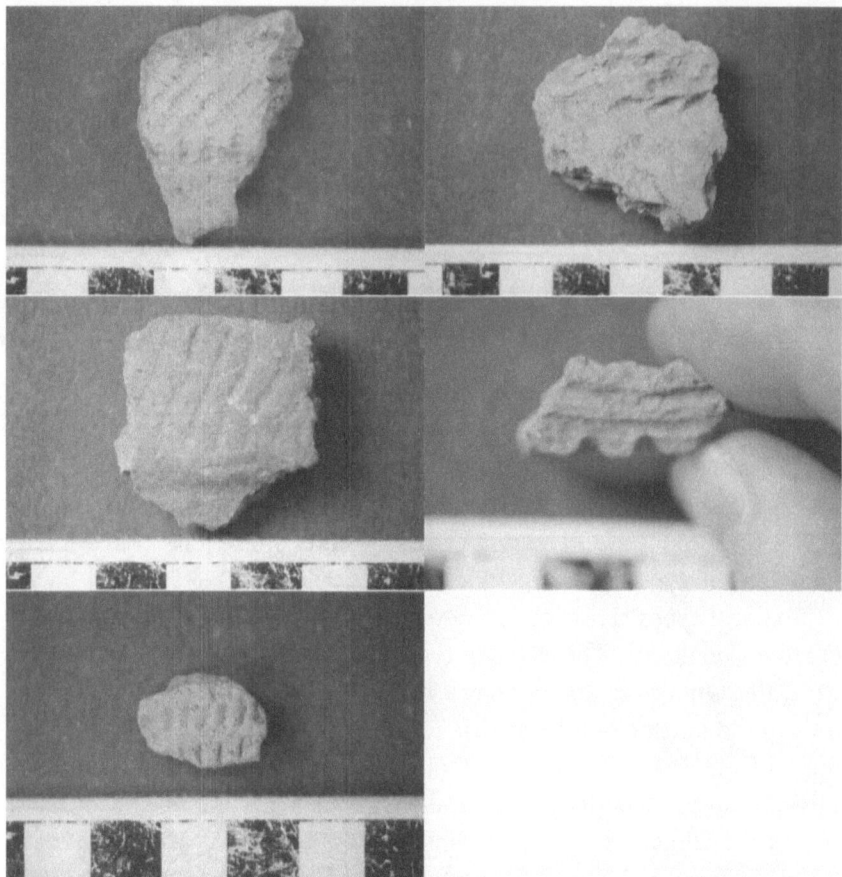

Figure 5.6. Myers Farm nonlocal ceramics. Swarthout Dentate (top left), Iroquois Linear (top right), Lawson Incised (middle left), Otsungo Notched (middle left), Uren Dentate (bottom left). Macy O'Hearn.

local Cayuga performing food preparation south of the cookhouse while visitors congregated more in the cookhouse.

Other oddities were noted among the Myers Farm ceramics. Two sherds appear to have remnants of pigment, one red and one black. The black pigmented sherd seems to have been decorated with diagonal stripes. Twelve sherds appear to have fabric pattern remnants ranging from a very fine mesh material with the woven squares barely one millimeter in size to larger netting (figure 5.8). The Haudenosaunee made fine textiles from several plant sources, including milkweed (*Asclepias syriaca*), nettle (*Urtica dioica*), Indian hemp (*Apocynum cannabinum*),

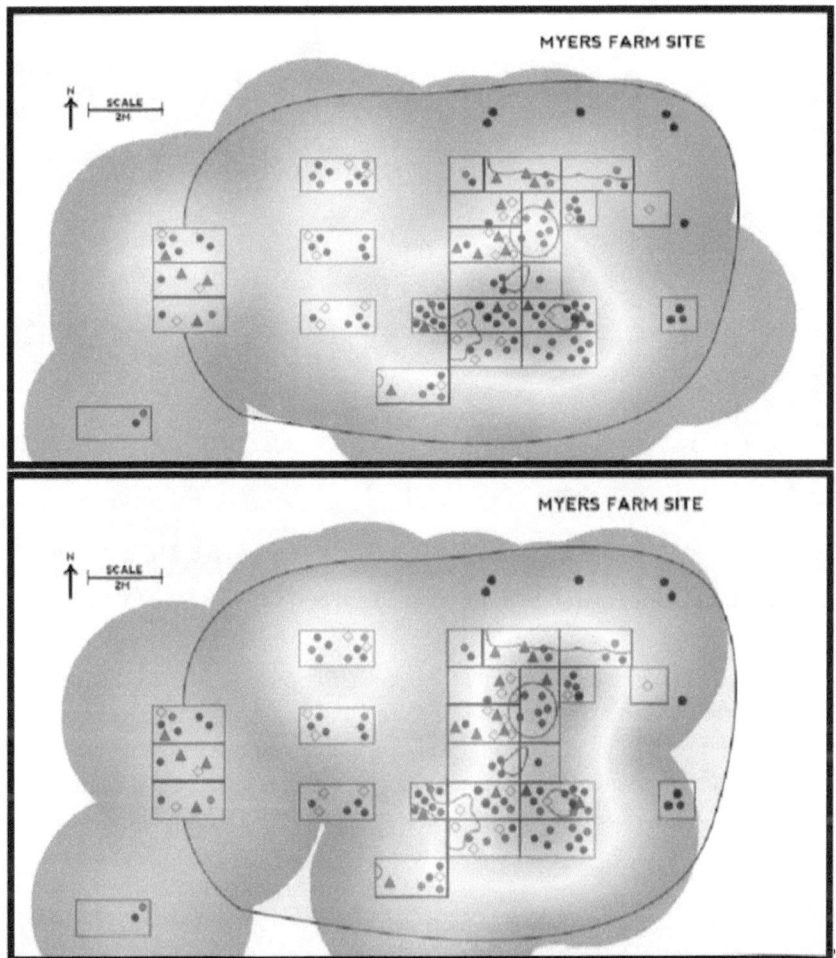

Figure 5.7. Myers Farm local (above) nonlocal (below) ceramic distribution heat map. Macy O'Hearn.

and slippery elm (*Ulmus rubra*) (Finnegan 2004). O'Hearn noted an ethnographic use of fine fabric in ceramic manufacture by the Tohono O'odham (Papago) of Southern Arizona:

> [The potter] removes a fistful of wet clay from its container. This she puts on the cloth in front of her and begins to pat it into a bun. As soon as the ball of clay is round and flat, she adds ashes or dirt to the stone anvil with which she pats the bun, or to the mold, to prevent the clay from sticking to her hand. The potter then places the bun over the base of the inverted

Figure 5.8. Myers Farm fabric-impressed ceramic sherd. Macy O'Hearn.

pot that is being used as a mold. She may first put ashes on the base of the mold to prevent the bun from sticking to it, or she may use dirt, water, or as one potter told us, nothing. Another potter, Rita Valenzuela, places a cloth over the base of the mold, with the result that the cloth imprints show in the interior of the base of the new pot even after it is fired. (Fontana et al. 1962, 58, cited in O'Hearn 2013a, 27)

Nine of these pottery sherds were brought to Edward Jolie of Mercyhurst University:

At 50x I'm seeing *possible* filaments that could be trace remains of fine plant fiber cordage. Indeed, although the fibers are very fine, the blurry sediment stain that borders them could indicate the former dimensions of the original cord *if* what we're seeing is the barest remains of decayed fiber. So, at this point I'm inclined to see this as something real on 5 out of 9 samples you sent. If we're looking at some incidental fabric pseudomorph, then it's showing a very fine mesh knotted fabric, likely a net bag or recycled fishing/hunting net. Its presence on vessel interiors would suggest use as a liner or as a step in the production process where it helps separate a still-drying ceramic vessel from the fabric of another vessel being used as a template—akin to a Hopi "puki" in the Southwest where a coiled basket made in the shape of the desired pot was used to help shape and start the pot—in this case you have a pot line with a fabric to help separate the wet or leather hard new vessel from its mold. (Jolie, personal communication, email 2016)

COMPLETE POT

A complete but heavily fragmented pot was recovered from the large cooking pit. A total of 193 sherds pertain to this single pot, which has a rounded body, a straight flaring neck and a rim diameter of twenty-eight centimeters. It could only be partially reconstructed (figure 5.9). The pot has elements of different types of the MacNeish typology:

> The neck and body bear general similarities to the Owasco Corded Oblique type, which is characterized by oblique, parallel impressed lines which sometimes extend down onto the neck . . . this vessel also possesses decoration on the rim and a high, incipient collar, and is characterized by blocks of opposing oblique incised lines. The incised decoration along the

Figure 5.9. Myers Farm complete pot, partially reconstructed. Macy O'Hearn.

rim and collar may represent a variation on Cayuga Horizontal or Richmond Incised. (O'Hearn 2013a, 20–21)

The complete pot raises the possibility that individual sherds from the same pot could be sorted into different types of the MacNeish typology. This is not to critique the typology, which has largely stood the test of time over sixty-five years. It merely highlights how ceramic typologies in general are basic organizational and heuristic devices with limitations. Whole pots are rare in Haudenosaunee/Iroquois territory, and thus decorated pottery style types were based on sherds.

As stated early, the replica made by Ada Jacques faithfully displayed the incised designs of the original, but not the pot shape, which she considered to be "not right." I wonder if her comment is due to the age of the site, when historic forms of ceramics and projectile points were gradually developing, leaving archaeologists to label some forms as "transitional." I also wonder if visitors to the site exerted stylistic influence on even local pottery styles.

One sherd from the complete pot was included in the residue analysis performed by Eleanora A. Reber and Didi el-Behaedi. It tested positive for Amyrin, a compound biomarker for plants (see chapter 4). Nothing more specific could be determined.

O'Hearn summarized the collection from Myers Farm:

> The ceramic assemblage at Myers Farm is extremely heterogeneous, a quality that has been argued by Engelbrecht (2007, 222–25) to be a correlate of conflict at Onondaga and Seneca sites. According to his study of ceramic decoration, the heterogeneity is seen as an indication of fusion that occurs when smaller groups form alliances during times of warfare. The argument can also be made, however, that the natural response to warfare between groups would be distrust of neighboring groups and a desire for community self-preservation, as indicated by the palisades that are often found on sites that are thought to be occupied during times of conflict. (O'Hearn 2013a, 17)

The variability of the Myers Farm ceramic assemblage supports the overall interpretation of the site as a feasting ground with outside visitors. The overall site contexts and artifact assemblages suggest that the variability pertains to peaceful interactions and not conflict-related aggregation.

GROUND STONE

In terms of quantity, perhaps the most astounding artifact assemblage is ground stone. A total of 1,798 ground stone artifacts were recovered. This does not include lightly ground or ambiguous pieces, but only clearly ground, shaped and beveled specimens. The size and diversity of ground stone is a direct testament to the scale of food processing and production at the site. Alison Armour analyzed the ground stone artifacts as a summer Ithaca College student intern. Hand grinders are most prevalent (n=584), followed by hammerstones (n=429) and then small pallets (n=395) (table 5.2). Grinding slabs are the heaviest, averaging 3,499 grams (7.7 pounds). One enormous grinding slab/table east of the structure weighs 133,000 grams (293 pounds). The assemblage also includes small ground stone implements with specialized uses, including abraders, polishers, spindle whorls, and precision grinders.

About half of ground stone artifacts (n=849) show evidence of lesser secondary uses, such as nutting marks on a hand grinder or smooth, ground patches on a hammerstone. Some of these tools appear to have up to four different uses. For example, a total of 273 specimens have battering as if secondarily used as a hammer. Another 192 specimens have small ground patches.

The most utilized raw material for ground stone is limestone (n=1215, 67.6 percent), followed by granite (n=347, 19.2 percent), a stone im-

Table 5.2. Myers Farm Ground Stone Tools

Tool Type	freq	avg wt (gm)	avg max length (mm)
Hand grinder	584	193	67
Hammerstone	429	142	61
Small pallet	395	127	79
Polisher	79	45	41
Abrader	87	53	50
Pestle	82	144	61
Grinding slab	70	2499	136
Nutting stone	26	206	72
Precision grinder	17	18	47
Bowl	4	882	148
Plummet	3	106	64
Pick-ax	1	715	196
Burin	1	49	54
Spindle whorl	1	—	—
Total	1798		

ported from sources in the Adirondack Mountains at least one hundred miles to the northeast, quartzite (n=80, 4.4 percent), and sandstone (n=77, 4.3 percent). Ground stone artifacts were also made of igneous rock, slate, siltstone, and quartz in low frequencies. Limestone is the most common material used in all ground stone categories except for hammerstones, where there was a preference for granite.

HOE BLADES

Hoe blades are relatively rare on most Haudenosaunee sites. The Levanna site produced only six hoe blades from the 2007–2009 excavations, so the forty-five hoe blades from Myers Farm was surprising. Sarah Ward of Ithaca College conducted a study of these specimens (Ward 2014a, 2014b). All are made from Tully limestone, present only in the exposed bottoms of the regional stream gorges. Hoe blades range from 9 to 23 centimeters in length, 6 to 17 centimeters in width, and 1.2 to 6.4 cm in thickness. Weights range from 140 to 2,917 grams. Ward subdivided the hoe blades into small (140–1,100 grams), medium (1,100–2,000 grams), and large (2,000–2,917 grams) categories. All hoes are rectangular and blocky, manufactured using the natural fracture planes of the limestone and exhibiting haft markings on the sides. Use edges are straight (n=25), convex (n=18), and concave (n=2), although the curved edges may be the result of heavy use and wear and are probably not a design element. Nearly all specimens (n=42) are heavily worn or exhausted. Twenty-seven hoes were found inside the large cooking pit. It appears they were used to help line the pit following the end of their original use-life (Ward 2014a, 2014b).

Studies of hoe blades in the eastern United States are rare. Some scholarship has been conducted on the chert hoes of the mound chiefdoms of the Mississippi Valley, contemporary to Myers Farm. In those cases, the management and organization of hoe manufacture and distribution is viewed as a mechanism of specialization and social stratification (Cobb 2010; Sussenbach 1993). The subsistence change from house gardening to full-scale corn-based agriculture depended on expanding agriculture into communal fields and working difficult prairie lands that were previously inaccessible. Experimental research with replicas of Mill Creek chert hoes showed their capabilities to work even the toughest soils (Hammerstedt and Hughes 2015). Hoe blades were removed from quarries as unfinished blanks and were finished at secondary locations in a complex production chain (Cobb 2010).

What does the large hoe blade collection from Myers Farm tell us? The Cayuga did not go through the same processes of intensification that affected other members of the Haudenosaunee Confederacy like the Mohawk and Onondaga. Instead of expanding their populations and settlement sizes, the Cayuga population remained stable for centuries. I have suggested that the Cayuga instead developed occupationally specialized villages, for purposes including healing and agricultural production, as an alternative pathway of culture change (Rossen 2015, 181–89). In this sense, hoe blade manufacturing appears to be related to a movement toward specialized agricultural stations, along with large-scale food production and feasting.

My visits to Taughannock Gorge near Trumansburg, New York, a gorge on the western side of Cayuga Lake across from Myers Farm and Levanna, with analysts Sarah Ward and Macy O'Hearn, located a Tully limestone hoe blade quarry site. On a talus slope, we noted numerous tabular fragments of limestone suitable as blanks, along with numerous limestone flakes and a few partially worked specimens. The absence of finished hoe blades at the quarry site suggests that, like in the Mississippian case, blanks were removed from the quarry with minimal working and were finished at other locations. Although gorge quarries nearer to Myers Farm east of Cayuga Lake have not been located, it is likely that they existed as the only local access to exposed Tully limestone. These quarries add another dimension to the emerging picture of a more complex Cayuga settlement pattern, including a variety of small special activity sites.

CHIPPED LITHICS: PROJECTILE POINTS AND SCRAPERS

The relatively small chipped lithic tools collection was analyzed by Shannon LaBelle (2016), an Ithaca College summer student intern. Sixteen projectile points were evenly divided between the Madison and

Figure 5.10. Myers Farm "transitional" type projectile points. Specimen at far left is bone. Jack Rossen.

"Transitional" types (Ritchie 1971). The Madison is a narrow triangular point with greater than two to one length-to-width ratio. Transitional points are wider than Madisons but not a fully equilateral triangle like the Levanna type (figure 5.10). Transitional points are diagnostic of the fifteenth century in New York. In addition, three point tips and two projectile preforms were recovered. All projectiles at Myers Farm are made of high-quality quarry cherts, in order of importance from Morehouse, Edgecliff, and Clarence cherts.

Twenty-one side scrapers (with use edges perpendicular to the primary striking platform) and twenty end scrapers (with use edges parallel to primary striking platform) are present in the collection. These are all hafted cutting and slicing tools with edge angles between twenty-five and thirty degrees. Most scrapers are made of the expedient Seneca chert, available in stream cobbles adjacent to the site, but a substantial minority of scrapers were made of Morehouse (n=8), Edgecliff (n=3), and Nedrow (n=3) cherts. These cherts are only available in the quarries located along the Onondaga Escarpment twenty-five miles north of Myers Farm. The variability in cherts used to make end and side scrapers suggests a variety of uses, with the scraping and cutting of not just plants but also harder materials such as bone requiring higher quality chert. Instead of being expedient, lightly used tools, many scrapers at Myers Farm were used for relatively heavy-duty communal food processing (LaBelle 2016).

FAUNAL REMAINS

Faunal remains from two key site contexts, Feature 3, the large cooking pit and Feature 13, a storage pit complex outside and just southwest of the structure, were analyzed by Jessica E. Watson of the University at Albany and the New York State Museum (Watson and Rossen 2016; tables 5.3 and 5.4). Watson found that unlike Levanna, large mammal bones,

Table 5.3. Myers Farm Faunal Remains

Taxa	NISP	%Total	MNI	Weight (g)	%Total
Aves	20	4.85		6.3	1.63
Passeniformes	5	1.21		0.37	0.10
cf Columba livia	6	1.46		1.23	0.32
Columba livia	4	0.97	1	0.99	0.26
Buteo jamaicensis	2	0.49	1	1.5	0.39
cf Buteo jamaicensis	1	0.24		0.18	0.05
Total Bird	**38**	**9.22**	**2**	**10.57**	**2.73**
Rodentia	10	2.43		1.22	0.31
Sciurus carolinensis	6	1.46	3	2.44	0.63
Tamiasciurus hudsonicus	5	1.21	1	0.95	0.25
Tamias straitus	4	0.97	1	0.22	0.06
Sciuridae	3	0.73		0.13	0.03
cf Sciuridae	1	0.24		0.09	0.02
Total Rodent	**29**	**7.04**	**5**	**5.05**	**1.30**
Odocoileus virginianus	46	11.17	2	203.88	52.64
cf Odocooileus virginianus	24	5.83		51.61	13.33
Total Deer	**70**	**16.99**	**2**	**255.49**	**65.97**
Small mammal	17	4.13	2	2.13	0.55
S-M mammal	5	1.21	1	0.72	0.19
Medum mammal	40	9.71	2	8.14	2.10
M-L mammal	20	4.85	1	7.83	2.02
Large mammal	93	22.57	2	87.42	22.57
Mammalia	33	8.01		4.1	1.06
Total Mammal	**208**	**50.49**	**8**	**110.34**	**28.49**
Osteichythyes	66	16.02	1	4.81	1.24
Total Fish	**66**	**16.02**	**1**	**4.81**	**1.24**
Testudines	1	0.24	1	1.05	0.27
Total Turtle	**1**	**0.24**	**1**	**1.05**	**0.27**
Grand Total	**412**	**100**	**19**	**387.31**	**100**

Table 5.4. Myers Farm Faunal Remains

Activity	Modification	Taxa	Feature 3	Feature 13	Total
Cooking	burned	Ococoileus virginianus	3		3
		mammal	1		1
		Medium mammal	3		3
		Large mammal	6		6
	calcined	Odocoileus virginianus	2		2
		cf Odocoileus virginianus	1		1
		m-l mammal	2	2	4
		Large mammal	14	2	16
	cutmark	Odocoileus virginianus	2		2
	heated bone	Odocoileus virginianus	1		1
	kitchen butchering	cf Odocoileus virginianus	1		1
		Large mammal		1	1
Marrow extraction	spiral fracture	Aves	2		2
		Odocoileus virginianus	2		2
		m-l mammal		1	1
		Large mammal	7	1	8
	spiral fracture, calcined	Large mammal	2		2
Carnivore scavenging	gnawed	Odocoileus virginianus	1		1
Tool manufacture	bone flake	Large mammal	4		4
	bone tool	Medium mammal	1		1
	spiral fracture / bone flake	Large mammal	2		2
	square fracture	Large mammal	3		3
Tool use	burnished	Odocoileus virginianus	1		1
	spiral fracture, utilized	Odocoileus virginianus	1		1
Total			62	7	69

particularly white-tailed deer, dominate the assemblage. In addition, medium-to-large mammal is almost equally present in Feature 13. Small mammals, birds, and rodents were identified in the large cooking pit.

Squirrels and chipmunks in this assemblage are probably not intrusive, especially the Eastern fox squirrel (*Sciurus carolinensis*), which doesn't burrow. Pigeon (*Columba livia*) and red-tailed hawk (*Buteo jamaicensis*) are present but rarely modified. Watson also analyzed bones for various modifications. In Feature 3, the cooking pit, 16 percent of bone was modified. As expected, these are mostly cooking and other food-related modifications, including marrow extraction from green bones. In the storage pit complex, Feature 13, 30 percent of bone was modified, all related to cooking or marrow extraction. Only Feature 3 had worked bone, including several bone flakes, an awl, and a utilized spiral fractured long bone.

A few bone, tooth, and antler effigies were recovered (figure 5.11). Two are nearly identical animals carved crudely from deer vertebrae. They superficially resemble moose, though Dan Hill of the Cayuga believes they may represent mastodons. The simplicity of the carving leads me to speculate if these were children's toys. Another is an animal face (bear or fox) carved into deer antler. Also recovered is a bear tooth pendant with one root removed to form the shape of a foot with lines cut into the tapered base that may represent toes. The bottom is flat with a slight arch toward the heel. Bear tooth foot effigies are common on Cayuga sites during the sixteenth century (Sanft 2013). The Myers Farm specimen may be a precursor of these later effigies.

The pattern of bone fragmentation and heating, especially in Feature 3, the large cooking pit, indicates marrow extraction and bone grease production (Fisher 1995; Noe-Nygaard 1977; Outram 2005; Outram et al. 2014). Bone grease and marrow could have been used for many purposes, including dietary supplement and flavoring (Binford 1978; Karr et al. 2008) and crafting, medicinal, and ritual contexts (Jordan 2008, 286; Tooker 1964). There is also evidence of carnivore scavenging.

In summary, faunal remains from Myers Farm showcase its use as a feasting ground for agriculturalists. The predominance of large game animals contrasts sharply with the faunal assemblages from nearby village sites like Corey and Levanna, which are dominated by small mammals, birds, and fish (Rossen 2015; Watson and Rossen 2016).

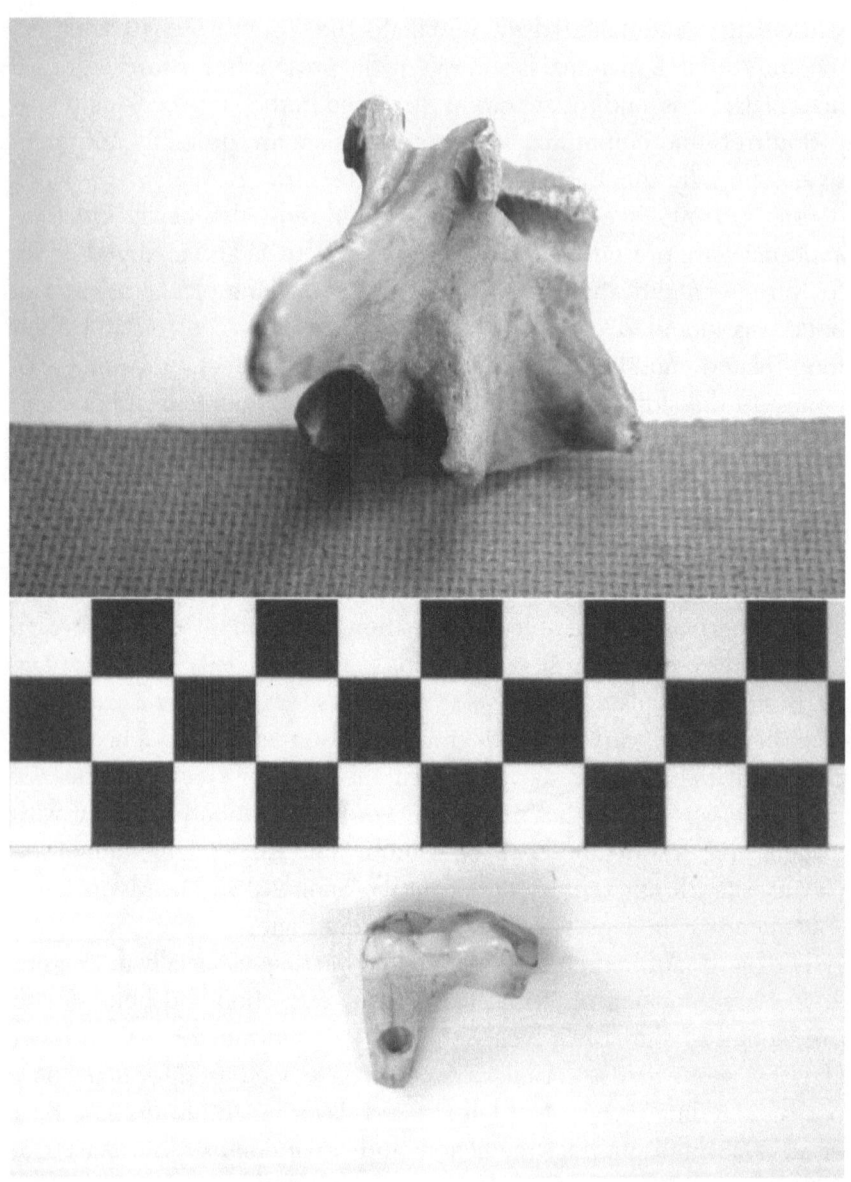

Figure 5.11. Myers Farm animal carving from deer vertebrae, a possible child's toy and bear tooth pendant. Jack Rossen.

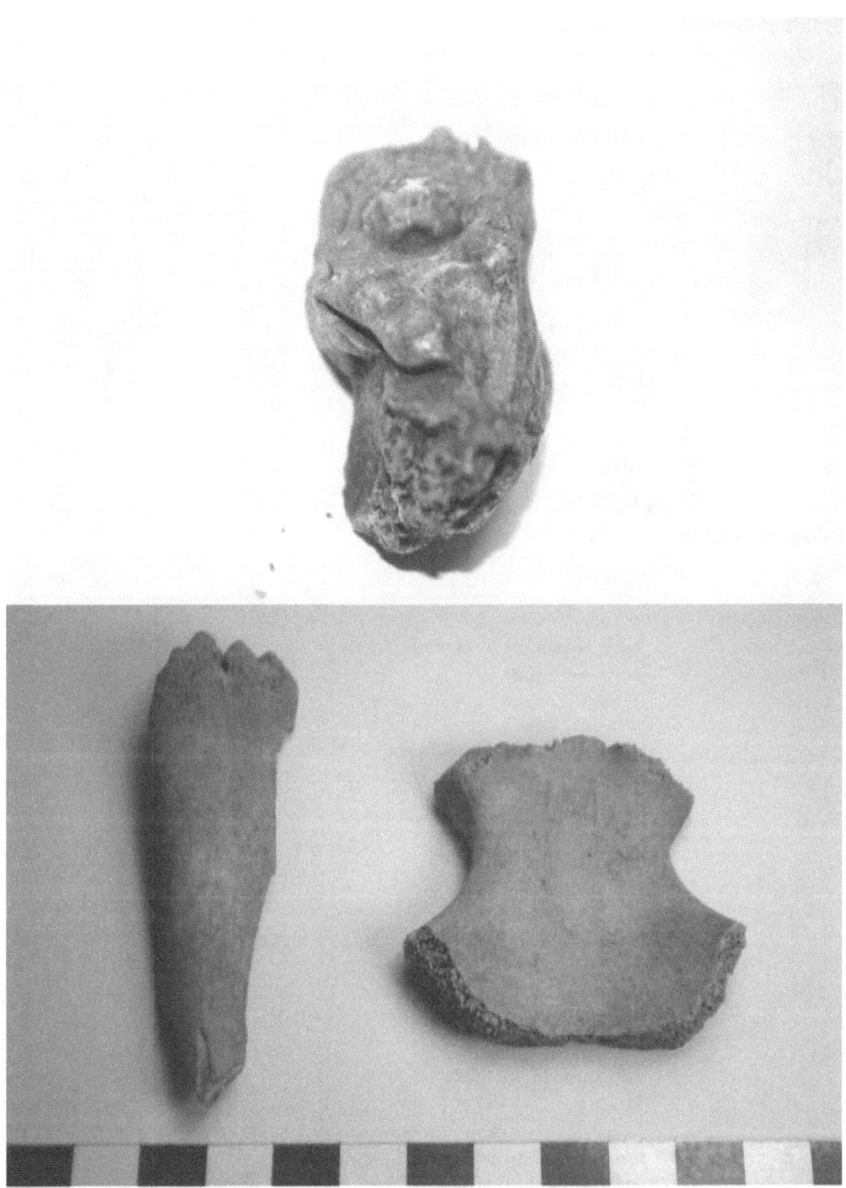

Figure 5.11 (continued). Worked bone pendants from Myers Farm and animal face carved into deer antler (top). Jack Rossen.

BOTANICAL REMAINS

The large cooking pit (Feature 3) and the honey-combed storage pit complex (Feature 13) provided archaeobotanical data through water flotation of the complete feature fill (table 5.5). A total of six samples and 120 liters of soil was analyzed, including four samples I analyzed with assistance from Erika Bucior and two samples analyzed independently by Natalie Mueller of Washington University, St. Louis (in table 5.5 the analyst is identified for each sample). Corn (*Zea mays*), both kernels and cupules, the inedible outer structural layer of the cobs, are present in abundance. Other cultigens are common bean (*Phaseolus vulgaris*), squash rind and seeds (*Cuccurbita pepo*), gourd rind (*Lagenaria* sp.),

Table 5.5. Myers Farm Botanical Remains (analyst for each sample listed in parentheses)

Sample	Species	freq	gm wt
Feature 3 west	wood: American beech (*Fagus grandifolia*)	5,110	56.2
48–53 cm	corn (*Zea mays*)—kernels	89	1.4
20 liters	corn—cupules	45	.1
(Rossen)	squash (*Cucurbita pepo*)—seeds	5	—
	squash—rind	4	—
	sunflower (*Helianthus anuus*)	3	—
	gourd (*Lagenaria* sp.)	2	—
	blackberry/raspberry (*Rubus* sp.)	15	—
	sumac (*Rhus* sp.)	11	—
	hickory (*Carya* sp.)	1	—
Feature 3 east	wood (not identified)	—	76.2
48–53 cm	corn (*Zea mays*)—kernels	172	2.0
20 liters	corn—cupules	80	.9
(Mueller)	corn—glumes	18	.1
	sunflower (*Helianthus anuus*)	1	—
	sumac (*Rhus* sp.)	25	—
	chenopod (*Chenopodium* sp.)	7	—
	hickory (*Carya* sp.)	6	.3
	acorn (*Quercus* sp.)	1	.0
	American chestnut (*Castanea dentata*)	1	.0
	nightshade (Solanaceae)	1	—
	fungus	2	.0
Feature 3 west	wood (maple 55%, Am beech 45%)	5,688	922
60–65 cm	corn (*Zea mays*)—kernels	119	2.4
20 liters	corn—cupules	25	1.6
(Bucior)	sunflower (*Helianthus anuus*)	6	—
	bean (*Phaseolus vulgaris*)	2	.0
	sumac (*Rhus* sp.)	13	—
	silnese	3	—

Sample	Species	freq	gm wt
Feature 3 west	wood: maple (Acer sp.)	2,426	46.1
Bottom 78 cm	corn (Zea mays)—kernels	21	.3
20 liters	corn—cupules	3	.0
(Rossen)	bean (Phaseolus vulgaris)	2	.0
	sunflower (Helianthus anuus)	2	—
	gourd (Lagenaria sp.)	1	—
	sumac (Rhus sp.)	8	—
	blackberry/raspberry (Rubus sp.)	6	—
	acorn (Quercus sp.)	1	.0
Feature 3 west	wood (not identified	—	140.1
Bottom 65–81 cm	corn (Zea mays)—kernels	57	.7
20 liters	corn—cupules	18	.1
(Mueller)	squash—rind	6	.0
	squash—seed	2	—
	bean (Phaseolus vulgaris)	2	.0
	sumac (Rhus sp.)	30	—
	copperleaf (Acalypha sp.)	2	—
	chenopod (Chenopodium sp.)	2	—
	grass (Poaceae)	2	—
	mulberry (Morus sp.)	1	—
Feature 13	wood (maple 60%, Am beech 15%, Am elm 10%, unid 15%)	3,818	54.8
20 liters	corn (Zea mays)—kernels	79	1.8
(Rossen / Bucior)	corn—cupules	48	1.2
	bean (Phaseolus vulgaris)	7	.7
	blackberry/raspberry (Rubus sp.)	15	—
	sumac (Rhus sp.)	11	—
	acorn (Quercus sp.)	4	.2
	sunflower (Helianthus anuus)	3	—

and sunflower (*Helianthus anuus*). Like at Levanna, the cultivation and use of tobacco (*Nicotiana* sp., probably *N. rustica*) is indicated by the smoking pipes even though the plant was not directly recovered.

Corn, beans, and squash are the famed "three sisters" of Haudenosaunee lore and diet (Mt. Pleasant 2009). There is strong evidence that they were introduced separately to the northeast, with squash first, followed by corn and last, beans (Hart 2008). The Myers Farm collection shows that the Three Sisters suite of interrelated plants, grown together in mounds and symbiotic in the maintenance of soil chemistry and fertility, was established by the middle of the fifteenth century. The histories and attributes of eight-row "Eastern Eight" corn, squash, gourds, and tobacco were discussed in chapter 4 in connection with the Levanna site materials.

Wild berries present at Myers Farm are blackberry/raspberry (*Rubus* sp.) and mulberry (*Morus* sp.). Sumac berries are best known for their use in a Vitamin C-rich tea and as a high-energy food source and medicine (Gilmore 1931, 47–48; Vogel 1982, 378). The high frequency of sumac seeds further supports the concept of managed and manipulated wild resources.

Acorn (*Quercus* sp.) and American chestnut (*Castanea dentata*) are edible nuts present in minor frequencies, as are the wild plants chenopod (*Chenopodium* sp.), catchfly (*Silene* sp.), nightshade (Solanaceae) and grass (Poaceae). Chenopod has edible greens and starchy seeds and one species (*Chenopodium berlandieri*) was cultivated throughout the Midwest and southeast as part of the "Eastern Agricultural Complex" (B. Smith 2011). The catchfly, nightshade, and grass specimens may be natural intrusions indicative of local flora during the site occupation.

SMOKING PIPES

Fifty-one smoking pipe fragments were recovered, a high density for such a small site. Haudenosaunee pipe smoking is associated with both sacred and secular uses. Smoking connected people with the spirit and supernatural world and was used in aspects of trade, politics, diplomacy, and leisure. One notable use of pipe smoking was in the creation of alliances with both other Native and later with non-Native groups (Rafferty and Mann 2004).

Alison Armour (2016) conducted an analysis of the Myers Farm smoking pipes for an Ithaca College Senior Honors Thesis. She used pipe diagrams to categorize specimens by pipe cross-section (Rutsch 1973, 50). Her analysis documented a variety of bowl types, including trumpet pipes with flared bowls, straight-sided bowls, and basket bowls. More than half are finely decorated, including stamped, incised, stamped and incised, herring-bone, and cordmarking (figure 5.12, table 5.6).

Despite being a plowed site, the spatial distribution of smoking pipes was distinctive. Pipe fragments were concentrated around the large cooking pit and along the structure walls, where materials could easily be lost. Nineteen pipe fragments came from an apparent toss zone just outside the southeast corner of the structure. No effigy pipes were

Figure 5.12. Myers Farm pipe decorations, after Armour 2016. Alison Armour.

Table 5.6. Myers Farm Smoking Pipes (after Armour 2016)

Bowl Type	Percentage
Trumpet with flared rim	52
Straight-edge undecorated	18
Basket-bowl	12
Straight-edged decorated	12
Straight-edged ring bowl	3
Modified trumpet, no flared rim	3

Decoration	Percentage
None	45
Incised	23
Stamped and incised	16
Stamped	12
Herring-bone	2
Cording	2

found like those at Levanna. This supports a secular feasting and alliance interpretation of these materials.

GAME PIECES

One of the most remarkable assemblages from Myers Farm is the game pieces. Our understanding of this collection is due to the ingenuity and analytical creativity of Lydia Bailey, then a Wells College student (Bailey 2015, 2016). As a summer intern, she picked through bags of faunal remains and discovered that what we thought was a small collection of game pieces was large and diverse. These include seventy-five bone game pieces, forty-two bone claw shaped dice, and three ceramic disks.

Some game pieces are deer humerus or femur heads repetitively cut and shaped to consistent forms. Bailey formed a typology of these, including large and small "whole heads" (a complete sphere with carved eye socket-like holes in the side), "half heads" (n=16) which were split and notched, and "head tops" (n=19) which may be fragmented examples of the other types.

Bone claw dice are common (n=42), all very similar in size (ca 15 mm in length). Eighteen dice are marked with a dotted pattern along the bottom edge (figure 5.13), twelve of these have their dots on the left side (using the narrow "claw" end to orient), and six have dots on the right side. Four specimens have a white slip and one a series of short lines (figure 5.13).

Perhaps the most extraordinary specimen is a deer phalange carved into a ring and pin (or ball and cup) game piece (figure 5.13). This piece has a tapered and smoothed neck and a drilled hole. In use, the worked phalange would be a cup and another piece connected to the drilled hole by a string would be swung and caught in the cup (Beauchamp 1901, 316). Also unusual are the three ceramic incised disks, which all have one red and one black side. One has a ray pattern, a second has two parallel incised lines, and the third one side that is half red and half black (figure 5.13).

Specifically interpreting archaeologically recovered game pieces is difficult. The Haudenosaunee have both secular (daily) and sacred dice games. Several Cayuga friends remember playing dice games in their homes as children. The Haudenosaunee peach stone toss game was

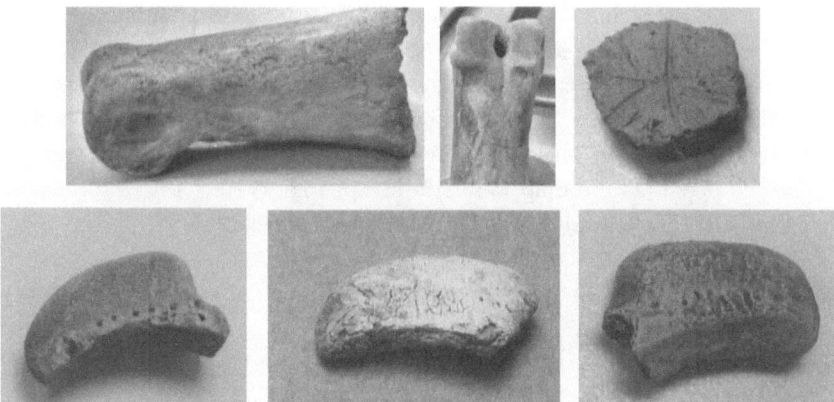

Figure 5.13. Myers Farm game pieces, after Bailey 2016. Lydia Bailey.

played with a set of six pieces, blackened on one side. This game closed major gatherings such as the Green Corn and Harvest Festivals and the New Year's Jubilee (Kimm 1900, 42). The game is played today at the traditional Mohawk community of Kanatsiohareke with a wooden eight-piece set (Porter 2006).

There is a version of the game known as "ghost gamble," which was described by Harry C. Yarrow (1880, 101–3) for the Sioux. This is essentially a game with the dead, played with recently departed relatives. Through the game, the life possessions of the deceased were distributed among relatives, creating a spiritual bond between living and dead and removing redistribution decisions from the living. The pieces used were sets of eight peach stones, some plain, some blackened, and some with crosses. The pieces were tossed with particular combinations winning. Yarrow had a set of game pieces that he described as one hundred years old, or dating to approximately 1780 (Yarrow 1880, 103). My Cayuga friends tell me that a version of ghost gamble is still played, but it is looked down on by the present-day Cayuga as superstitious. None would admit to playing it themselves.

Rebecca Hawkins of the Cherokee differentiates dice from peach pit games and describes their Indian dice game and the Myers Farm specimens:

> The fact that four of them are painted is most telling. Ours are either two tokens painted differently or two not like the others. Usually the other

tokens are just round and are either painted on one side or with different markings on one side. I have seen the two different ones be turtles (most common) and otters (custom-made set). I think there is an odd number, maybe nine. You bang a wooden bowl with the tokens in it on a pillow and then count based on which and how many tokens are turned painted side up. We play it all the time. But with live people. We even have tournaments. (R. Hawkins, personal communication, email 2015)

In most accounts, six to twelve dice are used, some of which are restricted to either men or women. This type of secular dice toss game was widespread in the Americas (Macfarlan and Macfarlan 1958[1958], 105–9). In any case, numerous dice sets were present at Myers Farm and game playing must have been a common site activity. Game playing was a key component of forging and maintaining friendships and peaceful relationships. It may also have been a means to include the spirit ancestors in the proceedings.

DISCUSSION

The fifteenth-century Myers Farm site is unusual in the catalog of Cayuga archaeology. It is very small and undefended, but with an intensive use. The artifacts are as unusual as its size. The amazing variety of ceramic styles include several types not typical of the region. The large cooking pit feature and rectangular structure together represent a cookhouse. The prodigious amount of ground stone indicates food production on a scale far outpacing the site size. The frequency of limestone hoe blades is simply unheard of in the northeast. The high frequency of smoking pipes and bone game pieces further suggests regional gatherings of people.

Faunal and botanical analyses reinforce the idea that the site was a feasting ground, especially the fauna with its unusual emphasis on large mammals. Even the raw materials used to make expedient lithic tools like scrapers are different at Myers Farm. Despite the high artifact densities and the black midden, there is no good evidence that the site was regularly inhabited. At most there might have been a caretaker family living there. Given its hilltop location amid a present-day complex of hay, corn and, soybean fields, and especially the hoe blades, it can also be postulated that Myers Farm was an agricultural station. That is, the feasting ground was located at a centrally located place near a large area of fertile food production.

WHY FEASTING?

Archaeologists and ethnographers have globally documented feasting in many cultural contexts (Dietler and Hayden 2001a). There are two primary ways that feasting has been explained. First, feasting has been viewed as a nearly universal ecological imperative—that is, a strategy to gain social power, produce leaders, and provide a communal social safety net for the less fortunate (the "ecological materialism" view). Second, feasting has been viewed as an activity related to specific political strategies and especially processes of social change. That is, feasting produces leadership and provides stability during the uncertainties of political change or upheaval (the "culture and power" view). In either type of explanation (which are not necessarily mutually exclusive), feasting must be understood within the specific cultural context of its time (Dietler and Hayden 2001b).

Feasting has been documented throughout the prehistoric eastern United States. It is often associated with earthen mound building, especially the platform mounds of the Late Prehistoric Mississippian chiefdoms of the Mississippi Valley and more tribal-level Fort Ancient people living in the central Ohio Valley (Kelly 2001; Knight 2001). In these cases, social status and power were being built through feasting within both more and less formalized political offices and structures of power. Near Levanna and Myers Farm in central New York, the Cayuga occasionally built burial mounds but not platform mounds. It is tempting to speculate on the use of the hilltop location of Myers Farm, with its panoramic views, as a natural substitute for a mound.

What might be the cultural and social purposes of feasting at Myers Farm? It appears that Cayuga populations remained relatively stable from the tenth to fifteenth centuries while neighboring groups like the Onondaga, Seneca, and Mohawk were undergoing substantial population increase. Intensification processes of the period included village growth, growth of longhouse size, fusion of villages, and increased settlement crowding. These neighboring groups experienced a need for greater formalization of power and the need for greater organization of growing settlements, while maintaining the established ideals of communalism and egalitarianism (Birch 2008, 2010; Creese 2011; Kapches 1990, 1994). In contrast, the Cayuga moved more toward occupational specialization of their small villages (Rossen 2015, 185–89). Feasts at Myers Farm may have helped to maintain relations with neighboring tribes who were becoming larger and more powerful, both within and beyond the confederacy. Feasts could have had an important role in reinforcing the power of clan mothers and chiefs for the relatively sparsely populated Cayuga.

CAYUGA SETTLEMENT PATTERNS

It is noteworthy that Myers Farm is located five miles east of Cayuga Lake and is the easternmost of a site cluster (including Levanna and Corey) that I have referred to as the Cayuga Heartland. The Cayuga settlement pattern thus looks more complex than was previously believed. Instead of an open countryside with palisaded two-acre villages, the landscape included those two-acre villages—undefended according to our evidence—and also a variety of smaller sites. These include gorge quarries for procuring Tully Limestone, outlying longhouses (like the Eagle Cottage site excavated in an Aurora village backyard), and of course, feasting ground/agricultural station sites. Is Myers Farm just one of a string of feasting grounds and agricultural stations stretched out along the eastern periphery of the Cayuga heartland? This is unproven but I would consider it possible (figure 4.1). These smaller sites would be much less visible to archaeologists and much more difficult to locate than larger sites. They might also be less likely to garner research attention.

How do the Myers Farm excavations support and reinforce the research and interpretations of Levanna? Although occupied 250 years after the later occupation of Levanna, Myers Farm alerts us to a greater variety of Cayuga site types, far beyond the old stereotype of two-acre palisaded villages (Niemczycki 1984). The site presents a vivid picture of multicultural gatherings, with people smoking tobacco, playing games, and producing and consuming large amounts of food. In general, the Myers Farm artifacts, particularly the ceramics and especially the "transitional" projectile points, provide a smooth sequence from the tenth to the sixteenth centuries. The Levanna ceramics, demonstrating long and gradual style shifts and changes (both increases and decreases) in style popularities, suggest that smooth transitions predated the early Levanna occupation back hundreds of years into Point Peninsula times. As I have previously argued (Rossen 2015), there is no evidence for archaeological correlates of warfare in all these sites. Myers Farm stands out clearly as a small, undefended place where people traveled in peace to eat, play, smoke, and mingle.

6

CONCLUSIONS

Chasing the Ghosts of the
Old-Time New York Archaeologists

When I began test excavations at the Levanna site at the urging of Betty Pangburn, I barely knew the outline of the multidimensional story of the site and its early investigators. In time I would become immersed and obsessed with the people and their complex motives and emotions. I was literally chasing the ghosts of the old-time New York archaeologists. From the mid-1920s through the late 1940s, Levanna was a major center of archaeological research, public display, cultural revitalization efforts, entrepreneurship, and professional dispute and intrigue.

The characters are larger than life: Arthur C. Parker, the powerful father figure and mentor, the museum director holding the purse strings in an age of apprentice training, the first major Native American (Seneca) figure in archaeology, a burial excavator who incited the wrath of his own people as early as 1903, the future president of the fledgling Society for American Archaeology! Parker depended on a network of interested amateurs to alert him to the discovery of major sites, and E. H. Gohl, a landscape artist, performed that role in central New York.

Then there are Parker's two apprentices, Harrison C. Follett and William A. Ritchie, bitter rivals forced together at the 1927 Levanna excavations. One (Ritchie) from a well-to-do background and socially polished, and the other (Follett) from the hardscrabble working class, a telephone company employee. One (Ritchie) an erudite writer, with a natural talent for analyzing and organizing artifacts, the other (Follett) a dedicated field man with a tough outdoors demeanor. When the ongoing Great Depression forced Parker to retain only one, the rejected Follett tenaciously became an entrepreneur, opening the Levanna Museum to finance himself and his excavations. Parker and Ritchie turned away from Levanna (or according to Follett, he kicked Ritchie off the site), refusing to recognize its scientific importance. They were angered by the commercialism, yet they were never personally forced to raise funds for research. The accusations, countercharges, affidavits, and investigations that followed have all been discussed. Innocent, well-meaning, and respected academics like Carter Woods and President Kerr MacMillan of nearby Wells College could not avoid becoming entangled in the maelstrom.

As the years passed, Follett's site became famous all the way to Hollywood. The animal effigies captured the imagination of thousands. The bear! The thunderbird! The salamander! Betty Pangburn described them to me as magical. Alas, Ritchie and James B. Griffin called them out as fakes in 1936. The evidence is indeed strong that the effigies were falsified, as were similar ones at Spanish Hill in Waverly, New York, and other sites in Pennsylvania. Local people from commoners to professors, a prominent lawyer, and a college president remained true believers. Yet we cannot convict Follett of more than surrounding himself with con men. There is no smoking gun to connect Follett to the forgeries. Yet shouldn't a dedicated field archaeologist like him be able to recognize the con? Did he hold suspicions but couldn't stop as the quarters rolled in every summer?

Parker and Ritchie blocked all Follett's attempts at publication of the Levanna materials. Follett pushed on in the face of almost universal professional ridicule. Simultaneously, Follett spoke to every club and organization in the region and carried his crusade to the people. His museum attracted an interesting and strange assortment of celebrities, oddly enough including white actors who played cowboys (Douglas Fairbanks Sr. and Mary Pickford) and Indians in the movies and a bogus barnstorming Indian chief.

Then in another strange turn, the local Cayuga and Onondaga used Levanna as a forum for an early cultural revitalization movement. This

CONCLUSIONS

Figure 6.1. Cayugas, Onondagas, and Senecas performing smoke dance at Levanna, August 20, 1936. Homer St. Clair Archive.

came at a low moment of Native American history in New York, a time referred to by Haudenosaunee Confederacy historian Rick Hill as the Dark Age. The functioning Confederacy was operating in secret, and the Haudenosaunee were looking to Plains Indians for ideas on dress. Yet the photos of the Haudenosaunee Smoke Dance performed in 1932 are unmistakable, identical to those that the revitalized Haudenosaunee perform today on the powwow and festival circuit every summer and fall (figure 6.1). Gas rationing that began as the United States entered World War II ended the museum endeavor, though there is some evidence that Follett continued his work sporadically on a small scale at Levanna until 1947.

For all their confidence, institutional support, leadership of the profession, and publication outlets, Parker and Ritchie saddled us with an untenable historical model. Levanna and other sites represented the 3rd Period Algonkian. That is, Levanna, Owasco, and other major sites of central New York were not the matriarchal Haudenosaunee (the confederacy originally including the Seneca, Cayuga, Onondaga, Oneida, and Mohawk) at all, but culturally were affiliated with the Native peoples of New England, Canada, and the Great Lakes who spoke a different language and were patrilineal and patrilocal. Parker and Ritchie promoted the idea that the Haudenosaunee had recently migrated into the region, displacing these Algonkian peoples. How strange that a prominent Seneca archaeologist would promote a historical model that disconnected his own people from their past! Indeed the in-migration versus in situ or in place local development debate continued. Richard "Scotty" MacNeish, who would go on to be a globetrotting archaeologist of great fame in places like Mexico, Peru, Honduras, and China, effectively nixed the in-migration idea with his 1952 ceramic typology. Yet periodically the in-migration idea rises from the ashes, most notably in the 1990s writings of Dean Snow (1995, 1996).

Follett's imagery of Native Americans was dark, lurid, and disturbing. He saw a brutal, violent Native existence of deprivation, disease, fear, and desperation, which led to the superstitious spectacle of effigies. His reconstructions showed a life of crude technology and discomfort. The people of Levanna lived behind their palisade walls, facing death at any moment they ventured out. The subtext of his museum was to show how good the museum visitor life was by comparison. This may have been a resonant theme during the darkest days of the Great Depression, when people lived lives of well . . . deprivation, fear, and desperation.

Staring at his photographs and reading his letters and manuscripts, I have tried to imagine the life of rejection, heartbreak, and determination that Harrison C. Follett experienced. He lived long enough to see William A. Ritchie ascend to the position of New York State Archaeologist in 1949, but not long enough to see the publication of Ritchie's *Archaeology of New York State* (1965), long considered the Bible for archaeology of the region. Ritchie would outlive Follett by forty-one years and publish some 150 articles, monographs, and books. Facing a publication blockade, Follett would be able to publish almost nothing. His long, rambling, handwritten manuscripts sit archived.

What would Follett think of the new excavations at Levanna? What would he say about this book? Would he take some comfort from his rehabilitation as a folk hero of the avocational archaeologists of New York (DeOrio 1999)? At least we must respect the gritty determination of a reviled archaeologist who loved his work enough to continue on a shoestring against tremendous odds during the worst economic crisis of American history.

Follett's Levanna displayed both the brightest and most difficult sides of archaeology. It is a filter through which we see some of the great issues facing contemporary archaeology. These include (1) the commercialization of archaeology, (2) the integrity of field archaeologists, and (3) the power of major institutions to control research and paradigms (that is, to define knowledge and "truth") versus marginalized and second-rank institutions and scholars. Furthermore, Levanna highlighted (4) public archaeology and the difficulties and ramifications of representation to the public, and (5) Native American revitalization and the role of archaeology in this process. All these issues remain today. Archaeologists have begun to address some of them through Indigenous Archaeology (see chapter 3), but issues of collaboration, revitalization, and representation remain convoluted and complex.

The Levanna site lay dormant until 2007, when I tested excavated there, fully believing that, as reported, it had been destroyed. Other sites in the region have succumbed to that fate. The contemporary site of Lakeside, or Owasco, in Auburn, New York on Owasco Lake is probably one of them. The massive earth-moving and rechanneling of a river bed in Emerson Park probably destroyed the site or buried it under many meters of fill. I know because I spent serious field time looking for it.

Somehow, like archaeology itself, Levanna endured. Despite the effigies and the distorted public portrayal, it is a real site, spectacularly unusual because two farmers (Fred Sherman and then Homer St. Clair) refused to plow and plant there. I consider the survival and intactness of Levanna to be nothing less than a miracle. It hid in plain sight, rusty historical plaque and all, waiting for another round in another era of archaeology.

What did the new excavations from 2007 to 2009 tell us? Evidence is good for two relatively brief occupations, the first in the late tenth century and the second at the cusp of the twelfth and thirteenth centuries. The people of Levanna practiced a mixed subsistence economy of farming, fishing, hunting, snaring, trapping, wild plant system management, and wild plant collecting. They were not hunter-gatherers as Follett believed. Despite its two brief occupations, ceramic analysis shows the development, peak, and decline in use of decorative styles. During its occupations, a variety of ceramic styles were made and used. Some reflected the old ways, while others represented the dynamic present and the coming styles of the future. Richard S. MacNeish remains the hero of Native ceramics analysis in New York. His

1952 typology is still serviceable, although we continue to push the temporal limits of individual styles and the stylistic boundaries of his individual types (see Adams and Adams 1991 for the philosophy of this sort of "practical reality" approach to artifact typologies). MacNeish gave us the foothold for the in situ development of the Haudenosaunee that is now accepted by a wide majority of archaeologists. MacNeish thus gave Haudenosaunee history back to the Haudenosaunee, and the Levanna research supports that idea. Unlike what is stated on the rusty historical plaque, Levanna was Haudenosaunee, and we may more specifically label it as "Early Cayuga." It is not "Algonkian." It is no longer "Owasco," the term given by Parker and Ritchie based on the Lakeside site on Owasco Lake as a generic marker for the time period (Ritchie, Lenig, Miller 1953). Levanna reconnects the Cayuga with its history in stark contrast to the way archaeologists have often disconnected it overtly (Algonkian) or covertly (Owasco).

Special studies were one of the great contributions of the scientific revolution and "New" or "Processual Archaeology" of the 1970s (Clarke 1973; Malone and Stoddart 1998). In this case, the detailed analysis of ceramic paste, fauna, and botanical remains (based on systematic water flotation) added surprising information about subsistence. Levanna corroborates the sixteenth-century Cayuga site of Corey Village in disputing the "deer hunter" stereotype of the Cayuga. From the tenth to the sixteenth centuries, the Cayuga clearly relied on fish and small fauna such as squirrels, and deer was an occasional and welcomed supplemental treat.

All indications are that the Levanna people lived in peace (twice) in a village without palisades or defensive positioning. I previously discussed this as a long-term trend in the Cayuga heartland east of Cayuga Lake from the tenth to the sixteenth centuries (Rossen 2015, 177–81). The sixteenth-century Corey Village, a triangular-shaped site set high above two gorges, had a double earthen embankment and ditch, but only along the steep western cliff. The level eastern side remained open and undefended. As suggested by the Cayuga and Onondaga clan mothers, I concluded that the embankment was protection for children living at the site from the cliff.

Investigations at the fourteenth-century Myers Farm site brought several surprises. The small size, intensive occupation, and specialized

CONCLUSIONS   165

nature of the site were all unexpected. The excavations and analyses all pointed to site use as a small feasting ground and agricultural station (not a habitation site), including evidence of large-scale food production, game playing, pipe-smoking, and substantial visitation from outsiders. Despite being located on a hilltop, there is no evidence of palisades or defense. It seems more likely that the hill represented a raised exalted place in the manner that earthen mounds did to the south and west. There is in short no evidence of the endemic warfare that has so often been used to describe the Cayuga. For example, William N. Fenton wrote, "The roots of Iroquois warfare extend deep into their culture. The persistent theme of requickening the living in the name of the dead flows through these roots as the sap of society and nourishes a concern for ongoing generations" (Fenton 1998, 259–60). In contrast, it is now evident that the major heartland area of Cayuga territory managed to live in peace for centuries. Levanna appears to push a peaceful scenario back to the twelfth and tenth centuries.

Is this peaceful landscape evidence of an early Haudenosaunee Confederacy, as oral histories state? This case was made earlier (Rossen 2015). For Levanna, the amazing and striking face and animal effigy smoking pipes must be considered. Pipe smoking at Levanna appears to have been both a secular and sacred practice. If the face pipes are indeed medicine society pipes, and if medicine societies existed then as now to promote peaceful intertribal relations and were indeed part of the Peacemaker's program for the Great Peace, then Levanna is an early Confederacy village. This conclusion will be controversial among archaeologists who have long struggled with the age of the Haudenosaunee Confederacy, and who have been unable to reconcile their archaeological and historic evidence with oral traditions.

I remember my early presentation of Levanna and the early Confederacy thesis at an annual meeting of the Iroquois Studies Conference in Cornwall, Ontario (Rossen 2010b). Following a rough and tumble question and answer session, I sat alone, stunned, nibbling lunch at the convention venue. Rick Hill, the Confederacy historian, sat down with me. After a period of silence, he told me that, yes, he had been told by his grandparents that the Confederacy began sometime in the 900s. Rick Hill believes that the formation of the Confederacy, similar to the journey of the Peacemaker, Hiawatha, and Jigonsaseh across the land, was a long process. He spoke of an "original wampum string" of villages along the journey route. These were villages that first accepted the message of the Peacemaker and formed the core of the developing Confederacy. He thought that Levanna could have been one of the original "wampum string of villages" along the path.

This anecdote encompasses so much that it is almost overwhelming to contemplate, as I have over the years since Rick Hill sat down with me that day. Archaeologists and anthropologists have been very hesitant to accept oral history as historical fact (Henige 2009). In addition, archaeologists are conservative by nature. Yet there is multisite evidence for a peaceful landscape, the early gradual development of longhouse architecture, matrilocality, and corn-based agriculture. The dominance of small fauna likewise suggests the importance of women in food production beyond agriculture, and the gender balance so prominent in Haudenosaunee society (Venables 2010). The Peacemaker did not expect tribes who had been at terrifying war with each for centuries to instantly live in peace within the Confederacy. We know that new institutions providing cross-cutting social ties were put in place, possibly including revitalization of and adjustments to the preexisting clan system and medicine societies (Porter 2008).

FINAL THOUGHTS

Levanna has given so many stories. There is the window into the personalities, conflicts, grit, and determination of archaeologists working in the 1920s and 1930s. The letters and manuscripts were written with vivid grace, passion, and fury from all perspectives. Archaeologists fought to maintain the integrity of the discipline, bring the past to the public, include Native people, and be heard while controlling the message. Levanna certainly opened a new episode in the amazing life of Arthur C. Parker that is not discussed in his biographies (Colwell-Chantapough 2009; Porter 2001). The early professional life and struggles of William A. Ritchie come to life. We usually know him as the accomplished and self-assured author and state archaeologist. Harrison C. Follett comes out of the shadows as a figure important enough to push the archaeological establishment to spend enormous time and energy to discredit him.

CONCLUSIONS

The 2007–2009 reexcavations were closely associated with the nearby Cayuga-SHARE Farm. A group of citizens and academics including myself had purchased the Union Springs farm in 2001 and after operating it as an educational center, transferred it to the Cayuga Nation in 2005 with substantial help from the Haudenosaunee Confederacy (Hansen and Rossen 2007; Rossen 2008). The Cayuga thus reestablished a foothold in their ancestral homeland shortly after the long-running Cayuga Indian Land Claim (1980–2005) was dismissed from court on appeal. Many of us knew that the courts could never ultimately help the Cayuga people, and that their return would have to be accomplished in a community, grassroots manner. The Cayuga-SHARE Farm was a symbol of the Cayuga return, a place where the Three Sisters (corn-beans-squash) could be planted and where important meetings of Confederacy committees could be held. It truly became Indian country when informal lacrosse games were held during the Cayuga Nation Picnics.

In regard to the archaeological research, the Cayuga-SHARE Farm and its proximity to the investigated sites provided a constant backdrop, as the stories in this volume suggest, allowing constant communication to occur as research progressed. Several days of service learning at the farm was one component of all the archaeological field schools. Students planted crops and maintained the gardens and grounds. Field school crews were integral in preparing the farm for the annual Cayuga Nation Picnic that occurred there each summer after 2005. Native and non-Native visitors to the site and participants in the excavations were able to work at the farm and sometimes reside there. The farm was a place where dialogue on issues was often conducted, and where the relationships of archaeology to sovereignty and cultural revitalization were discussed. College classes were taught and meetings of Haudenosaunee organizations were held there on a range of issues. This led to corollary projects such as the GPR study of the Onondaga cemetery behind their longhouse, which pinpointed unmarked burials to prevent accidental future disturbance of the ancestors. The Cayuga-SHARE Farm continues to this day to be an important symbolic and practical center for the Cayuga people, who are returning to their homeland after two centuries but largely remain displaced. It is also an important place to visit for non-Native people to reconnect with nature and find some measure of healing the troubled past and racist present of the region.

The Cayuga have much business to conduct, and among them are environmental protection and cultural resource management. The high profile and media saturated Cayuga Land Claim trials had muddied local history when an "expert" for New York State testified that the Cayuga homeland was really in Canada. The thirty-year absence of professional archaeology in the heartland east of Cayuga Lake even left locals wondering. The archaeological excavations at Corey Village (2003–2005), Levanna (2007–2009), and Myers Farm (2011–2014) helped to reestablish the Cayuga history of the heartland. In reestablishing the cultural significance of the area, we came to confront established paradigms and stereotypes. Archaeologists had established ideas of incessant warfare, a nation of deer hunters and warriors, a landscape of scattered palisaded two-acre villages, and a brief Confederacy, established either just before European contact or after, or even well after Europeans arrived. I believe there is now evidence to reconsider these stereotypes. I also think that Levanna brings a case to pay more careful attention to oral traditions and to incorporate them into our testable research designs.

Levanna is a testament to the power of ordinary people. The site exists because hardscrabble farmers thought it was not right to plow and plant there. The same family that hosted and received Parker and Follett welcomed me back to conduct fieldwork nearly seventy years later. When Homer St. Clair, the bridge between the Follett days and mine, passed on in 2012, and Betty Pangburn, who badgered me to test excavate the site, followed in 2013, I was shaken. Ada Jacques, the Onondaga potter who re-created traditional designs and replicated the Myers Farm pot, left us in 2016. Chief Irving Powless Jr., who urged me to share the Levanna face pipes with the world, passed in 2017. It troubles me that these great friends, key facilitators, and inspirations are gone without having seen the published results.

Finally, what is the role of archaeology in the present-day struggles and triumphs of Native people like the Cayuga and Onondaga? We reexamine the specters of the past in hopes of finding the truer stories and guiding our actions and interpretations in the future. In this case, the specters were multidimensional, the people and their relationships with each other and the environment in the tenth, twelfth, and fifteenth centuries, as well the activities, agendas, and struggles of the early twentieth-century investigators. This research should end any specula-

CONCLUSIONS

tion or "expert testimony" that central New York was not the Cayuga homeland. Indigenous archaeology emphasizes a questioning of what constitutes knowledge and how we achieve understanding. If we can reconcile Native wisdom with Western science, perhaps through that synergy we can find a greater path to knowledge. I hope the new stories help us achieve some measure of greater understanding of the past or better communication between Native and non-Native people. Foremost, it is hoped that the research helps the Cayuga people reconnect with their past and walk steadily into the future.

REFERENCES

Adams, David W. 1995. *Education for Extinction: American Indians and the Boarding School Experience, 1875–1928.* Lawrence: University Press of Kansas.

Adams, William Y., and Ernest W. Adams. 1991. *Archaeological Typology and Practical Reality: A Dialectical Approach to Artifact Classification and Sorting.* Cambridge: University of Cambridge Press.

Akwesasne Notes. 2005. *Basic Call to Consciousness.* Summeaown, TN: Book Publishing Co.

Amick, Daniel S. 2014. "Reflections on the Origins of Recycling: A Paleolithic Perspective." *Lithic Technology* 39, no. 1:64–69.

Anderson, Thomas J. 2013. "The Net Weight Site: A 1,000-year-old Native American Occupation in Schoharie County, New York." Paper presented at annual meeting, New York State Archaeological Association, Watertown, NY, April.

Anonymous. 1916. "Double Auto Show for Selden Cars." *New York Times.* Feb. 23.

Anonymous 1926. "Edward H. Gohl, Artist and Archaeologist, Succumbs." *Auburn Citizen.* Tuesday, May 11.

Anonymous. 1939. "Cayuga Indians May Buy Site Near Levanna for their Tribal Territory." *Auburn Citizen*, Auburn, NY. August 17.

Anonymous. 1949. "D. Sands Titus Called by Death." *Syracuse Post-Standard.* Syracuse, NY. August 20.

Anonymous. 1954a. "In Memory of Harrison C. Follett." *The Archaeological Society of Central New York Bulletin* 9(6). June.

Anonymous 1954b. "Harrison Colvin Follett's Death." *The Bulletin, New York Stat Archaeological Association*. No. 2, 1–2. December.

Anonymous. 1984. "Traditional Teachings." Cornwall, ON: North American Travelling College.

Anonymous. 1986. "Theft from the Dead." In *Art from Ganondagan, the Village of Peace*. Waterford, NY: State Office of Parks, Recreation, and Historic Preservation, Bureau of Historic Sites.

Anonymous. 2016. Adelaide "Ada" Jacques. Obituary. *Syracuse Post-Standard*. Syracuse, NY. June 16-17.

Anyon, Roger, T. J. Ferguson, Loretta Jackson, Lillie Lane, and Philip Vicenti. 1997. "Native American Oral Tradition and Archaeology: Issues of structure, Relevance, and Respect." In *Native Americans and Archaeologists: Stepping Stones to Common Ground*, edited by Nina Swidler, Kurt E. Dongoske, Roger Anyon, and Alan S. Downer, 77–87. Walnut Creek, CA: Altamira Press.

Armour, Alison. 2016. "Cayuga Smoking Pipes and Peaceful Relations: A Fifteenth Century Case Study from the Myers Farm Site." Senior Honors Thesis, Anthropology Department. Ithaca, NY: Ithaca College.

Asch, David L. 1994. "Aboriginal Specialty-Plant Cultivation in Eastern North America: Illinois Prehistory and a Post-Contact Perspective." In *Agricultural Origins and Development in the Midcontinent*, edited by William Green, 25–86. Report 19, Office of the State Archaeologist. Iowa City: University of Iowa.

Asch, David L., and Nancy B. Asch. 1985. "Prehistoric Plant Cultivation in West-Central Illinois." In *Prehistoric Food Production in North America*, edited by Richard I. Ford, 149–203. Anthropological Papers no. 75. Ann Arbor: Museum of Anthropology, University of Michigan.

Atalay, Sonia. 2012. *Community-based Archaeology: Research with, by, and for Indigenous and Local Communities*. Berkeley: University of California Press.

Bailey, Lydia. 2015. "Myers Farm Site Game Piece Typology." Ms. in possession of the author.

———. 2016. "Game Pieces at Myers Farm: A Fifteenth Century Cayuga Site." Student Internship Poster presentation, Wells College, Aurora, NY. September 21.

Barnes, Joseph W. 1981. *Rochester and the Automobile Industry*. Rochester History 43(2 & 3):1–39. July.

Bartram, William. 1955[1791]. *Travels through North and South Carolina, Georgia, East and West Florida*. Reprinted. Mineola, NY: Dover Books.

Baugher, Sherene, and Sara Clark. 1998. *An Archaeological Investigation of the Indian Fort Road Site, Trumansburg, New York*. Ithaca, NY: Cornell University.

Beauchamp, William M. 1898. *Earthenware of the New York Aborigines*. Bulletin of the New York State Museum, Vol. 5, no. 22. Albany: University of the State of New York.

———. 1901. *Wampum and Shell Artifacts Used by the New York Indians*. Bulletin of the New York State Museum, no. 41, Vol. 8. Albany: University of the State of New York.

Beisaw, April M. 2014. "Levanna Faunal Assessment." Ms. In author's possession.

———. 2015. "Faunal Remains." In *Corey Village and the Cayuga World: Implications from Archaeology and Beyond*. Syracuse: Syracuse University Press.

———. 2016. "Notes on Levanna Faunal Analysis." Ms. in author's possession. Benedict, Salli M. Kawennotakie. 2004. "Made in Akwesasne." In *A Passion for the Past: Papers in Honour of James F. Pendergast*, edited by J. V. Wright and J. Pilon, 435–54. Gatineau, Quebec: Canadian Museum of Civilization.

Benedict, Salli M. Kawennotakie. 2004. "Made in Akwesasne." In *A Passion for the Past: Papers in Honour of James F. Pendergast*, edited by J. V. Wright and J. Pilon, 435–54. Gatineau, Quebec: Canadian Museum of Civilization.

Berkhofer, Robert F. 1979. *The White Man's Indian: Images of the American Indian from Columbus to the Present*. New York: Vintage Books.

Binford, Lewis R. 1977. *For Theory Building in Archaeology: Essays on Faunal Remains, Aquatic Resources, Spatial Analysis, and Systemic Modeling*. New York: Academic Press.

———. 1978. *Nunamiut Ethnoarchaeology*. New York: Academic Press.

———. 1980. "Willow Smoke and Dogs' Tails: Hunter-Gatherer Settlement Systems and Archaeological Site Formation." *American Antiquity* 44(3):4–20.

———. 1983. "People in Their Lifespace." In *In Pursuit of the Past: Decoding the Archaeological Record*, by L. R. Binford, 129–143. New York: Thames and Hudson.

Birch, Jennifer. 2008. "Rethinking the Archaeological Application of Iroquoian Kinship." *Canadian Journal of Archaeology* 32(2):194–213.

———. 2010. "Coalescence and Conflict in Iroquoian Ontario." *Archaeological Review from Cambridge* 25(1):29–48.

Birch, Jennifer, and Ronald F. Williamson. 2013. *The Mantle Site: An Archaeological History of an Ancestral Wendat Community*. London: Altamira Press.

Bird, S. Elizabeth. 1996. *Dressing in Feathers: The Constitution of the Indian in American Popular Culture*. Boulder, CO: Westview.

Boggs Jr., Sam. 2006. *Principles of Sedimentology and Stratigraphy*. Englewood Cliffs, NJ: Prentice Hall.

Bonaparte, Darren. 2006. *Creation and Confederation: The Living History of the Iroquois*. Ahkwesahsne, Mohawk Territory: Wampum Chronicles.

Borofsky, Robert. 2005. *Yanomami: The Fierce Controversy and What We Can Learn from It*. Berkeley: University of California Press.

Bradbury, John F. 2005. "Tie Hackers, Tie Rafting, and the Railroad Crosstie Industry at Arlington and Jerome." *Old Settlers Gazette* 4–13. Fort Leonard Wood, MO.

Bruchac, Margaret M., Siobhan M. Hart, and H. Martin Wobst. 2010. *Indigenous Archaeologies: A Reader on Decolonization*. Walnut Creek, CA: Left Coast Press.

Campbell, Jon. 2015. "Old Name Officially Returns to Nation's Highest Peak." U.S. Board of Geographic Names. Washington, DC: U.S. Geological Survey.

Canfield, William Walker (Cornplanter). 1904. *The Legends of the Iroquois, Told by "the Cornplanter."* New York: A. Wessels Co.

Carlson, Douglas M., Robert A. Daniels, and Jeremy J. Wright. 2016. *Atlas of Inland Fishes of New York*. New York State Museum Record no. 7. Albany: New York State Education Dept.

Chernela, Janet, Fernando Coronil, Ray Hames, Jane H. Hill, Trudy Turner, and Joe Watkins. 2002. *Papers of the American Anthropological Association El Dorado Task Force*. Washington, DC: American Anthropological Association.

Clarke, David. 1973. "Archaeology: The Loss of Innocence." *Antiquity* 47:6–18.

Cobb, Charles R. 2010. *From Quarry to Cornfield: The Political Economy of Mississippian Hoe Blade Production*. Tuscaloosa: University of Alabama Press.

Colwell-Chanthaphonh, Chip. 2009. *Inheriting the Past: The Making of Arthur C. Parker and Indigenous Archaeology*. Tucson: University of Arizona Press.

Colwell-Chanthaphonh, Chip, and T. J. Ferguson. 2008. *Collaboration in Archaeological Practice: Engaging Descendant Communities*. New York: Altamira Press.

Cook, Frederick. 2000[1887]. *Journals of the Military Expedition of Major General John Sullivan against the Six Nations of Indians in 1779 with Records of Centennial Celebrations*. Bowie, MD: Heritage Books.

Crawford, Gary W., and David G. Smith. 1996. "Migration in Prehistory: Princess Point and the Northern Iroquoian Case." *American Antiquity* 61(4):782–90.

Creese, John L. 2011. "Deyughnyonkwarakda—At the Wood's Edge: The Development of the Iroquoian Village in Southern Ontario, A.D. 900–1500." PhD dissertation, Department of Anthropology, University of Toronto.

Cruz, M. Dores. 2011. "Pots Are Pots, Not People: Material Culture and Ethnic Identity in the Banda Area (Ghana), Nineteenth and Twentieth Centuries." *Azania: Archaeological Research in Africa* 46(3):336–57.

Cusick, David. 2004[1825]. *Sketches of Ancient History of the Six Nations*. Bristol, PA: Evolution.

David, Nicholas, and Carol Kramer. 2001. *Ethnoarchaeology in Action*. Cambridge: Cambridge University Press.

DeBoer, Warren. 1990. "Interaction, Imitation, and Communication as Expressed in Style: The Ucayali Experience." In *The Uses of Style in Archaeology*, edited by M. Conkey and C. Hastorf, 82–104. Cambridge: Cambridge University Press.

Deloria, Philip J. 1998. *Playing Indian*. New Haven, CT: Yale University Press.

DeOrio, Robert N. 1999. "Harrison Calvin Follett: In Recognition of His Contribution to Cayuga Archaeology." Ms. in author's possession.

Dieckmann, Jane Marsh. 1995. *Wells College: A History*. Aurora, NY: Wells College Press.

Dietler, Michael and Brian Hayden. 2001a. *Feasts: Archaeological and Ethnographic Perspectives on Food, Politics, and Power*. Washington: Smithsonian Institution Press.

———. 2001b. "Digesting the Feast—Good to Eat, Good to Drink, Good to Think." In *Feasts: Archaeological and Ethnographic Perspectives on Food, Politics, and Power*, edited by Michael Dietler and Brian Hayden, 1–22. Washington: Smithsonian Institution Press.

Dobson, G. B. 2015. "Wyoming Tails and Trails." Wyomingtalesandtrails.com. Accessed 6/25/2015.

Dowie, Mark. 2017. *The Haida Gwaii Lesson: A Strategic Playbook for Indigenous Sovereignty*. Oakland: Inkshares.

Drooker, Penelope B. 2004. "Pipes, Leadership, and Interregional Interaction in Protohistoric Midwestern and Northeastern North America." In *Smoking and Culture: The Archaeology of Tobacco Pipes in Eastern North America*, edited by Sean Rafferty and Rob Mann, 73–123. Knoxville: University of Tennessee Press.

Echo-Hawk, Roger. 1997. "Forging a New Ancient History for Native America." In *Native Americans and Archaeologists: Stepping Stones to Common Ground*, edited by Nina Swidler, Kurt E. Dongoske, Roger Anyon, and Alan S. Downer, 88–102. Walnut Creek, CA: Altamira Press.

———. 2009. "An Unspeakable Past." Roger-Echo-Hawk.com.

Facing Hawai'i's Future: Essential Information about GMOs. 2012. Koloa, HI: Hawai'i SEED.

Fenton, William P. 1998. *The Great Law and the Longhouse: A Political History of the Iroquois Confederacy*. Norman: Univ. of Oklahoma Press.

Ferguson, T. J., Joe Watkins, and Gordon L. Pullar. 1997. "Native Americans and Archaeologists: Commentary and Personal Perspectives." In *Native Americans and Archaeologists: Stepping Stones to Common Ground*, edited by Nina Swidler, Kurt E. Dongoske, Roger Anyon, and Alan S. Downer, 237–52. Walnut Creek, CA: Altamira.

Finnegan, Timothy. 2004. "Art." In *The Greenwood Encyclopedia of American Regional Cultures: The Mid-Atlantic Region*, edited by Robert P. Marzec. Westport, CT: Greenwood.

Fisher, John W. 1995. "Bone Surface Modifications in Zooarchaeology." *Journal of Archaeological Method and Theory* 2(1): 7–68.

Flenniken, J. Jeffrey. 1985. "Stone Tool Reduction Techniques as Cultural Markers." In *Stone Tool Analysis: Essays in Honor of Don E. Crabtree*, edited by Mark G. Plew, James C. Woods, and Max G. Pasevic, 91–131. Albuquerque: University of New Mexico Press.

Flenniken, J. Jeffrey and Anan W. Raymond. 1986. "Morphological Projectile Point Typology: Replication Experimentation and Technological Analysis." *American Antiquity* 51(3): 603–614.

Flink, James J. 1990. *The Automobile Age*. Cambridge, Ma: MIT Press.

Follett, Harrison C. 1952. "Field Notes," handwritten version. Rochester Museum and Science Center Archives.

———. 1952. "Field Notes," typed version. Rochester Museum and Science Center Archives.

———. 1957. "The Algonkian Site of Levanna, N.Y. on Cayuga Lake. *Yesteryears*, Supplement no. 1.

———. n.d.a. "Early Levanna Notes." Handwritten manuscript. Rochester Museum and Science Center Archives.

———. n.d.b. "The Algonquin Indian Village Site near Levanna New York: Excavating Since 1932, 1932–1942," vol. 1. Unpublished typed manuscript. Homer St. Clair Archive.

———. n.d.c. Foreword by the Author. Handwritten and partially typed manuscript, Homer St. Clair Archive.

Fontana, Bernard L., William J. Robinson, Charles W. Cormack, and Ernest E. Leavitt Jr. 1962. *Papago Indian Pottery*. American Ethnological Society Monographs; no. 37. Seattle: University of Washington Press.

Ford, James A. 1954. Spaulding's Review of Ford. *American Anthropologist* 56, no. 1: 109–14.

Ford, James A., and Julian H. Steward. 1954. "On the Concept of Types." *American Anthropologist* 56(1): 42–57.

Franklin, Benjamin. 1938[1736]. "A Treaty of Friendship, Held with the Chiefs of the Six Nations at Philadelphia in September and October, 1736." In *Indian Treaties Printed by Benjamin Franklin, 1736–1762*, edited by Carl Van Doran and Julian P. Boyd. Philadelphia: Historical Society of Pennsylvania.

Freestone, Ian. 1995. "Ceramic Petrography." *American Journal of Archaeology* 99:111–15.

Funk, Robert. 1977. "An Archaeologist for All Seasons: A Biographical Sketch of William A. Ritchie." In *Current Perspectives in Northeastern Archaeology*, edited by Robert E. Funk and Charles F. Hayes, xiii–xxv. Rochester: New York State Archaeological Association.

Gazin-Schwartz, Amy, and Cornelius Holtorf. 1999. *Archaeology and Folklore*. London: Routledge.

George-Kanentiio, Doug. 2000. *Iroquois Culture and Commentary*. Santa Fe, NM: Clear Light Publishers.

Gibson, John Arthur, Hanni Woodbury, Reginald Henry, Harry Webster, and Alexander Goldenweiser. 1993. *Concerning the League: The Iroquois League Tradition as Dictated by John Arthur Gibson*. Algonquian and Iroquoian Linguistics Series, Vol. 9. Winnipeg: University of Manitoba.

Gilmore, Melvin R. 1931. *Uses of Plants by the Indians of the Missouri River*. Lincoln: University of Nebraska Press.

Gohl, Edward H. 1914. "The Effects of Wild Westing." *Quarterly Journal of the Society of American Indians* 2:226–9. Washington, DC: Society of American Indians.

Gonyea, Ray. 1986. "Introduction." In *Onondaga: Portrait of a Native People*, by Fred R. Wolcott and Dennis Connors. Syracuse, NY: Syracuse University Press.

Greenleaf, William. 1961. *Monopoly on Wheels, Henry Ford and the Selden Automobile Patent*. Detroit, MI: Wayne State University Press.

Grenander, M. E. n.d. "Biographical Sketch." In *Finding Aid for the Papers of Vincent J. Schaefer*, M.E. Albany, NY: Grenander Department of Special Collections and Archives, University at Albany Libraries.

Griffin, James B. 1943. *The Fort Ancient Aspect: Its Cultural and Chronological Position in Mississippi Valley Archaeology*. Ann Arbor: University of Michigan Press.

———. 1945. "Review: The Pre-Iroquoian Occupations of New York State, by William A. Ritchie." *American Antiquity* 10(4):401–7.

———. 1953. *Archaeology of Eastern United States*. Chicago: University of Chicago Press.

Griffin, James B., and Volney B. Jones. 1976. "Carl Eugen Guthe, 1893–1974." *American Antiquity* 41(2):168–77.

Grifone, Francis V. 1957. Preface. In "The Algonkian Site of Levanna, N.Y. on Cayuga Lake." *Yesteryears*, Supplement no. 1.

Haberman, Thomas W. 1984. "Evidence for Aboriginal Tobaccos in Eastern North America." *American Antiquity* 49(2):269–87.

Hammerstedt, Scott W., and Erin R. Hughes. 2015. "Mill Creek Chert Hoes and Prairie Soils: Implications for Cahokia Production and Expansion." *Midcontinental Journal of Archaeology* 40(2):149–65.

Hansen, Brooke, and Jack Rossen, 2007. "Building Bridges through Public Archaeology in the Haudenosaunee Homeland." In *Past Meets Present: Archaeologists Partnering with Museum Curators, Teachers, and Community Groups*, edited by John H. Jameson Jr. and Sherene Baugher, 127–48. New York: Springer.

———. 2017. Activist Anthropology with the Haudenosaunee: Theoretical and Practical Insights from the Two Row Wampum Renewal Campaign. *Anthropology in Action* 24, no. 3:32–44.

Harlan, Jack R. 1992. *Crops and Man*. Madison: American Society of Agronomy, Crop Science Society of America.

Hart, John P. 2008. "Evolving the Three Sisters: The Changing Histories of Maize, Beans, and Squash." In *Current Northeast Paleoethnobotany II*, edited by John P. Hart, 87–100. Bulletin Series 512. Albany: New York State Museum.

———. 2012. "Pottery Wall Thinning as a Consequence of Increased Maize Processing: A Case Study from Central New York." *Journal of Archaeological Science* 39(11):3470–74.

Hart, John P., and Hetty Jo Brumbach. 2003. "The Death of Owasco." *American Antiquity* 68(4):737–52.

———. 2005. "Cooking Residues, AMS Dates and the Middle-to-Late Woodland Transition in Central New York." *Northeast Anthropology* 69:1–33.

———. 2009. "On Pottery Change and Northern Iroquoian Origins: An Assessment from the Finger Lakes Region of Central New York." *Journal of Anthropological Archaeology* 28:367–81.

Hart, John P., Robert A. Daniels, and Charles J. Sheviak. 2004. "Do *Cucurbita pepo* Gourds Float Fishnets?" *American Antiquity* 69(1):141–48.

Hart, John P., and William Engelbrecht. 2012. "Northern Iroquoian Ethnic Evolution: A Social Network Analysis." *Journal of Archaeological Method and Theory* 19: 322–49.

Henige, David. 1999. "Can a Myth Be Astronomically Dated?" *American Indian Culture and Research Journal* 23, no. 4:127–57.

———. 2009. Impossible to Disprove Yet Impossible to Believe: The Unforgiving Epistemology of Deep-Time Oral Tradition. *History of Africa* 36:127–234.
Hill, Richard W., Sr. 2006. "Making a Final Resting Place Final: A History of the Repatriation Experience of the Haudenosaunee." In *Cross-Cultural Collaboration: Native Peoples and Archaeology in the Northeastern United States*, edited by Jordan E. Kerber, 3–17. Lincoln: University of Nebraska Press.
———. 2013. "Between the Two Rows: Reflecting on the Linked Vessels." Paper presented at American Indian Program Thirtieth Anniversary Recognition and Two Row Wampum Renewal Conference. Ithaca, NY, Apr.
Hirsch, Mark G. 2014. "The Two Row Wampum Belt." In *Nation to Nation: Treaties Between the United States and American Indian Nations*, edited by Suzan Shown Harjo, 59–60. Washington, DC: National Museum of the American Indian.
Hodder, Ian. 1991. "The Decoration of Containers: An Ethnographic and Historical Study." In *Ceramic Ethnoarchaeology*, edited by William A. Longacre, 71–94. Tucson: University of Arizona Press.
Hudson, Jean L. 2004. "Additional Evidence for Gourd Floats on Fishing Nets." *American Antiquity* 69(3):586–87.
Hurley, Jensen. 2016. "Levanna Net Sinkers." Ms. in possession of the author.
———. 2016. "Cayuga Fishing Technology: An Analysis of Tenth Century Net Sinkers from the Levanna Site, Central New York." Paper presented at James J. Whalen Academic Symposium, Ithaca, NY.
"Indian Tenor to Sing for Church Benefit." 1948. *Palm Beach Post*. February 2.
ICT Staff. 2011. "Tracing the Peacemaker's Journey." *Indian Country Today*. July 6.
Jacques, Frieda. 1991. "Discipline of the Good Mind." *Northeast Indian Quarterly*. Ithaca: Cornell University.
Johannessen, Sissel. 1984. "Paleoethnobotany." In *American Bottom Archaeology*, edited by Charles J. Bareis and James W. Porter, 197–224. Urbana: University of Illinois Press.
Johansen, Bruce E. 2000. "Education—The Nightmare and the Dream: A Shared National Tragedy, A Shared National Disgrace." *Native Americas* 17(42): December 31.
Johnson, Elias. 2010[1881]. *Legends, Traditions and Laws of the Iroquois, or Six Nations, and History of the Tuscarora Indians*. London: Forgotten Books.
Johnson, Frederick. 1944. "Review: The Pre-Iroquoian Occupations of New York State, by William A. Ritchie." *American Anthropologist* 46(4):530–35.

Johnston, Charles M. 1964. *The Valley of the Six Nations: A Collection of Documents on the Indian Lands of the Grand River Valley*. Toronto: University of Toronto Press.

Jordan, Kurt. 2008. *The Seneca Restoration, 1715–1754: An Iroquois Local Political Economy*. Gainesville: University Press of Florida, Gainesville.

Kapches, Mima. 1990. "The Spatial Dynamics of the Ontario Iroquoian Longhouses." *American Antiquity* 55(1):49–67.

———. 1994. "The Iroquoian Longhouse: Architectural and Cultural Identity." In *Meaningful Architecture: Social Interpretations of Buildings*, edited by M. Locock. Worldwide Archaeology Series, no. 9. Avebury: Aldershot.

Katchmer, George A. 1991. *A Bibliographic Dictionary of Silent Film Western Actors and Actresses*. Jefferson, NC: McFarland.

Karr, Landon, L. Adrien Hannus, and Alan K. Outram. 2008. "Bone Grease and Bone Marrow Exploitation on the Plains of South Dakota: A New Perspective on Bone Fracture Evidence from the Mitchell Prehistoric Indian Village." *South Dakota Archaeology* 26:33–62.

Kearns, Rick. 2015. "Yanomami of Brazil Honor Return of Stolen Blood." *Indian Country Today*. April 10.

Kelker, Luther Reilly. 1907. *History of Dauphin County, Pennsylvania*. New York: Lewis Publishing Co.

Kelly, Lucretia S. 2001. "A Case of Ritual Feasting at the Cahokia Site." *Feasts: Archaeological and Ethnographic Perspectives on Food, Politics, and Power*, edited by Michael Dietler and Brian Hayden, 334–367. Washington, DC: Smithsonian Institution Press.

Kerber, Jordan, ed. 2006. *Cross-Cultural Collaboration: Native Americans and Archaeologists in the Northeastern United States*. Lincoln: University of Nebraska Press.

Kimm, S. C. 1900. *The Iroquois, A History of the Six Nations of New York*. Middleburgh, NY: Pierre W. Danforth.

Kistler, Logan, Alvaro Montenegro, Bruce D. Smith, John A. Gifford, Richard E. Green, Lee A. Newsom, and Beth Shapiro. 2014. "Transoceanic Drift and the Domestication of the African Gourds in the Americas." *Proceedings of the National Academy of Sciences* 111, no. 8: 2937–41.

Kistler, Logan, Lee A. Newsom, Timothy M. Ryan, Andrew C. Clarke, Bruce D. Smith, and George H. Perry. 2015. "Gourds and Squashes (*Cucurbita* spp.) adapted to Megafaunal Extinction and Ecological Anachronism through Domestication." *Proceedings of the National Academy of Sciences* 112(49):15107–12.

Kleinberg, Eliot. 2010. "Chief Ho-To-Pi: Greek-turned-'Indian' Wowed Kids." *Palm Beach Post*. June 18.

Knight, Vernon J. 2001. In *Feasts: Archaeological and Ethnographic Perspectives on Food, Politics, and Power*, edited by Michael Dietler and Brian Hayden, 311–33. Washington, DC: Smithsonian Institution Press.

Kovach, Margaret. 2010. *Indigenous Methodologies: Characteristics, Conversations, and Contexts*. Toronto: University of Toronto Press.

Kuhn, Robert D., and Martha L. Sempowski. 2001. "A New Approach to Dating the League of the Iroquois." *American Antiquity* 66(2):301–14.

LaBelle, Shannon. 2015. "Levanna Lithic Tool Assemblage." Ms. in possession of the author.

———. 2016. "Cayuga Lithic Tools: An Analysis of 15th Century Projectile Points and Chipped Lithic Tools from the Myers Farm Site, Central New York." Paper presented at James J. Whalen Academic Symposium, Ithaca, NY.

LaDuke, Winona. 2005. *Recovering the Sacred: The Power of Naming and Claiming*. Cambridge, MA: South End Press.

Lajewski, C. K., H. T. Mullins, W. P. Patterson, and C. W. Callinan. 2003. "Historic Calcite Record from the Finger Lakes, New York: Impact of Acid Rain on a Buffered Terrane." *Geological Society of America Bulletin* 115(3):373–84.

Little, Elbert. 2004. *National Audubon Society Field Guide to North American Trees*. New York: Alfred A. Knopf.

Linton, Ralph. 1924. *Uses of Tobacco among North American Indians*. Fieldiana, Popular Series, no. 15. Chicago: Field Museum.

Lomawaima, K. Tsianina, and Brenda J. Child. 2000. *Away from Home: American Indian Boarding School Experiences, 1879–2000*. Phoenix: Heard Museum.

MacNeish, Richard S. 1952. *Iroquois Pottery Types: A Technique for the Study of Iroquois Prehistory*. Bulletin 124, Anthropological Series, no. 31. Ottawa: National Museum of Canada.

Mann, Barbara A. 2000. *Iroquois Women: The Gantowisas*. New York, NY: Peter Lang.

———. 2005. *George Washington's War on Native America*. Westport, CT: Praeger.

Mann, Barbara A., and Jerry L. Fields. 1997. "A Sign in the Sky: Dating the League of the Haudenosaunee." *American Indian Culture and Research Journal* 21(2):105–63.

Mann, Rob. 2004. "Smokescreens: Tobacco, Pipes, and the Transformational Power of Fur Trade Rituals." In *Smoking and Culture: The Archaeology of Tobacco Pipes in Eastern North America*, edited by Sean Rafferty and Rob Mann, 165–83. Knoxville: University of Tennessee Press.

McAssey, Edward V., Jonathan Corbi, and John M. Burke. 2016. "Range Wide Phenotypic and Genetic Differentiation in Wild Sunflower." *BMC Plant Biology* 16(1):1–8.

Macfarlan, Allan, and Paulette Macfarlan. 1985[1958]. *Handbook of American Indian Games.* New York: Dover.

Malone, Caroline, and Simon Stoddart. 1998. "Special Section: David Clarke's "Archaeology: The Loss of Innocence (1973) 25 Years Later." *Antiquity* 72:676–77.

McConaughy, Mark A. 2008. "Current Issues in Paleoethnobotanical Research from Pennsylvania and Vicinity." In *Current Northeast Paleoethnobotany II*, edited by John P. Hart, 9–28. Bulletin Series No. 512. Albany: New York State Museum.

McKeown, C. Timothy. 1995. "Special Issue: The Native American Graves Protection and Repatriation Act." *Federal Archaeology* 7(3).

McKern, W. C. 1945. "Review: The Pre-Iroquoian Occupations of New York State, by William A. Ritchie." *American Anthropologist* 47(1):140–42.

Means, Bernard K. 2007. *Circular Villages of the Monongahela Tradition.* Tuscaloosa: University of Alabama Press.

Minderhout, David J. 2013. *Native Americans in the Susquehanna River Valley, Past and Present.* Lewisburg, PA: Bucknell University Press.

Miroff, Laurie E., and Timothy D. Knapp. 2009. *Iroquoian Archaeology and Analytic Scale.* Knoxville: University of Tennessee Press.

Mitchell, Ammie. 2015. "A New Look at Old Traditions: A Petrographic Examination of the Point Peninsula and Owasco Ceramic Categories of the Levanna Site." Ms. submitted to the author.

———. 2017. "The Symbolism of Coarse Crystalline Temper: A Fabric Analysis of Early Pottery in New York State." PhD dissertation, Department of Anthropology, University at Buffalo, Buffalo, NY.

Moncrief, Nancy D., and Alton C. Dooley Jr. 2013. "Using Fluorescence of Bones and Teeth to Detect Remains of the Eastern Fox Squirrel *Sciurus niger*) in Archaeological Deposits." *Southeastern Archaeology* 32:46–53.

Morgan, Lewis Henry. 1851. *The League of the Ho-de-no-sau-nee.* Rochester, NY: Sage and Brothers.

Mt. Pleasant, Jane. 2009. "The Science Behind the Three Sisters Mound System: An Agronomic Assessment of an Indigenous Agricultural System in the Northeast." In *Histories of Maize: Multidisciplinary Approaches to the Prehistory, Linguistics, Biogeography, Domestication, and Evolution of Maize*, edited by John Staller, Robert Tykot, and Bruce Benz, 529–37. Walnut Creek, CA: Left Coast Press.

Murray, Louise Wells. 1908. *A History of Tioga Point and Early Athens, Pennsylvania.* Wilkes-Barre, PA: Reader Press.

National Park Service. 2018. "Denali or Mount McKinley?" www.nps.gov/dena/learn/historyculture/denali-origins.htm

REFERENCES

Niemczycki, Mary Ann Palmer. 1984. *The Origin and Development of the Seneca and Cayuga Tribes of New York State*. Rochester, NY: Rochester Museum and Science Center Research Records, no. 17.

Noe-Nygaard, Nanna. 1977. "Butchering and Marrow Fracturing as a Taphonomic Factor in Archaeological Deposits." *Paleobiology* 3(2):218–37.

O'Hearn, Macy. 2013a. "A Critical Examination of the Existing Typology for Haudenosaunee Ceramics and an Analysis of the Decorated Ceramics Assemblage from the Myers Farm Site, King Ferry, New York." Senior Honors Thesis, Anthropology Dept., Ithaca College.

———. 2013b. "Emerging Issues in the Ceramics Analysis of Myers Farm, a Fifteenth Century Cayuga Farmstead." Paper presented at annual meeting, New York State Archaeological Society. Watertown, NY, April 29.

———. 2016. "Notes on Ceramics from the Levanna Site." Ms. in author's possession.

O'Hearn, Macy, and Sarah Ward. 2015. "Other Artifact Assemblages." In *Corey Village and the Cayuga World: Implications from Archaeology and Beyond*, 104–9. Syracuse, NY: Syracuse University Press.

Orton, Clive, and Michael Hughes. 2013. *Pottery in Archaeology*. Cambridge: Cambridge University Press.

Outram, Alan K. 2005. "Distinguishing Bone Fat Exploitation from Other Taphonomic Processes: What Caused the High Level of Bone Fragmentation at the Middle Neolithic site of Ajvide, Gotland?" In *The Zooarchaeology of Fats, Oils, Milk and Dairying*, edited by J. Mulville and A. K. Outram, 32–43. Oxford: Oxbow.

Outram, Alan K., L. P. Karr, E. G. Short, and L. A. Hannus. 2014. "A Bone Grease Processing Station at the Mitchell Prehistoric Indian Village: Archaeological Evidence for the Exploitation of Bone Fats," *Environmental Archaeology: The Journal of Human Palaeoecology*, 1–12.

Parker, Arthur C. 1910. *Iroquois Uses of Maize and Other Food Plants*. Education Department Bulletin, no. 482. Museum Bulletin 144. Albany: New York State Museum.

———. 1920. *The Archaeological History of New York*. Bulletins 235, 236. Albany: University of the State of New York.

Parmenter, Jon. 2010. *The Edge of the Woods: Iroquoia, 1534–1701*. East Lansing: Michigan State University Press.

Peacock, D. P. S. 1970. "The Scientific Analysis of Ancient Ceramics: A Review." *World Archaeology* 1:357–89.

Pollack, David. 2015. "Ceramic Artifacts." In *Corey Village and the Cayuga World: Implications from Archaeology and Beyond*, edited by Jack Rossen, 41–70. Syracuse, NY: Syracuse University Press.

Porter, Joy. 2001. *To Be Indian: The Life of Iroquois-Seneca Arthur Caswell Parker*. Norman: University of Oklahoma Press.

Porter, Tom. 2006. *Kanatsiohareke: Traditional Mohawk Indians Return to Their Ancestral Homeland*. New York: The Kanatsiohareke Community.

———. 2008. *And Grandma Said: Iroquois Teachings as Passed Down through the Oral Tradition*. Xlibris Corporation.

Rafferty, Sean M., and Rob Mann. 2004. *Smoking and Culture: The Archaeology of Tobacco Pipes in Eastern North America*. Knoxville: University of Tennessee Press.

Reber, Eleanora, and Didi el-Behaedi. 2015. "Residue Analysis of Six Visible Pottery Residues from the Levanna and Myers Farm Sites." Anthropological Papers 29. Papers of the UNCW Residue Lab 22. Wilmington, NC: University of North Carolina at Wilmington.

Reynolds, Katie. 2008. "Levanna Net Sinker Analysis." Ms. in possession of the author.

Rice, Prudence. 1987. *Pottery Analysis: A Sourcebook*. Chicago: University of Chicago.

Ritchie, William A. 1928. *An Algonkian Village Site Near Levanna, N.Y. Research Records of the Rochester Municipal Museum*, no. 1. Rochester Municipal Museum, Rochester, NY.

———. 1932. "The Algonkin Sequence of New York." *American Anthropologist* 34(3): 406–14.

———. 1944. *The Pre-Iroquoian Occupations of New York*. Museum Memoir, no. 1. Rochester, NY: Rochester Museum of Arts and Sciences.

———. 1945. *An Early Site in Cayuga County, New York: Type Component of the Frontenac Focus, Archaic Pattern*. Research Records, no. 7. Rochester, NY: Rochester Museum of Arts and Sciences.

———. 1969. *The Archaeology of Martha's Vineyard: A Framework for the Prehistory of Southern New England: A Study in Coastal Ecology and Adaptation*. New York: Natural History Press.

———. 1971. *New York Projectile Points: A Typology and Nomenclature*. Bulletin 384. Albany: New York State Museum.

———. 1981[1965]. *The Archaeology of New York State*. Harrison, NY: Harbor Hill Books.

Ritchie, William A., Donald Lenig, and P. Schuyler Miller. 1953. *An Early Owasco Sequence in Eastern New York*. Circular 32. Albany: The University of the State of New York.

Ritchie, William A., and Richard S. MacNeish. 1949. "The Pre-Iroquoian Pottery of New York State." *American Antiquity* 15(2):97–124.

Roche, Mark. 2012. "WPA Project Uncovers Borough's Early Residents." *CARE Newsletter*, 4–6. December.

Rogers, Nina. 2014. "Rethinking Levanna Ceramics: A Short-Term Occupation Site in Central New York." Master's Thesis, University of Denver.

Rossen, Jack. 1992. "Botanical Remains." In: *Fort Ancient Cultural Dynamics in the Middle Ohio Valley*, edited by A. Gwynn Henderson, 189–208. Madison: Prehistory Press.

———. 1999. "The Flote-Tech Flotation Machine: Messiah or Mixed Blessing?" *American Antiquity* 64(2):370–72.

———. 2000. "Archaic Plant Utilization at the Hedden Site, McCracken County, Kentucky." In *Current Archaeological Research in Kentucky, Volume Six*, edited by David Pollack and Kristen J. Gremillion, 1–24. Frankfort, KY: Kentucky Heritage Council.

———. 2006. "Research and Dialogue: New Vision Archaeology in the Cayuga Heartland of Central New York." In *Cross-Cultural Collaboration: Native Peoples and Archaeology in the Northeastern United States*, edited by Jordan E. Kerber, 250–64. Lincoln: University of Nebraska Press.

———. 2008. "Field School Archaeology, Activism, and Politics in the Cayuga Heartland of Central New York." In *Collaborating at the Trowel's Edge: Teaching and Learning in Indigenous Archaeology*, edited by Stephen W. Silliman, 105–20. Tucson: University of Arizona Press.

———. 2010. "Archaeology, Tourism, and Intrigue at the Levanna Site, 1922–2009." History's Mysteries Lecture Series, Susquehanna River Archaeological Center, Waverly, NY, May 4.

———. 2010b. "Can Archaeologists Learn How Old the Haudenosaunee (Iroquois) Confederacy Is?" Paper present at the annual Conference on Iroquois Research, Cornwall, Ontario, October 2.

———. 2011a. "Las Pircas Phase (9,000–7,000 B.C.)," In *From Foraging to Farming in the Andes: New Perspectives on Food Production and Social Organization*, edited by Tom D. Dillehay, 95–116. Cambridge: Cambridge University Press.

———. 2011b. "Preceramic Plant Gathering, Gardening, and Farming," In *From Foraging to Farming in the Andes: New Perspectives on Food Production and Social Organization*, edited by Tom D. Dillehay, 177–92. Cambridge: Cambridge University Press.

———. 2013. "Longhouse, Cookhouse, Smoking Pipes, Eclipse: Archaeology of the Cayuga Heartland and the Origins of Confederacy." Invited presentation at Colgate University, Hamilton, NY, September 18.

———. 2015. *Corey Village and the Cayuga World: Implications from Archaeology and Beyond*. Syracuse, NY: Syracuse University Press.

———. 2016. "Remembering the Archaeology on the Farms Project (1991–1993) or Growing Up on the Farm." *Vermont Journal of Archaeology* 14:1–8.

Rossen, Jack, and April M. Beisaw. 2016. On Cayuga Faunal Remains: Reply to Somerville. *New York State Archaeological Association Newsletter* 12(1):11–14.

Rossen, Jack and Richard Edging. 1987. "East Meets West: Patterns in Kentucky Late Prehistoric Subsistence." In *Current Archaeological Research in Kentucky, Volume One*, edited by David Pollack, 225–34. Frankfort: Kentucky Heritage Council.

Rossen, Jack, and James Olson. 1985. "The Controlled Carbonization and Archeological Analysis of Southeastern U.S. Wood Charcoals." *Journal of Field Archaeology* 12:445–56.

Rossen, Jack, W. Mahealani Pai, Brooke Hansen, and J. Keonelehua Kalawe. 2017. "Enhancing Heritage Management and Food Security through Cultural Revitalization at Maluaka, Hawai'i Island." Paper presented at Hawai'i Conservation Conference, Honolulu, July.

Rossen, Jack, W. Mahealani Pai, and J. Keonelehua Kalawe. 2017a. "Social Organization and Engineering of Agriculture at Maluaka, Kona Field System, Hawai'i Island." Paper presented at Society for American Archaeology Conference, Vancouver, March.

———. 2017b. "Further Archaeological Investigations into the Social Organization of Ancient Hawaiian Agriculture at Maluaka, Hawai'i Island." Paper presented at the Society for Hawaiian Archaeology Conference, Kapolei, Hawai'i, September.

Rossen, Jack, María Teresa Planella, and Rubén Stehberg. 2010. "Archaeobotany of Cerro del Inga, Chile at the Southern Inka Frontier." In: *Distant Provinces in the Inca Empire*, edited by Michael Malpass and Sonia Alconini, 14–43. Iowa City: University of Iowa Press.

Rossen, Jack, and Jocelyn C. Turner. In press. "Plant Use Systems at the Falls of the Ohio: Boundary Maintenance and Interaction." In volume on the Falls of the Ohio, edited by David Pollack.

Rutsch, Edward S. 1973. *Smoking Technology of the Aborigines of the Iroquois Area of New York State*. Rutherford, NJ: Farleigh Dickinson University Press.

Sanft, Samantha M. 2013. "Beads and Pendants from Indian Fort Road: A Sixteenth Century Cayuga Site in Tompkins County, New York." Master's thesis, Cornell University.

Schoff, Harry L. 1937. "A Thunderbird Effigy." *National Archaeological News* 1(1):16–19.

———. 1938. "Archaeological Report of the Opening of Three Indian Graves on the Old Heydrick Farm at the Junction of Deer and French Creeks, Venango County, Pennsylvania." (tDAR ID: 118981). *National Archaeological Database Reports Module.*

———. n.d.a. "Certain Marks on Pottery Pipes of the Historic Seneca."(tDar ID 118982). *National Archaeological Database Reports Module.*

———. n.d.b. "McFate Site: Report on Archaeological Excavations Conducted in Northwestern Pennsylvania by the Works Progress Administration." (tDAR ID 118987). *National Archaeological Database Reports Module.*

Schoolcraft, Henry R. 2002[1846]. *Notes on the Iroquois.* East Lansing: Michigan State University Press.

Schroeder, Marjorie. 2007. "Carbonized Plant Remains from the Caesars Archaeological Project, Harrison County, Indiana." In *Caesars Archaeological Project Overview: Geomorphology, Archeobotany and Other Specialty Analyses, Caesars Archaeological Project Report Volume 1,* edited by C. Russell Stafford, 258–374. Anthropology Laboratory Technical Report 36. Terre Haute: Indiana State University.

Schulenberg, Janet K. 2002. *New Dates for Owasco Pots. In Northeast Subsistence-Settlement Change, A.D. 700–1300,* edited by J. P. Hart and C. B. Rieth, 153–65. Bulletin 496. Albany: New York State Museum.

Silliman, Stephen, ed. 2008. *Collaborating at the Trowel's Edge: Teaching and Learning in Indigenous Archaeology.* Tucson: University of Arizona Press.

Simpson, Duane B., and Stephen T. Mocas. In press. "The Late Archaic at Riverpark and Its Implications on Analyzing Patterns of Change Within the Broader Falls of the Ohio Region." In volume on the Falls of the Ohio, edited by David Pollack.

Smith, Bruce D. 2009. Initial Formation of an Indigenous Crop Complex in Eastern North America at 3800 B.P. *Proceedings of the National Academy of Sciences* 106:6561–66.

———. 2011. The Cultural Context of Plant Domestication in Eastern North America. *Current Anthropology* 52, Supplement 4:S471–S484.

Smith, Erminnie A. 1994[1883]. *Myths of the Iroquois.* Ohsweken: Iroqrafts.

Smith, Hanley K. 1970. "The Biology, Wildlife Use and Management of Sumac in the Lower Peninsula of Michigan." PhD dissertation. Michigan State University, East Lansing.

Smith, Claire, and H. Martin Wobst. 2005. *Indigenous Archaeologies: Decolonizing Theory and Practice.* London: Routledge.

Smith, Linda Tuhiwai. 2012. *Decolonizing Methodologies: Research and Indigenous Peoples.* London: Zed Books.

Snow, Dean. 1995. "Migration in Prehistory: The Northern Iroquois Case." *American Antiquity* 60(1):59–79.

———. 1996. "More on Migration in Prehistory: Accommodating New Evidence in the Northern Iroquoian Case." *American Antiquity* 60(4):791–96.
Somerville, Kyle. 2015. "Faunal Exploitation in the Eastern Cayuga Sequence, Central New York State, c. 1275–1525." *The Bulletin, Journal of the New York Archaeological Association* 129:57–72.
Spaulding, Albert C. 1953. "Statistical Techniques for the Discovery of Artifact Types." *American Antiquity* 18(4):305–13.
———. 1954. Reply to Ford. *American Antiquity* 19(4):391–93.
Spears, Michael. 2010. "Microscopic Usewear Analysis of Lithics from the Levanna Site, Cayuga County, New York." Senior Honors Thesis, Anthropology Department. Ithaca College, Ithaca, NY.
Stafford, C. Russell, and Stephen T. Mocas. 2009. "The Middle, Late, and Terminal Archaic Occupations at the Caesars Archaeological Project, Harrison County, Indiana." In *Caesars Archaeological Project Vol 4. Archaeology and Quaternary Research Laboratory*. Technical Report 39. Terre Haute: Indiana State University.
Starna, William A. 2008. "Retrospecting the Origins of the League of the Iroquois." *Proceedings of the American Philosophical Society* 152(3):279–321.
Stevens, Peter F. 1993. *The Mayflower Murderer and Other Forgotten Firsts in American History*. New York: William Morrow and Co.
Stoltman, James. 1989. "A Quantitative Approach to the Petrographic Analysis of Ceramic Thin Sections." *American Antiquity* 54:147–60.
Stoner, Wesley D. 2015. Petrographic Analysis of Ceramics. In *Corey Village and the Cayuga World: Implications from Archaeology and Beyond*, edited by Jack Rossen, 71–81. Syracuse, NY: Syracuse University Press.
Sussenbach, Tom. 1993. "Agricultural Intensification and Mississippian Development in the Confluence Region of the Mississippi River Valley." PhD dissertation, Anthropology Department. Urbana-Champaign: University of Illinois.
Swanton, John R. 1946. *The Indians of the Southeastern United States*. Bulletin 137. Washington, DC: Bureau of American Ethnology.
Swidler, Nina, Kurt E. Dongoske, Roger Anyon, and Alan S. Downer. 1997. *Native Americans and Archaeologists: Stepping Stones to Common Ground*. Walnut Creek, CA: Altamira Press.
Teague, Lynn S. 1993. "Prehistory and Traditions of the O'Odham and Hopi." *Kiva* 58(4):435–54.
Tehanetorens. 1999. *Wampum Belts of the Iroquois*. Summertown, TN: Native Voices.
———. 2000. *Roots of the Iroquois*. Summertown, TN: Native Voices.
Thomas, Chief Jake. 1989. *Illustrations and Descriptions of Wampum Belts*. Wilsonville, ON: Sandpiper Press.

REFERENCES

———. 1994. *Teachings from the Longhouse*. Toronto: Stoddart Publishing.
Tibbetts, John C. 2011. "Arizona Jim: The Westerns of Douglas Fairbanks, Sr." *Journal of Popular Film and Television* 39(2):42–49.
Tibbetts, John C., and James M. Welsh. 2014. *Douglas Fairbanks, Sr. and the American Century*. Jackson: University Press of Mississippi.
Tobin, Dave. 2002. George Washington's Campaign of Terror. *Syracuse (NY) Post-Standard*, August 20, B1.
Tooker, Elisabeth. 1964. *An Ethnography of the Huron Indians, 1615–1649*. Smithsonian Institution Bureau of American Ethnology Bulletin 190. Washington, DC: US Government Printing Office.
Turner, Terence. 2001. *The Yanomami and the Ethics of Anthropological Practice*. Latin American Studies Program, Occasional Paper Series, Volume 6. Ithaca, Ny: Cornell University.
Twigg, Deborah. 2005. "Revisiting the Mystery of Carantouan and Spanish Hill." *Pennsylvania Archaeologist* 75, no. 2.
US Geological Survey. 2007. "Geologic Units Containing Green Slate." https://mrdata.usgs.gov/geology/state/sgmc-lith.php?text=slate.
Van Diver, Bradford B. 1985. *Roadside Geology of New York*. Sevierville, TN: Mountain Press.
Venables, Robert W. 2010. "The Clearings and the Woods: The Haudenosaunee (Iroquois) Landscape—Gendered and Balanced." In *Archaeology and Preservation of Gendered Landscapes*, edited by Sherene Baugher and Suzanne M. Spencer-Wood, pp. 21–55. New York: Springer.
Vogel, Virgil J. 1982. *American Indian Medicine*. Norman: University of Oklahoma Press.
Von Gelder, Sarah. 2008. "On Wild Rice, Wind Power, Thunder Beings, Self-reliance, and our Covenant with the Creator: An Interview with Winona LaDuke." *YES! Magazine*. Summer.
Wagner, Gail E. 2000. "Tobacco in Prehistoric Eastern North America." In *Tobacco Use by Native North Americans: Sacred Smoke and Silent Killer*, edited by Joseph C. Winter, 185–201. Norman: University of Oklahoma Press.
Waldman, Amy. 1999. "Iron Eyes Cody, 94, An Actor and Tearful Anti-Littering Icon." *New York Times*. January 5.
Wall, Steve. 2001. *To Become a Human Being: The Message of Tadodaho Chief Leon Shenandoah*. Charlottesville, VA: Hampton Roads.
Wallace, Paul A., and John Kahionhes Fadden. 1994. *White Roots of Peace: The Iroquois Book of Life*. Santa Fe, NM: Clear Light.
Ward, Sarah. 2014a. "Myers Farm Site: A Case Study in the Significance of Hoe Blades in Cayuga Culture." Independent Study Paper, Ithaca College.

Ward, Sarah. 2014b. "Myers Farm Site: A Case Study in the Significance of Hoe Blades in Cayuga Culture." Paper presented at the annual meeting, Northeast Anthropological Association, Pottsdam, NY.

Watkins, Joe. 2000. *Indigenous Archaeology: American Indian Values and Scientific Practice*. Walnut Creek, CA: Altamira Press.

Watson, Jennifer E., and Jack Rossen. 2016. "Tool Manufacturing Patterns and Bone Breakage at a Haudenosaunee Site in New York." Poster presented at Society for American Archaeology conference, Orlando, Fl, April 7.

Waugh, F. W. 1916. *Iroquois Foods and Food Preparation*. Memoir 86, Anthropological Series, no. 12, Canada Department of Mines, Geological Survey. Ottawa: Government Printing Bureau.

Weissner, Polly. 1983. "Style and Social Information in Kalahari San Projectile Points." *American Antiquity* 48(2): 253–76.

Welles, Mary L. 1908. *A History of Old Tioga Point and Early Athens, Pennsylvania*. Wilkes-Barre, PA: Raeder Press.

Whiteley, Peter M. 2000. "The Misappropriation of Cayuga Lands: A Brief History." For the US Department of Justice (Indian Resources), intervenors in *Cayuga Nation et al. vs. Pataki et al.* Syracuse, NY: US District Court.

Whyte, Thomas R. 2014. "Gifts of the Ancestors: Secondary Lithic Recycling in Appalachian Summit Prehistory." *American Antiquity* 79(4): 679–96.

Wiegand, Karl M., and Arthur J. Eames. 1926. *The Flora of Cayuga Lake Basin, New York: Vascular Plants*. Ithaca, NY: Cornell University Agricultural Experiment Station.

Wilbert, Johannes. 1987. *Tobacco and Shamanism in South America*. New Haven, CT: Yale University Press.

Williams, Paul. n.d. *Kayanerenkó:wa: The Great Law of Peace*. Ms. in author's possession.

Williams-Shuker, Kimberly. 2009. "Bottom-Up Perspectives of the Contact Period: A View from the Rogers Farm Site." In *Iroquoian Archaeology and Analytic Scale*, edited by Laurie E. Miroff and Timothy D. Knapp, 131–52. Knoxville: University of Tennessee Press.

Winiarz, Joseph F. 2015. "Lithic Raw Material Sources." In *Corey Village and the Cayuga World: Implication from Archaeology and Beyond*. Syracuse, NY: Syracuse University Press.

Woods, Carter A. 1934. "A Criticism of Wissler's North American Culture Areas." *American Anthropologist* 36(4):517–23.

———. 1976. "Postscript." Typed manuscript. Wells College Library, Wells College, Aurora, NY.

Wonderley, Anthony. 2002. "Oneida Ceramic Effigies." *Northeast Anthropology* 63:23–48.

———. 2005. "Effigy Pipes, Diplomacy, and Myth: Exploring Interactions between St. Lawrence Iroquoians and Eastern Iroquoians in New York State." *American Antiquity* 70(2):211–40.

Woods, Carter A., and Harrison C. Follett. n.d. "A Prehistoric Algonquin Village Site near Levanna, N.Y." Unpublished typed manuscript, Wells College Library, Wells College, Aurora, NY.

Yamada, Katherine. 2014. "Verdugo Views: The True Story of Iron Eyes Cody." *Los Angeles Times*. August 28.

Yarnell, Richard A. 1978. "Domestication of Sunflower and Sumpweed in Eastern North America." In *The Nature and Status of Ethnobotany*, edited by Richard I. Ford, 289–99. Anthropological Papers, no. 67. Ann Arbor: Museum of Anthropology, University of Michigan.

Yarrow, Harry C. 1880. *Introduction to the Study of Mortuary Customs of North American Indians*. Washington, DC: Bureau of American Ethnology.

Young, David E., and Robson Bonnichsen. 1985. "Cognition, Behavior, and Material Culture." In: *Stone Tool Analysis: Essays in Honor of Don E. Crabtree*, edited by Mark G. Plew, James C. Woods, and Max G. Pavesic, 91–131. Albuquerque: University of New Mexico Press.

INDEX

Algonkian, 3, 19, 41, 47, 51 53, 124, 161, 164
Algonquin, 4, 6, 8, 10
American Museum of Natural History, 100
Armour, Alison, 90, 139, 150, *151*
Auburn, New York, 4, 12, 24, 28, 54, 126, 163
Aurora, New York, 12, 17, 19, 50, 118, 156

Bailey, Lydia, 152, *153*
Beauchamp, William M., 12, 92
Beisaw, April M., 96, 98, 100, *101*, 102
Big Swede, 30
Binford, Lewis R., 74
Bomberry, Chief Blake, 49
botanical remains: analysis of, 6, 9, 74, 103–21, 148–50
Bucor, Erika, 148

Canfield, William Walker. *See* Cornplanter
Cayuga: land claim, 2, 19, 168; Lake, viii, 10, 19, 23, 32, 48, 50, 67, 92, 112, 118–19, 122, 126, 133, 141, 156, 164, 168; Nation, vii, 45, 50, 167; people, viii, 6, 10, 18, 48, 50, 120, 123, 124
Cayuga-SHARE Farm, vii, viii, 1–2, 45, 47, 49, 51, 61–62, 65, 167
ceramics: analysis of, 73, 76, 81–89, 132–38, 157, 179–80; chronology of, 54, 163–64, 179–80; coiling versus paddle-and-anvil, 82; fabric remnants on, 134–37; non-local, 133–35; petrography of, 86–89; replication of, 125–26; residue analysis of, 89; typology of, 51–54, 132–34
Chagnon, Napoleon, 61
Chittim, Ammie, 86–88

Chonodote site, *see* Peachtown site
Clarke, Noah, 33–35
Codzie, Sitsa, 94, *95*
corn, 4, 6, 54–57, 87–8, 106–14, 117–18, *121*, 123, 148–50, 153
Cornplanter (William Walker Canfield), 12, 56–57
Corey Village site, x, 2, 8, 67, 72, 80, 88, 92, 102, 114, 116, 119, 121, 125–26, 133, 145, 156, 164
Cowles, Ellsworth, 42

DeOrio, Robert, 13, 27, 39, 126–27
Drummond, Richard, 23–24, 33–35

Echo-Hawk, Roger, 57–59
effigies: animal, viii, ix, 1–2, 4, 10, 16, 18, 21–24, *26*, 73; controversy of, 32–44, 160–62
el-Behaedi, Didi, 89, 138
expanded identity, concept of, 49

Fairbanks, Douglas, Sr., 29, *31*
faunal remains: analysis of, 96–102, 143–47, 166; dietary stress and, 102
feasting, 127, 138, 141, 145, 152, 154–56, 165
Finger Lakes, viii, 32, 67
fishnet sinkers, 19, 93–95
Follett, Harrison C., viii–ix, 2, 11–14, 19, *20*, 20–28, *26*, 33–8, 41–44, 69, 93, 126, 159–63, 166, 168
Franklin, Benjamin, 60
Frontenac Island, 67, 118

Gaiwí:yo, Good Message of Handsome Lake, *see* Handsome Lake
game pieces, 152–54, *153*

George, Chief Sam, 49
Gibson, Chief John Arthur, 60
Gohl, E. H., 12, 19, 69, 159
Gonyea, Faithkeeper Tony, 46, 65
good mind, concept of, 49–50, 66
gourd, 113
Great Gully, 1, 18, 62, 67, 79, 94
Great Peace, x, 7–8, 45–46, 56, 165
Griffin, James B., 12, 17–18, 36–38, 41–43, 160
ground stone artifacts, 139–40, 154
Guthe, Carl E., 17, 36–37

Hado:ih, great healer and false face image, 6, 92, 96
Handsome Lake, Seneca prophet: Good Message of, 61, 66
Hansen, Brooke, 1, 2
Haudenosaunee Confederacy: age of, 10, 55–57, 62–63, 165–66, 168; eclipse story, 7, 56–58; faithkeepers of, 46, 60, 65; long versus brief chronology, 9–10, 55–57, 62–63, 118; models of development of, 6–8, 47; warfare versus peace in, x, 10, 55–57, 165–66
Hawkins, Rebecca, 153–54
Henige, David, 58–59
Hewitt, J.N.B., 12
Hiawatha, 45–46, 56, 165
Hill, Clan Mother Birdie, 62
Hill, Corrine, 65–66
Hill, Dan, vii, 145
Hill, Chief Norman, 62
Hill, Rick, 161, 165–66
Hill, Tadodaho Sidney, 45
hoe blades, 67, 122, 128, 131, 140–41, 154
Ho-To-Pi, Chief, 29–30, *31*
Hurley, Jensen, 27, 93

INDEX

indigenous archaeology, viii, 3, 5–6, 9, 13, 47–51, 62–63, 65, 163, 169
Iroquois Confederacy, *see* Haudenosaunee Confederacy
Ithaca, City of, 28, 50, 61, 67, 118

Jacobs, Chief Chuck, 49
Jacques, Adeliade "Ada," 125–26, 138, 168
Jigonsaseh, 45, 56, 165

Kanickhungo, Chief, 60
Kopenawa, Yanomami headman Davi, 61–62

LaBelle, Shannon, 80, 141
LaDuke, Winona, 45–47, 51
Lakeside site, *see* Owasco site
Lamoka Lake site, 24
Levanna site: effigies, *see* effigies; museum, vii-viii, 2–4, 10, 13–34, 24–32, 38, 41, 44, 69, 124, 160–62; palisade, 6, 7, 10, 20, 24, 27, 73, 124, 132, 162, 164; re-excavation of, 65–124
Longhouse. *See* protolonghouse
Lyons, Oren, Jr., 32, 46
Lyons, Oren, Sr., 30, 32, 46

MacMillan, Kerr, 12, 17, 27, 160
MacNeish, Richard S., 52–54, 81–6, 132, 137–38, 162–64
microscopic use-wear, 80–81
Mohawk Nation, 7, 9, 45, 55, 61, 90, 132, 141, 153, 155, 161
Mueller, Natalie, 148
Myers Farm site, x, 9, 55, 63, 67, 78–79, 89, 92–93, 104, 119, 122, 125–58, 164, 168

NAGPRA (Native American Graves Protection and Repatriation Act), 4, 58
National Museum of the American Indian, 4, 14
Neel, James, 61
Net Weight site, 94
New York State Museum, 17, 74, 76, 143

O'Hearn, Macy, 52, 83, 85–87, 132–38, 141
Onondaga Nation, viii, 3–4, 9, 12–13, 30, 32, 43–46, 57, 65, 67, 80, 126, 132–33, 138, 141, 155, 160–61, 164
oral traditions: comparison to archaeology, ix–x, 8–9, 18, 47, 49, 55–63, 165–66, 168
Owasco: Lake, 4, 19, 54, 163–64; Phase or Culture, ix, 3–4, 6, 9, 12, 41, 47, 51, 54–55, 74, 76, 81, 83, 85–90, 92, 124; Site, 3–4, 163

palisade: presence or absence of, 6, 10, 20, 24, 27, 73, 124, 132, 138, 156, 162–65, 168
Pangburn, Betty, 1, 51, 159–60, 168
Parker, Arthur C., viii–ix, 5, 11–14, 16–17, 19, 23–24, 33–37, 47, 53, 69, 74, 80, 119, 123, 159–61, 164, 166, 168
Peacemaker, the: epic of, 45, 56–57, 60–61, 165–66
Peacemaker's Journey, *see* Peacemaker
Peachtown site, 18
Pickford, Mary, 29, *31*
pipes. *see* smoking pipes
Powless, Chief Irving, 65–66, 168

projectile points, 19, 52, 78–80, 79, 141–43, *142*, 157
protolonghouse, 6, 76–77, 88, 118 figure
Putnam, Frederic Ward, 12

radiocarbon dates, 74–78, 129
Reber, Eleanora A., 89, 138
Ritchie, Donald, 19–20, 42
Ritchie, William A., viii–ix, 11–12, 14, 16, 19–21, 32, 35–43, 47, 52–54, 67, 69, 74, 78, 80, 82, 83, 85–86, 90, 159–62, 164, 166
Rochester Municipal Museum (now Rochester Museum and Science Center), 13, 20, 23, 35, 38
Rogers, Nina, 54, 73, 76, 81–88
Rogers Farm site, 92

Savishinsky, Joel, 94
Schaefer, Vincent, 13, 19
Schoff, Harry L., 14–16, 39–42
Selden, George B., Jr., 16, 19, 32–33, 36, 38–39
Seneca Nation, 4, 7, 9, 13, 16, 18, 30, 39, 43–45, 50, 55–57, 60–62, 66, 92, 117, 119, 132–33, 138, 155, 161
settlement patterns, 7–8, 53, 56, 63, 68, 81, 126, 141, 155–57
SHARE Farm. *See* Cayuga-SHARE Farm
Sherman, Fred, 2, 19, 21, 24, 69, 163
Silversmith, Donna, vii, 6, 50, 65
Smoke, Percy, 32, *32*
smoking pipes: *see* analysis of, chronology of, decoration of, typology of
Snow, Dean, 53, 162
Spanish Hill site, 18, 42–43, 160

squash, 113
St. Clair, Homer, ix, 2, 12, 19, 21, 29, 69, 73, 168
St. Clair, Randy, xiii, 2
sunflower, 113
Swamp, Chief Jake, 61

Tadodaho, 45, 46
Third Period Algonkian, *see* Algonkian
Thomas, Nick, 32, *32*
Three Sisters (corn-beans-squash agriculture), 4, 149, 167
Titus, David Sands III, 14
toss zones, 74, 75, 77–78, 86, 90, 98, 104–5, 108, 115–16, 118, 120, 122–23
Two-Row Wampum: concept, 49–50; Treaty, 50

use-wear analysis, *see* microscopic use-wear
Uticone, Julie and Jim, 2

Venables, Robert, 66

Ward, Sarah, 140–41
Watson, Jessica E., 143–45
Watson, Patty Jo, 103
Wells College, 12, 17, 24, 27, 36, 152, 160
wild rice, 67, 105, 112, 118
Woods, Carter A., 12, 17, 24, 33 41, 160

Yanomami: blood samples, 61; Chief Davi Kopenawa, *see* Kopenawa, Davi; visit to the SHARE Farm, 61–62
Yarrow, Harry C., 153

ABOUT THE AUTHOR

Jack Rossen received his PhD from the University of Kentucky. He was professor of anthropology and co-founder of Native American Studies at Ithaca College, Ithaca, New York, and taught in the master's program in Heritage Management at the University of Hawai'i at Hilo. He has conducted archaeological research in Peru, Chile, Argentina, and Hawai'i and has analyzed archaeobotanical materials from throughout South America, the Ohio Valley, and the northeastern United States.

He began work in 1998 on collaborative archaeology and community projects with the Cayuga and Onondaga Nations in what is now central New York. He recently directed teaching and research collaborations with Kamehameha Schools and Lili'uokalani Trust, working with high school students and at-risk youth, to better understand the social organization and engineering of agriculture at Maluaka in the Kona field system of Hawai'i Island. He currently works with the nonprofit History Flight in the Republic of Kiribati, supervising excavations of MIA US Servicemen from the Battle of Tarawa.

www.ingramcontent.com/pod-product-compliance
Lightning Source LLC
Chambersburg PA
CBHW021849300426
44115CB00005B/76